Praise

"This is a great read! The stories are totally engaging. DeLong nails it. A very timely book. Insights on language challenges, "compassion fatigue" and the role of humor in successfully hiring marginalized workers are among dozens of lessons learned."

–Michael Tamasi, CEO, AccuRounds

"A crucial resource for communities addressing workforce challenges, *Hidden Talent* illustrates actionable strategies for businesses to tap into valuable talent pools. The stories are rich with practical lessons and include helpful checklists to drive positive change in organizations."

–Jaimie Francis, head of Talent Pipeline Management® initiative, U.S. Chamber of Commerce Foundation

"I loved this book! Its resources and the stories can go a long way helping businesses like mine access the hidden talent we need to grow. Packed with new research, DeLong provides incredible insights and lessons from leaders already accessing the types of employees my industry—life sciences and medical devices—normally overlooks. I can't wait to share this with my partners, colleagues and friends who continually struggle to find talent."

–John Konsin, Co-founder & CEO, Prapela, Inc.

"The structural labor shortage is not only here to stay, it will get worse. DeLong's *Hidden Talent* offers important and practical remedies, all revolving around fully employing those who have become marginalized from the workforce. Based on the actual experiences of employers, DeLong's highly readable work covers a host of opportunities for those seeking talent from refugees, to the neurodiverse to the justice impacted."

–Jeffrey Korzenik, economist and author of "Untapped Talent: How Second Chance Hiring Works for Your Business and the Community"

"As a business leader, how would you feel if finding good workers was no longer a problem? What if you were able to hire candidates who not only turned out to be your best employees, but who also improved the morale and productivity of your entire company? You can start to achieve this seeming miracle by using the proven approaches in *Hidden Talent*. This book is fantastic! It will make a huge difference for companies, challenged individuals and their families."

—**Dr. Ivan Rosenberg, founder and president,
The Uniquely Abled Project**

"The demographic trends shaping our future workforce present both obstacles and opportunities. This unique book is full of examples of companies engaging workers who face inordinate challenges. *Hidden Talent* shows creative ways to reinvent your culture so it serves everybody by sustaining high performance while also meeting the needs of individual employees."

–**John Cain, CEO, Scot Forge**

"Countless employers across New England tell us how valuable refugees are to their companies. The stories in *Hidden Talent* are supported by our experiences at IINE. This book shows how great partnerships and innovative leaders can benefit from employing new arrivals eager to enter the US workforce."

–**Jeff Thielman, CEO, International Institute of New England**

Hidden Talent

Hidden Talent

How to Employ Refugees, the Formerly Incarcerated & People With Disabilities

David DeLong

Copyright © 2025 David DeLong

All rights reserved. No part of this book may be reproduced or used in any manner without the prior written permission of the copyright owner, except for the use of brief quotations in a book review.

This book is designed to provide accurate and authoritative information in regard to the subject matter covered. It is sold with the understanding that the author and publisher are not engaged in rendering legal, accounting, or other professional services. If legal advice or other expert assistance is required, the services of a competent professional should be sought.

Published by Longstone Press
60 Thoreau St., Suite 284
Concord, MA 01742

ISBN(paperback): 978-0-9888686-2-5
ISBN (ebook): 978-0-9888686-3-2

Book design and production by www.AuthorSuccess.com

Printed in the United States of America

DEDICATION

For my wife, Sue, who after 35 years
still listens to my dreams, and always says "Yes!"

Contents

INTRODUCTION	1
Author's Note on Language: What Should I Call You?	11
CHAPTER 1: Starting From Scratch: What Does It Feel Like to Be Marginalized in the Workplace?	15
SECTION 1: HIRING THE FORMERLY INCARCERATED	**21**
CHAPTER 2: Precisely: The Education of a Second-Chance Champion	23
CHAPTER 3: The Body Shop and the Power of Open Hiring	41
CHAPTER 4: JBM Packaging's Fair Chance Program: "It's not about the alarm clock"	58
CHAPTER 5: Lessons Learned from Second-Chance Companies	79
SECTION 2: RECRUITING AND EMPLOYING REFUGEES	**109**
CHAPTER 6: Boston Children's Hospital: How Partners Build a Talent Pipeline of Foreign-Born Workers	111
CHAPTER 7: Clampco Products: Betting on Refugees to Build a Sustainable Business	133
CHAPTER 8: Main Street Gourmet: A United Nations of Food That Says "Eat Dessert First!"	155
CHAPTER 9: How to Translate Lessons Learned from Employing Refugees	167

SECTION 3: HOW TO EMPLOY PEOPLE WITH DISABILITIES — 183

CHAPTER 10: Minnesota Diversified Industries: How a Mission Makes Money When Hiring Workers with Disabilities — 185

CHAPTER 11: Classic Wire Cut: Finding Gold in Neurodiverse CNC Machinists — 203

CHAPTER 12: How Heartland Systems Corporation Maintains Data Quality Across the Spectrum — 218

CHAPTER 13: Lessons Learned From Employing People with Disabilities — 238

SECTION 4: A PRACTICAL PATH FORWARD: WHICH MARGINALIZED WORKERS TO EMPLOY AND HOW TO DO IT — 259

CHAPTER 14: Finding Your "Why": Three Stories to Inspire and Clarify Who You Might Hire — 261

CHAPTER 15: "Yes, You Can Work Here": A Practical Framework for Employing Marginalized Workers — 271

Acknowledgments — 293
Notes — 295
Index — 305

Introduction

A small machine shop outside of Los Angeles can't find skilled machinists to make precision parts needed by its customers. A major Boston hospital has excessive turnover in its research operations department, threatening its ability to carry out potentially lifesaving medical research on schedule. Meanwhile, a leading-edge technology company strives to hire and retain experienced sales development specialists to grow revenues from its complex cloud-based products.

If you're an employer, you've probably dealt with similar challenges. There's a shortage of workers you can hire who will stick around and produce at a high level, leaving many entry-level jobs unfilled. Constant turnover puts extra pressure on existing staff who may quit due to burnout. At the same time, the chronic shortage of people needed to fill higher-skilled jobs limits productivity and growth.

Buckle up. This shortage of workers is going to be with us for a long time. The Bureau of Labor Statistics is forecasting about 12 million new jobs in the US by 2030, but predicts only 9 million new entrants coming into the workforce.[1] You do the math.

At a state level, for example, workforce experts in Connecticut say if their state had *0 percent unemployment*, it would still have 22,000 job openings![2] Nationwide, there will be an especially acute shortage of lower-skilled workers for positions not requiring a college degree with about 7 million relevant job openings but only 3 million unemployed individuals without a degree.[3] And please don't assume all these jobs can be handled with artificial intelligence solutions.

In short, there are fewer working-age people participating in the labor force, a declining number of young people entering the workforce, and more aging Baby Boomers retiring. To complicate matters, there will be more jobs requiring special skills training that workers are not prepared for coupled with plenty of low-skill, entry-level jobs people aren't interested in.

Being "Employer of the Year" Won't Be Enough

So, where's the good news—or at least a path forward? Today most companies focus on two solutions for critical workforce shortages. The first is to strive to be the ideal employer and attract reliable talent with great recruiting, onboarding, training, and retention practices. (Spoiler alert: this is an exhausting and virtually impossible task.) The second, which more and more companies are adopting, is to seek technology solutions that automate as many tasks as possible, thereby reducing the need for hard-to-find labor. These solutions seem like logical responses, but they aren't enough to address a shrinking labor pool if your business is going to continue to grow. I suggest there is a third often overlooked solution, one with potentially incredible economic and social payoffs. It looks like this.

Tucker, who is autistic, is an enthusiastic computer numerical controlled (CNC) machinist in that California machine shop, where he produces precision machined parts. Solange, a recent immigrant from the Republic of Congo, is a dedicated research operations technician at Boston Children's Hospital, working long hours to help find life-saving treatments for childhood diseases. Luisa, who spent six years in an Arizona prison, today is a business development specialist, selling cloud-based software for a major tech firm. She spends her days talking to senior IT leaders about complex data management services her company offers, building the sales pipeline to grow the business.

These employees perform hard-to-fill jobs at a high level. But if you're someone with a disability like Tucker, a refugee like Solange, or a job candidate with a criminal record like Luisa, you face major barriers in landing a quality job that pays a living wage.

In fact, the US has an incredible number of adults ages 18 to 65 who have been sidelined, ignored, or marginalized—you pick the term—from the workforce. This group includes the formerly incarcerated, immigrants, and people with disabilities. *(See next section "What Should I Call You?")* **The premise of this book is that many employers can benefit from tapping into one or more of these underused talent pools to fill key jobs or create new talent pipelines for roles with natural turnover.** This book will also help those who have tried hiring from these groups, but would like to do it more effectively. Here are some numbers that show this untapped potential:

The Formerly Incarcerated Are Shut Out of Most Job Opportunities

The current US prison population is a staggering two million inmates, but that is only about one-tenth of the total population of convicted felons in America. Best estimates are that 19 million Americans bear the weight of a felony conviction.[4] **About one in eight men in the US has a felony conviction.** For Black men that number is disproportionately high—almost one in three.[5] These citizens face inordinately difficult obstacles to sustainable employment. Most notably, many companies automatically screen out convicted felons from consideration for employment.

Failing to tap into this potential labor source is both a lost opportunity and has huge costs for society—and individuals. For instance, while states spend a median of about $64,000 annually to house a single prisoner, the cost to the individual is even greater. On average, because they were incarcerated, those with a felony conviction lose an estimated $500,000 in taxable income over a lifetime. While in prison, inmates earn an average of 86 cents an hour, and many of them are not doing work that builds useful skills.[6]

Immigrants, Refugees, or Asylum Seekers Want Opportunities

The United States is home to 46 million immigrants—those not US citizens at birth. Today they comprise more than 14 percent of the total US population—nearly double the proportion of immigrants in 1990 and the highest percentage in over 100 years. The US Census Bureau projects that these percentages will continue to set records in the years ahead, assuming legal immigration levels remain high, an uncertainty in the near term. Although by some estimates, 78 percent of foreign-born labor has legal work status, the employment potential for this group has remained stubbornly underutilized.[7]

And the pool of this talent just continues to grow. Unless you have been living under a rock the last few years, you know that major US cities like New York, Miami, Houston, and Los Angeles have been hit by waves of new asylum seekers who are putting a major strain on city and state budgets. Over two million asylum cases are now pending in US courts. But asylum seekers are eligible for work permits after waiting 180 days, and it could be years before their applications for lawful permanent residence are decided. Of course, the dynamics and the politics of migration are continually evolving. But the consensus is the flow of migrants into the US is not going to stop anytime soon because of increasingly intense wars, natural disasters, crime, and political repression.[8]

People with Disabilities Are Overlooked

More than 11 million working-age adults in the US have disabilities ranging from physical to cognitive limitations. Although people with disabilities have increasingly entered the workforce,[9] only about 41 percent of those who are prime working age (ages 25–54) are currently employed.[10] Another 26 percent are interested in working, and this doesn't count those who have given up looking for work.

Demographic Changes Drive Long-Term Worker Shortages

If you're a leader in almost any organization, you don't need a tutorial about the cause of the chronic labor shortage. But if you want to know more, here are three trends that help explain why the number of US workers looking for jobs is not going to grow in the next decade.

First, not counting retirees, the rate of participation in the US labor force continues its long-term decline. An increasing number of working-age individuals choose not to hold or search for a job for a variety of reasons. This is partly due to the long-term decline in the participation of working-age men in the workforce.[11] In addition, there are 1.7 million fewer workers in the US labor pool than before the COVID-19 pandemic.[12] Some working mothers have struggled to return to work after the COVID pandemic, as preschool childcare has become more expensive and harder to find. And some estimates are that 3 million people chose early retirement because of the pandemic.

Second, the long-term decline in US birth rates means there will be fewer 16- to 24-year-olds entering the workforce in the next 30 years. The birth rate in this country has declined dramatically since the Great Recession in 2007, suggesting the future labor pool will continue to shrink.[13] By the way, the declining fertility rate is a global phenomenon.

Third, the silver tsunami has finally crashed over us. The youngest

> Baby Boomers turn 65 in 2029. Although some will work well beyond age 65, about 75 million Boomers are expected to stop working by 2030. That's 10,000 people a day leaving their jobs for good![14]

What "Good" Looks Like

This is a book of stories and practical advice you can use in your business. *Hidden Talent* shows how other organizations are successfully recruiting, hiring, and retaining the formerly incarcerated, refugees, and workers with disabilities. It is filled with real-life examples of how leaders have developed workers who are key assets to the business.

> **If hiring marginalized workers was easy, every organization would be doing it.**

But more than anything, this book is realistic and practical. If hiring marginalized workers was easy, every organization would be doing it. But it's not simple! Tapping these talent pools takes courage, patience, finesse, and flexibility. The payoffs, however, can be incredible.

When you create employment for a person from one of these marginalized groups, not only are you likely to hire a productive, loyal, high-potential employee, but you're changing that person's life and, possibly, their family's lives. That's why *Hidden Talent* focuses both on the lessons employers have learned from hiring these marginalized workers as well as the stories of those impacted by these jobs. It's a strategy that can be a win for everyone.

Getting the Most Out of This Book

Hidden Talent is the culmination of over two decades of my work helping executives find broader solutions for chronic skill shortages and a changing workforce. This has given me a deep understanding of shifting workforce demographics and the changing skill sets that challenge businesses today. In the process, I've written three books on the rapidly changing talent pool. This book, however, focuses on the opportunity—and challenges—of harnessing the strengths of marginalized workers. *My primary goal with this book is to convince more employers to take a chance on hiring individuals who have traditionally been overlooked or excluded.*

I don't promote a single path for doing this. Since my days as a case writer at Harvard Business School, I've always tried to let stories reveal the lessons we can learn about effective problem-solving in business. The actionable knowledge you take away from this book will come from the stories themselves, which are the result of my interviews with hundreds of business leaders and people whose lives have been changed by innovative hiring programs. On a very personal level, for six years, I've watched my wife's nonprofit organization strive to help young adults—often first-generation immigrants—with a criminal history find jobs and stay employed. I've seen firsthand what a struggle it is for ex-offenders and immigrants to secure and succeed in good jobs.

From a national perspective, my work with the US Chamber of Commerce Foundation has shown me the complexities of regional workforce ecosystems. I've learned what is essential for building successful partnerships between employers and workforce development agencies and other NGOs in solving talent supply problems. I also know how mind-numbing these conversations can be for busy managers. I want to help you short-circuit this complexity.

Hidden Talent has three primary audiences:

- Business leaders will gain insights into new talent strategies that will improve organizational performance. Top executives will also learn about the critical role they must play in these initiatives.

- Human resource and line managers will learn practical lessons to accelerate talent acquisition from refugees, people with disabilities, and the formerly incarcerated. It is particularly relevant for leaders responsible for diversity, equity, inclusion, and belonging (DEI+B) goals in their organization.

- Leaders in nonprofits and workforce development agencies will learn how they can build more productive partnerships with employers to create effective talent pipelines that change the lives of the people they serve.

Read on if you want to be inspired by others who have tackled these challenges to make powerful changes in their organization. And if you don't think you have the resources for these innovative talent solutions, see the box in chapter 15: "*Investing In Marginalized Workers When You Have Limited Time and Resources.*" *Hidden Talent* is organized into four sections. Here is an overview that will help you decide where to start.

This introduction and chapter 1 will orient you on the journey your business could take to address chronic staffing shortages. It will help you decide which parts of the book will be most helpful to get started. It also offers deeper insights into the lived experiences of marginalized workers. Throughout the book, I provide brief stories that reflect the background, motivation, and commitment of individual employees who are either formerly incarcerated, refugees, or people with disabilities. (The names of these individuals have all been disguised to protect their privacy.)

Your organization, however, presents a unique context for leveraging these overlooked assets, given its size and critical staffing needs. You may be in a very large or a tiny organization and situated in an urban, suburban, or rural area. Variables like these heavily influence the number and types of marginalized workers you may want to hire.

Section 1 includes stories and lessons learned from three companies who have gone all in on hiring formerly incarcerated individuals, often called "second-chance hiring." The Body Shop, Precisely, and JBM Packaging are very different businesses that have invested in talent management practices to make second-chance hiring successful. These stories also reveal the challenges businesses must overcome to mine this hidden talent. Chapter 5 summarizes the lessons learned from these companies, while also integrating insights from my other research on hiring the formerly incarcerated.

Section 2 follows a similar pattern highlighting the untapped potential of foreign-born workers. You will learn from the experiences of three organizations—Boston Children's Hospital, Clampco Products, and Main Street Gourmet, who have invested heavily in training and employing immigrants or refugees. Chapter 9 ties together the lessons learned from these initiatives, as well as highlighting significant obstacles to address.

Section 3 reports on organizations that have discovered the advantages of training and hiring workers with disabilities in staffing hard-to-fill roles. Minnesota Diversified Industries, Heartland Systems Corporation, and Classic Wire Cut are three businesses committed to hiring from this overlooked talent pool. Chapter 13 ties together the lessons and unexpected obstacles that must be addressed when leveraging the skills of this often-marginalized group.

Section 4 shares three individual stories to help you reflect on why you would consider these nontraditional hires. One goal is to help fuel a conversation within your organization. The final chapter summarizes the critical success factors that must be managed, along with pitfalls to avoid in the process. The book ends with a detailed review of the business benefits that can come from employing refugees, the formerly incarcerated, and people with disabilities. It is a reminder that this workforce strategy is not charity. This is good for your business.

You can read *Hidden Talent* from start to finish, or choose topics you're particularly interested in. It's up to you. But nothing you read will impact your business performance or culture unless you take action and start doing things differently.

As you will see, other companies are doing it. So can you. Employing historically marginalized workers may be one of the most challenging workforce initiatives you've ever tried. But the rewards can be huge. Let's get started on a journey that can change lives. This could include yours!

AUTHOR'S NOTE ON LANGUAGE

What Should I Call You?

One of the hardest parts of writing *Hidden Talent* was choosing the right labels or terms to describe different types of marginalized workers. There are many ways to characterize people who fit into the three categories of marginalization that are central to this book. Those who identify with these categories or work with people in those categories rightly have strong opinions about the language used.

My intention is not to offend or aggravate anyone. But the primary audience for this book is potential employers, so decisions about what language to use strike a fine balance between honoring the lived experiences of marginalized workers and communicating concisely with busy managers. Still, people have different preferences, and no single term resonated for everyone I spoke with.

For example, people with a criminal record favor different terms, such as formerly incarcerated, former inmates, justice-involved, and returning citizens. These labels are used to describe an individual with a criminal conviction who will most likely be flagged in background checks during the employment process. I will use a mix of these terms, some of which are considered pejorative in some circles and preferred in others. The term

> **"Formerly incarcerated" is a term that everyone seems to understand.**

"justice-involved" will be used frequently, although it will be unfamiliar to some readers. It has become increasingly accepted among those advocating for "second-chance" employment opportunities. "Formerly incarcerated" is a term that everyone seems to understand, which is why I used it in the book's title.

On the other hand, foreign-born workers fall into several different categories influenced by specific legal terminology. The most common confusion is related to the terms immigrants and refugees. In a nutshell, "immigrants" in the US means a person who by choice has relocated permanently to this country, usually for economic reasons, by obtaining a green card, which allows unrestricted employment and can be renewed indefinitely.

"Refugees," however, have been forced to flee their native country to escape persecution, violence, wars, or natural disasters. A related category is "asylum seekers" (or asylees) who apply for resettlement in the US once they are in this country. They, too, are fleeing life threatening situations, but their status as a refugee has not yet been legally determined. Most businesses I studied focused on employing refugees who are more likely to struggle finding work because of language barriers and the time pressure they feel to generate income.

This book does *not* address employment barriers related to undocumented immigrants who lack the legal papers to work in this country. All the stories in *Hidden Talent* refer to people who are legally authorized to reside in the US and to work here.

Note that the label "migrant" has been used a lot in recent years, particularly in the press, as an umbrella term for people who have moved into the US (or other countries). But their immigration status after they arrive and their future plans are unclear. "Migrant" can technically refer to people who move either within their own country or internationally. It is too vague to be useful for employers and will not be used here.[15]

Finally, the world of disabilities is also vast and very complex. Workers with disabilities include individuals with a wide range of impairments that make it more difficult to perform certain activities or to interact with the world around them. Potential job candidates may have a physical disability, such as impaired vision or mobility. Or they may be diagnosed with autism spectrum disorder (ASD) or have an intellectual disability.

The list of potential disabilities is long. Stories in this book focus on employees who have developmental disabilities. I will often use the term "neurodiverse," which is increasingly used to describe people with a range of cognitive conditions or disorders, such as autism spectrum disorder, ADHD, and Down syndrome. The informal term "neurotypical" describes individuals with typical neurological development.[16]

> ...there is wide disagreement within this community about what language to use.

"Person first" is a common theme in discussions of language used to describe people with disabilities. An individual may have a disability, but it should not define them. Thus, I will avoid references like "disabled workers." Nevertheless, there is wide disagreement within this community about what language to use. Ultimately, the purpose of this book is to encourage managers to explore how they might hire and employ people with a wide range of disabilities. Language is continually changing and by the time you read this book, other terms will no doubt be in vogue or widely disparaged.

I use the term "marginalized" throughout the book as a catchall concept for all three groups I studied. Of course, marginalized is often used more broadly to describe much larger segments of the population, such as people of color, those of lower socioeconomic status, and those who identify as LGBTQ. My focus on these smaller more clearly defined talent pools is in no way intended to discount the employment challenges experienced by individuals in these broader groups. It is just that refugees, the formerly incarcerated, and people with disabilities face more conspicuous bias and explicit systemic obstacles to employment.

CHAPTER 1

Starting From Scratch: What Does It Feel Like to Be Marginalized in the Workplace?

Charles was nervous when he came out of that Ohio prison. He knew he was starting from scratch. Living in the halfway house was mandatory at first, and it gave him time to get his state ID and his social security card, things he needed to land a job. The programs focused on job readiness and anger management helped him too.

"Prison was the worst," he says with a nervous laugh. Charles knows he missed out on so much during his three years behind bars: the births of his two nieces, his sister's high school graduation—time with family and the people he cares about most. "Prison wasn't exactly a positive place." He speaks softly about it, as if worn down by the life he had created for himself.

> I did a lot of self-reflecting and soul searching in there. I laid everything out. The past five years of my life had been horrible. I was on drugs in the streets. The lifestyle I was living was nothing but pain every day. I was tired of it. When I went to prison, I knew I had to change. I wanted to go back to living my life positively and doing good things like I knew I could.

After leaving prison, Charles found life in the halfway house frustrating. Some residents were doing drugs. (Halfway houses are notorious for this.) It was noisy, and a few people from Charles's past tried to steer him in the wrong direction. He wasn't indulging in that lifestyle anymore, but he felt stuck, unable to move on. Even with a state ID, who would hire a man with a felony conviction? Recalling what he was feeling at the time, he says, "It's one thing to have a plan and expect to do this and that. But it's really about having patience. Sometimes things take time. I was afraid of losing my cool. But I was determined to surround myself with positive people."

After one interview, Charles thought he had landed a job through a reentry organization in Cincinnati. But then they told him they didn't have any work for him. He didn't know what to think. He had no experience with job searches. Released from the halfway house after four months, he moved in with his girlfriend and started looking for jobs in earnest. He applied for positions on Indeed, the jobs website. The first two weeks were tough. Nothing. Charles was trying to be patient, but he needed money—and a break. He needed an employer who would hire him despite his felony conviction and lack of work experience.

Charles is just one type of job applicant often overlooked by employers. As a former inmate, he faces many obstacles trying to find work after time in prison. He's highly motivated to change. But first he must deal with the penal system, which requires him to live in a stressful halfway house as part of his reentry process. He finished high school but has limited work experience and little practice looking for a job. He has a family that cares about him, but his confidence is fragile. He worries how employers will view his past.

The unemployment rate for the formerly incarcerated is at least 27 percent

More than 600,000 people are released from prison annually in the United States. But within three years, two-thirds will be rearrested and 50 percent reincarcerated.[17] The primary cause of recidivism is a lack of sustainable employment. The unemployment rate for the formerly incarcerated is at least 27 percent, and that doesn't take into account the underemployment of many justice-involved citizens who could be filling much higher-skilled jobs.

**From Bangladesh to Boston:
An Immigrant's Profile in Courage**

Bajra stared in disbelief as she opened the door to her apartment. It was empty. All the furniture was gone. Where would her kids sleep? Where would she sleep?

She had followed her husband to the US from Bangladesh three years ago with their two young children. Three days after she arrived in Boston, he insisted she start working at a local sandwich shop where he knew the owner. Bajra never saw a paycheck. Her husband collected her wages and threatened to get her deported if she complained. One day he left with the furniture.

For the next five years, Bajra worked two jobs to pay the rent and put food on the table. This meant up to 17 hours a day on her feet, first at Dunkin Donuts and then at a local grocery store. She often slept only three hours a night. Her doctor worried she was becoming dangerously thin. This was the price she paid to keep the family going. In the eight years since she'd come to the US, she'd only called out sick once.

Wearing her colorful hijab and a bright smile, Bajra began taking English language classes at Boston Jewish Vocational Service (JVS), hoping this would help her land a job that would sustain her family and her health. English-language proficiency is almost always an obstacle for immigrants, refugees, and asylees seeking work in the US. Other factors like level of education and work experience also come into play, but Bajra had an iron will and an unflappable work ethic. She relentlessly supported her children so that they might achieve a better life.

> ...as the size of the US-born labor pool continues to shrink...more effective recruiting of foreign-born workers becomes essential...

Immigrants, refugees, and asylees have traditionally taken lower-skilled jobs that US-born workers don't want, particularly in the service sector, agriculture, and construction. However, language and transportation are major barriers to sustainable employment. Many skilled immigrants end up seriously underemployed. But, as the size of the US-born labor pool continues to shrink, particularly in lower-skill jobs that resist automation, more effective recruiting and employment of foreign-born workers becomes essential for many businesses.

Stocking Shelves on the Spectrum

Harrison is a smart, talented guy who often speaks in staccato verbal flashes. An actor who loves community theater and music, he's been in over 40 shows, including *Sweeney Todd* and *West Side Story*. Five guitars hang on his bedroom wall at home. A high school graduate, he's articulate, thoughtful, and he smiles a lot.

Harrison is also on the autism spectrum and must manage his bipolar disorder. The only clue to his unique perspective on life comes when he regularly offers a double thumbs up or flashes a V-shaped peace sign—with both hands. You'd think he was running for president!

Despite his upbeat demeanor, Harrison had only worked in grocery stores in his six years after school. He was a bagger at one store, and then a cashier at Sam's Club. He also spent a month on the night shift there from 9:00 p.m. to 5:00 a.m. "That was horrible," he says. "I will never do that in my life ever again. But I got paid, so I couldn't complain."

He also worked in a café before moving to another major grocery chain, first as a bagger, then as a cashier, and then finally as a clerk in the deli and meat department. None of it went well, and Harrison looks at the ground and sounds apologetic when he describes the work experiences of someone on the autism spectrum.

> One thing gave me the most trouble. When someone like my supervisor said, 'Hey, do this,' they expect you to know right away what they want. But those words mean different things to different people on the spectrum. Bosses assume the words they say are what you'll do, like 'Straighten up that display case.' But we can't always understand what people mean by what they say. Oftentimes, in the store, I would do one thing based on the words they said to me, but they meant something different. That irritated them. And I'm confused about why they're mad at me. I thought I was doing what the supervisor asked me to do.

Harrison found complaining customers and screaming children particularly stressful. He needed a work environment that would be less emotionally demanding, where co-workers would patiently help him to understand what needed to get done. He was smart, reliable, anxious to do well, generally upbeat, attentive to detail and definitely underemployed. Harrison was anxious for a change in direction. But he had no idea where to look or where to apply his capabilities.

People with disabilities represent a third talent pool that is often overlooked or ignored by employers. Despite his intelligence, attention to detail, diligence, and dependability, for starters, Harrison requires some accommodations to be fully productive in the workplace. Like Charles and Bajra, he has limited work experience but also an unspoken drive to succeed. In the right setting, he would be a highly motivated and loyal employee.

Unfortunately, most employment opportunities create obstacles for people like Harrison. Statistics related to the employment of those with disabilities are tricky to interpret, but there is general agreement that the unemployment rate for this group is consistently about twice that of those with no disability.[18] Likewise, one advocacy group reported people with a disability and a bachelor's degree are three times less likely to be employed than those without a disability.[19]

Diamonds in the Rough

Of course, not everyone in these marginalized categories will be a good employee. Let's be clear about this. Many people in these groups would *not* be good candidates for jobs you need to fill. But plenty of them can be great employees—jewels—if just given the chance to shine.

The purpose of this book is to help you find candidates from these three talent pools who *can* be fantastic employees. The next section describes the experiences and lessons learned from three employers committed to actively hiring, supporting, and retaining workers who were formerly incarcerated.

SECTION 1
Hiring the Formerly Incarcerated

The next three chapters share the stories of companies committed to employing candidates who have been justice-involved. This section reveals the emotional experiences of investing in second-chance hires. Stories from Precisely, The Body Shop and JBM Packaging will also teach you practical lessons about the role of leadership, the organizational resources required, and the changes needed over time when trying to build a sustainable pipeline of second-chance talent. Chapter 5 looks across the experiences of multiple organizations—and goes deeper—to identify the most common critical success factors for benefiting from this group of marginalized workers.

CHAPTER 2

Precisely: The Education of a Second-Chance Champion

Initiatives that support second-chance hiring require an executive champion, someone with the organizational authority and budget to invest in what many see as a risky and nontraditional source of talent. But what are the requirements and challenges of being a champion? This chapter charts the journey of Brenda Kay, a veteran technology sales executive, who marched into an Arizona woman's prison with low expectations about the capabilities of inmates to sell her company's complex technology products. Over time, she realized how wrong her assumptions were. Kay has become a huge champion for justice-involved women whom she hires into entry-level sales roles at Precisely, the company she works for.

She knew the red power suit was a must. Anything to hide that Brenda Kay was nervous as hell. When you grow up with a father and brother working in law enforcement, you don't develop much empathy for people in prison. As she made her way to a prison 20 miles west of Phoenix, Arizona, Kay expected the worst.

Perryville Women's Prison was the home of Televerde, a sales and marketing organization that provides incarcerated women in five US prisons with telemarketing training to sell complex technology products for companies like SAP, Broadcom, and GE. The company Kay worked for, Pitney Bowes Software and Data (now known as Precisely), had contracted with Televerde to help sell geocoding, geolocation, and address-cleansing software to companies around the US.

But the seven Televerde business development reps (BDRs) weren't making their sales numbers. Three of the seven women were contacting potential customers from a large call center behind bars at Perryville. The other four had started their sales and marketing training while incarcerated and were hired to make calls from the Televerde headquarters in Phoenix upon their release.

Kay was visiting the prison to figure out the reason for the drop in sales. But even with more than 30 years of experience selling complex data software and SaaS solutions to large companies, Kay would never forget that day.

> When I walked in there, I was standing tall and owning it. But inside I was terrified. The whole experience was incredibly intimidating. I came in the door of the call center in the prison, and all the women were lined up in orange jumpsuits. They're in their bays with their headsets on and above their head is the name of the vendor they're supporting. They started taking off their headsets and gravitating towards me. You could tell they were nervous. I pretended I wasn't.
>
> We started to break the ice with simple questions like where I was from. I shared my career background and spoke about the work I had been doing at IBM and now at Pitney Bowes. I also shared personal details about my life, talking about how I was a proud mother and grandmother. They started to open up and tell me things. Then they started asking really good business questions.

This would be the first of many visits Brenda Kay made to the Televerde training center at the Perryville prison. She left the prison knowing that she had to do two things. First, she needed to ensure that her company spent more time properly training the Televerde reps hired to do sales prospecting. But, before that, she immediately called her two grown children. Sitting in the parking lot outside the prison after that first visit, the veteran sales exec fought back tears as she reached her daughter on the phone. Kay's questions poured out: "Was I a good mom? Was I there for you? Was I a good role model? Did I teach you the importance of making good decisions?"

"Mom, what happened in there?" asked her puzzled daughter. "Sounds like they really got to you."

Kay confessed, "There was this little blonde-haired, blue-eyed girl who reminded me of you, and another girl that reminded me of your cousin. My mother and nana feelings were boiling over. I realized, make one bad decision and you get caught—here's where you end up. It was an 'aha' moment for me. There was that emotional response. But the practical side quickly took over. How could I help these women use their skills to succeed in business outside of prison?"

Over the next year and a half, the armor of Kay's power suits and carefully coiffed hair became less important. She visited the Televerde operation many times, training and coaching the inmates to be more effective business development reps. She explains:

> We knew we had a problem developing promising sales leads and had to improve our processes. I found some training issues during my visits to the prison. The products being sold were complicated and we weren't giving our BDRs the right tools to effectively sell to clients or prospects.

Kay went into fix-it mode. She set up a new training process that helped the sales team in prison better articulate the value proposition of the solutions they were pitching. Soon the team at Televerde was showing results that were clearly increasing sales. But once that problem was solved, Kay wanted to stay involved and work even more closely with the women at Perryville. She was convinced that these inmates selling for different companies from call centers located behind bars had great potential when they left prison. She recalls her change of heart:

> When I went into Perryville in my red power suit, I didn't expect such rigor, disciplined process execution, strong metrics, and spectacular training. I really had to step back and check my assumptions. After going into the prison a few times, I got to know the ladies and built relationships with them. I did a lot of listening and asked a ton of questions.
>
> Once they got comfortable with me, they started telling me their stories and asking me for career advice and guidance. Clearly, there was mutual respect. I think they respected me as a businesswoman and as a mother. I respected them for what they had gone through, their perseverance, and how they were trying to change their lives. These women have amazing skills and are very smart. I wanted to help give them the second chance they deserved.

Finding Talent Behind Bars to Create a New Sales Organization

Organizational changes are inevitable. The software and data division of Pitney Bowes was acquired by another company and rebranded as Precisely. During the acquisition, all contracts with the Televerde sales operation were terminated. Kay lost her regular connections with the call centers at Perryville. But when she was named global senior vice president of business development, her new boss at Precisely had a challenging assignment for her. CEO Josh Rogers wanted Kay to create a new organization of 40 business development reps to feed the sales pipeline for the company's data integrity solutions.

Recruiting and training dozens of new staff was a tall order. The BDR role is essential for finding and engaging new clients, and it is a high-pressure job. It can pay well but, depending on the employer, can also burn employees out. BDRs must have great communication and organizational skills, the ability to build relationships quickly, and tremendous perseverance. Because they are in high demand across the technology industry, turnover is also a problem. Skilled BDRs often leave for other opportunities that pay slightly more. Finding qualified candidates and keeping this role filled with high-performing talent is a real challenge.

Televerde: The Path to a Second Chance

At the heart of Televerde's mission is a prison-to-workforce development program that has trained and employed close to 4,000 incarcerated women over 25 years. Televerde provides global call center outsourcing capabilities, partnering with companies such as SAP, Microsoft, Adobe and GE, to increase their volume of B2B sales leads, growing the sales pipeline. By providing education, job training and support, Televerde helps women in prison build skills that support meaningful careers when they re-enter their communities. This nonprofit works with the departments of corrections in Arizona, Florida, and Indiana, providing eight sophisticated call centers behind prison walls. And they're looking to expand to other states.[20]

Most organizations use prison labor for jobs they can't otherwise fill, such as picking up trash or to get labor at greatly reduced costs. But the women selected to participate in Televerde's prison program are compensated fairly and receive extensive on-the-job training in sales and marketing, business acumen, and the latest in-demand marketing technologies. After leaving prison, more than 90 percent of Televerde's graduates advance into professional career positions in sales, marketing, and technology fields.

Televerde helps those who have been incarcerated become thriving, skilled employees post-release. Other notable programs include the Last Mile, Prison Entrepreneurship Program, and Persevere Now.[21] Check your area to see if these and similar organizations can help you change lives while meeting your staffing goals.

Five Obstacles to Hiring Second-Chance Talent

Kay's experience at the Perryville prison gave her an idea of how to address her staffing problem: she would hire Televerde graduates who had finished their prison sentences. Since being released from prison, many were now working in Televerde's sales headquarters based in Phoenix. To hire those with a criminal record, Kay needed to overcome five obstacles:

1. Gain the support of the senior leadership team for the initiative.
2. Convince qualified Televerde graduates to apply for the BDR job openings at Precisely.
3. Design onboarding to meet the needs of second-chance new hires.
4. Provide extra support for challenges outside of work.
5. Be flexible enough to manage unexpected surprises.

1. Selling Senior Leadership

Kay met with CEO Josh Rogers, who had asked her to build the BDR organization. They needed people who could get up and running quickly to sell a complex portfolio of products. Kay reminded Rogers that she had seen firsthand the skills and work ethic of the women in the Televerde program at Perryville. Then she pitched the CEO:

> I want to hire Televerde grads who are out of prison to give them a second chance. Just let me offer them the opportunity to compete for a BDR job. They'll have to get through a pretty intense hiring process, interview with the hiring manager, then do a panel interview with my sales managers. If they make it that far, they still have to interview with me before they get an offer.

Kay told the CEO there would be challenges as they integrate Televerde graduates into Precisely's corporate structure. She knew they were going to have problems with background checks. The corporate environment could also be a challenge for second-chance hires. Kay ended her pitch saying, "We have a shot, Josh, at making a real difference in these women's lives."

Precisely's CEO took two seconds to respond, saying, "I'm with you on this. Talk to Lisa Crawford, [Chief Human Resource Officer at Precisely], and let's make it happen."

With Rogers's backing, Kay also quickly got the head of Human Resources on board. The sales managers were a different story. She told them, "We're going to try this, and I need you with me."

Predictably, some managers were skeptical. "Are you crazy?" was a common response.

But Kay knew that attitude would change once managers saw the new BDRs' product knowledge and sales prospecting skills.

2. Convince Formerly Incarcerated Candidates to Apply for the Jobs

Once Precisely's BDR jobs were posted, she contacted Televerde graduates who might be good candidates. She asked them to spread the word. But Kay underestimated the challenge of convincing these women to apply. The response was always the same. "I won't pass the background check!"

Kay reassured them she would take care of that. But they first had to compete for a job. Like every applicant, Televerde graduates had to come in ready to sell Precisely's managers on their skills in a convincing job interview.

Some were too nervous to apply. Others jumped at the opportunity. Televerde applicants got no breaks. When candidates applied, they had to follow the company's standard hiring process: fill out a job application online, then pass muster in an interview with a recruiter. Some never applied. Others applied and didn't make the cut. But when one of the Televerde grads was hired, the initiative suddenly gained momentum. "I don't know who was more nervous, me or her," Kay recalls. She'd stuck her neck out for this program. It had to work.

Along the way, there were difficult moments. Hiring second-chance individuals can create unexpected obstacles that demand creative responses. When they went to hire one particular candidate, the Televerde graduate's background check revealed a warrant out for the applicant's arrest. Most recruiters would have dropped the case right there. Instead, the HR manager—who knew this would be an issue—reached out to Kay to find out more.

"There's no way there's a warrant for her arrest," Kay told her. "She's been released from prison. She's meeting with her parole officer. They would have picked her up. They know where she is. I'm telling you; the paperwork didn't get filed. They just didn't close out the warrant."

The HR manager dug deeper and found that the warrants had been issued in a small county nearby. By contacting the office directly, HR confirmed that the court and police had never updated their records. A local official quickly closed out the warrant and cleared the record. It was no longer a barrier to employment.

"Do you know what would have happened to that young woman if she had gotten pulled over, even for a simple parking ticket?" Kay asked me during our interview. "A lot of companies would have walked away from that candidate as soon as the arrest warrant was flagged. But our HR team went above and beyond to get the problem fixed by city hall. And that candidate was hired."

Of course, not every applicant from Televerde succeeded. Some sent unpolished resumes or showed up for interviews unprepared and not ready to sell themselves. Kay explains why some candidates weren't hired:

> They didn't know the basics. They couldn't talk about what Precisely did or tell us what their strengths and their weaknesses were, or even why we should hire them. When we asked several applicants for questions, they didn't have anything to ask us. I mean, when you're applying for a sales role, you're in "sell mode." But they weren't closing us during the interview. We also waited for thank you notes after the interview. If we didn't get one, we took them off the list.

3. Adapt Onboarding Processes for Second-Chance Hires

Because there is so much to learn, it takes Precisely 90 days to get new BDRs onboarded and sufficiently trained to begin pursuing meetings on their own with clients or prospects. The goal is to convert these initial meetings into a sales opportunity that a more experienced account executive will then handle. Ironically, the applicants from Televerde were better trained than most new hires. Kay was surprised at how quickly Valerie, the first hire from Televerde, sailed through the onboarding process. She was already familiar with Precisely's products, and she was working on her own within two months.

> **Within a year, Kay's team had hired nine business development reps from the pool of talent that had been trained behind bars.**

With Valerie's success, word spread among Televerde grads that Precisely was a real opportunity. New hires would talk to their old colleagues and tell them about the job's benefits: a good base salary plus commission, paid time off, health care benefits, a 401K, and so on. This was a level of compensation these women had never experienced.

Slowly, grads started referring each other and encouraging colleagues to apply. Within a year, Kay's team had hired nine business development reps from the pool of talent that had been trained behind bars. But these second-chance hires needed other types of support when they joined Precisely's sales team.

Valerie's Story: Making the Best of a Bad Situation

Valerie was the oldest of seven children and she was always the problem solver in her family. "Let Valerie fix it," was the family saying. She would figure it out. Until one day she couldn't.

Years passed, and as a mother of five young children, Valerie found herself in an abusive marriage. Her partner, who would disappear for days, had multiple affairs and had friends who threatened Valerie and her children. She feared for their safety and had to get away. But she couldn't show the world she was falling apart. She was the dependable one, the person who could fix anything. But she had no idea what to do. As a working mother with kids to feed and a nightmare of a husband, she made an impulsive decision.

At her accounting job, she stole from her employer, adding money to her payroll check. Things quickly got worse. Before she knew it, Valerie had lost her job and was sentenced to prison, separating her from her children and family. The woman who could solve everyone else's problems no longer had any answers.

Finding a New Path

Landing at the Perryville women's prison, Valerie put her head down and worked, first as a kitchen helper. She often took on two shifts, working from 4:00 a.m. to 7:00 p.m. She knew that despite her love of numbers, no one would ever hire her for accounting work because of her felony conviction. Still, she was determined to leave prison with skills she could use to rebuild her life.

Valerie was accepted into Televerde's sales and marketing training program after three years at Perryville. After months of training, she sat at a computer workstation in the prison, developing new business leads on the phone five days a week for major firms like SAP and Pitney Bowes.

One day the Televerde call center had a visitor. Brenda Kay, senior vice president of sales for Pitney Bowes, sat next to Valerie to watch her work. For many nerve-racking minutes, Valerie tried to concentrate on the task at hand, as Kay listened in on her calls. Kay seemed impressed. Hope kindled in Valerie. Brenda Kay might be a lifeline to future employment.

Who Knows My Story?

Valerie had something to prove."I'd seen so many women leave Perryville and then come right back to prison. Part of the redemption process for me was to come out of prison and be a success story."

Shortly after she was released, Valerie tugged on her lifeline and applied to Precisely, Kay's new company, for an entry-level sales development position. Even though Brenda Kay knew Valerie's capabilities, she still had to go through the full interview process like other candidates. Valerie worried how the conversation would go with managers who didn't know her story.

"I hadn't interviewed in years! How do I sell myself to someone who has no idea about me and my past? And when they see Televerde on my resume, are they going to research it and see its mission is to work with women in prison? That was my fear."

The first time she applied to Precisely they chose another candidate. She started questioning herself: "What did I do? What should I not have said?"

But Valerie persisted. Another job was posted and, finally, an offer came through to start as a business development rep. Today, Valerie is thriving at Precisely, and one day she hopes to lead a team of sales reps to share what she has learned.

Admitting Mistakes and Building Confidence

Valerie will tell you the most important benefit of her job has been the impact on her family and her relationships with her children. Once again, she can provide for others, which includes four daughters and a son. She says: "This job has been a great confidence builder because I know what I'm capable of doing. And for management to see what I'm capable of and for them to trust that I'm managing my book of business in the right way—that's huge."

Valerie has thought deeply about her prison experience, saying:

"There are those of us who know we made a mistake. And we're mentally strong enough to be able to acknowledge that, but not sit in it. We admit it, but we're determined not to be defined by that. We want to do everything humanly possible to not go back to prison. We learned our lesson the first time."

Protect Confidentiality: Whose Story Is It to Tell?

One of the challenges Kay anticipated was protecting the privacy of BDR new hires with a criminal record. From the beginning, she told new hires that nobody except the management team knew anything about their past. "We're not telling your story to anyone," she said. "If you want to, that's your decision. But it's your story to tell."

> **"We're not telling your story to anyone. …It's your story to tell."**

Kay presented the opportunity at Precisely as a fresh start. Her goal was to build the self-esteem of her new BDRs.

As it turned out, most account executives for whom the BDRs worked were just happy to have a productive sales colleague feeding their pipeline with qualified leads. Kay recalls:

> When we hire someone, we say, 'This is your BDR. Their name is…and they're going to cover your territory. They're trained and ready to go.' That's it. Basically, we didn't make a big deal about it. The account executives working with these BDRs were thrilled with their performance. What they saw was the skill set they were getting. Some BDRs have since told their account executives their story. Others, to this day, still don't know. And I don't think it matters one bit.

Address Challenges of Working from Home

Precisely has a remote-first work culture, with most employees operating from home full time. When Kay began Precisely's second-chance hiring program, she hadn't worked in an office for more than 17 years. Likewise, new hires would have to demonstrate they had the discipline needed to work remotely. They didn't have a local office available to them, and it wasn't all smooth sailing, Kay confessed:

> In the beginning, we had some issues with onboarding new BDRs because they got easily distracted at home. We had challenges with meetings that were being missed,

BDRs that weren't adequately prepared for calls, and reps showing up not dressed appropriately for client meetings. These issues were dealt with swiftly as they arose, but there was a definite learning curve as the team adjusted to a new way of working.

Be Explicit About Performance Standards and Career Paths

Kay's sales managers became huge supporters of second-chance hiring. But this wasn't always the case. As a champion of the program, she initially had to educate her managers on the positives of this hiring approach, while staying transparent about the potential challenges.

"In some cases, I had to say, 'This is going to be tough. It's a different kind of hire for you and me. We can work through this together with communication and teamwork. I need you with me on this. But understand these BDRs must perform and make their numbers.'"

Kay knew opportunities for growth and promotion would be critical for the long-term success of Precisely's second-chance initiative. New hires, especially second-chance hires, need to see others getting promoted so they know it is possible. New employees can progress to more senior BDR roles, then onto an inside sales role before potentially becoming an account executive. This job progression is the same for everyone on the team. Kay ensured BDRs had a promising career path at Precisely if they kept making their sales goals—and at least one second-chance employee has made it all the way to an inside sales job within three years.

4. Provide Extra Support for Challenges Outside of Work

We all face time-consuming and sometimes emotionally challenging issues in our non-work lives, but having a criminal record creates an extra layer of difficulties. Second-chance hires often face obstacles outside of the workplace that can undermine their ability to stay employed, including finding housing.[22]

For the first time in her career, Kay found herself taking calls from landlords who wanted information about her new BDRs—and not just the basic, "Is this person employed at your company?"

Instead, landlords were looking for a detailed reference: "We did a background check, and I understand she was in prison. I'm not sure about this. Can I really trust this person?"

Kay quickly learned the weight of her employees' felony convictions, even when a Televerde graduate had been employed for a year and earned a good salary, their transition into an apartment or buying a car could still be very stressful.

On top of this, many of the women who Precisely hired from Televerde had children who were taken care of by others while they were in prison. Now those women had to go through the process of trying to regain custody. Kay says:

> People say to leave your personal life at home. That doesn't happen. As I tell my team, we're all human beings. People bring their personal lives to work. Sometimes, employees have a lot of personal issues all going on at once. These women were fighting to get their kids back, struggling to get into an apartment or buy a home, and still trying to make their sales numbers. You must be prepared to be there for them in all aspects.
>
> Believe me, I've got our employee assistance program number on speed dial. Because sometimes they need counseling, and I'm not a counselor. I know my limits. My managers are very smart, caring people. If they run into a roadblock, they'll come to me, and we'll see if we can help fix the problem or provide guidance. If not, we help them access the professional help they need.

5. Be Flexible Enough to Manage Unexpected Surprises

Hiring women who had been justice-involved has created some unanticipated challenges. Kay has had to remind her sales managers that their new BDRs might need extra coaching on how to handle certain work situations and tasks that often get taken for granted—such as guidance on dressing professionally or creating an expense report.

Soon after they started work, Kay wanted to send several BDRs on out-of-town trips to industry trade shows to make contacts and learn more about their products and customers. She confesses she didn't anticipate that these women wouldn't have credit cards. (Prison doesn't exactly boost your credit rating.) Additionally, some reps had no experience flying, much less navigating airports. Kay and her managers had to help BDRs from Televerde work through these obstacles, including booking their hotels, helping to submit expense reports, and providing travel guidance.

Kay was particularly proud of the fact that out of 40 BDRs, two of her top performers this year are second-chance hires from the Televerde program. This qualified them to attend special annual sales meetings, inevitably held in some cool foreign resort. Suddenly, personal passports became a work issue. Kay recalls, "There are steps these women are required to take to get a passport that are different than the steps that the rest of us take. We got it all worked out, but it's things like that you don't initially think through."

Benefits of the Second-Chance Initiative

It's been a few years since Brenda Kay's first visit to that prison in the desert west of Phoenix. Her company's decision to pursue talent from the pool of justice-involved women has had benefits that surpassed her expectations.

First, Precisely has had lower turnover among BDRs. In a job that often sees 30 percent turnover industry-wide, Precisely has less than 8 percent of its BDRs leaving in a year. These entry-level sales jobs are notoriously hard to fill. They require strong communication skills, perseverance, and the ability to master complex products. Decreasing turnover creates tremendous cost savings by cutting recruiting and onboarding expenses. It also reduces the impact of lower performance among new BDRs who are less experienced in selling the company's products.

Precisely's second-chance hires have been among the highest-performing members of the sales organization. Two of the three most productive BDRs in 2022 were Televerde graduates. "And they didn't just barely qualify as top performers," Kay says. "They blew their sales goals out of the water."

Justice-involved employees at Precisely have also created their own kind of quality control in recruiting for BDR jobs. "The nine women that have worked for me from Televerde are very guarded about encouraging others to apply to the company," says Kay. "They think they've been given a spectacular opportunity—a second chance—by Precisely, and they don't want anybody to screw that up."

Another benefit of the program is that it has actively supported Precisely's commitment to diversity, equity, inclusion, and belonging by increasing the racial, ethnic, and socioeconomic diversity of the salesforce.

Kay likes to tell a story that illustrates the intangible benefits of giving people a second chance. Maria, one of Kay's BDR team, had recently met with CEO Josh Rogers.

Maria said she had told Josh, "You changed my life. I have a home. I got my kids back. I have a car. I love this company. And I'm gonna stay here for life. I just want you to personally know that." And the

CEO got emotional. Then she paused and said to Kay, "Maybe I shouldn't have told him all that."

"No, that's fine," said Kay. "You talked from your heart. You didn't go in with an agenda like most people do with CEOs. You just told your story, and he wasn't prepared for you to look at him and say, 'You changed my life.'"

CHAPTER 3

The Body Shop and the Power of Open Hiring

Like all retailers, The Body Shop, an iconic beauty brand, had struggled to staff its stores and distribution centers in recent years. In keeping with its non-conforming culture, in 2020 the company rolled out a radical staffing practice known as Open Hiring. This approach dramatically reduced the company's recruiting and hiring costs, while creating opportunities for many populations traditionally ignored as a viable part of the US labor pool, including second-chance hires. Unlike Precisely, which sought out well-trained candidates, The Body Shop's Open Hiring initiative targeted entry-level candidates who could learn the necessary skills while on the job. This innovative approach upended many traditional human resources practices, but as leaders at The Body Shop discovered, the payoffs can be tremendous. Unfortunately, major changes in the retail industry led the company to cease operations in the US in 2024. They continue to use Open Hiring practices in their UK operations. Companies like IKEA have also begun experimenting with the practice. Lessons from The Body Shop's experience are still highly relevant.

Jennifer Crespo, manager of a Body Shop store in Fort Lauderdale, Florida, awaited the arrival of her newest employee. It was Victor's first day, and when he entered The Body Shop, he was carrying a huge backpack. Jennifer greeted him and found a place to store his backpack, then asked if he could bring a smaller bag tomorrow. The store's employee lockers couldn't hold Victor's large bag. Looking down at his sneakers, Victor mumbled, "I don't have a place to stay. Everything I own is in that backpack." Jennifer didn't know what to say. Welcome to the world of Open Hiring.

In an era when labor shortages threaten business performance and recruiting costs are through the roof, Open Hiring is a counterintuitive approach to staffing. New hires are simply offered a position in order of their application date. The first person to apply is the first person to get the opportunity—no resume, job interview, background check, or drug test required. In practice, this creates opportunities for many people who have a criminal record, but Open Hiring also benefits those experiencing homelessness, survivors of domestic abuse, recovering substance abusers, and people from other marginalized groups.

Open Hiring, from an employer's viewpoint, translates to reduced recruitment expenses and greater exposure to an extensive range of potential talent. However, hiring individuals who are usually excluded from standard hiring procedures presents additional difficulties. The Body Shop, a global company specializing in cosmetics and skincare products, had to overcome these obstacles to implement this innovative approach effectively.

In late 2019, The Body Shop piloted Open Hiring in a centralized distribution warehouse in North Carolina. The goal was to remove barriers to employment by aligning staffing practices with the company's mission: "to fight for a fairer, more beautiful world." (Remember, they're in the business of making people feel and look better, so this vision isn't as fluffy as it might sound.) The COVID pandemic in 2020 made it even more difficult to hire and retain entry-level staff in distribution centers and retail stores. The Body Shop needed a different approach that aligned with its mission and helped meet its staffing needs. Leaders at The Body Shop had to overcome four challenges to build a company that could effectively recruit, train, and employ traditionally marginalized job candidates.

- **Confront employee bias**
- **Design an effective pilot project**
- **Learn to decode the different needs of marginalized workers**
- **Reinvent training to support diversity**

1. Confront Biases and Win Employee Support

As head of HR at The Body Shop's US distribution center, Jennifer Wale (not the Jennifer at the Fort Lauderdale store) had to sell management on Open Hiring. She had to convince her colleagues Open Hiring wasn't some crazy idea that would create chaos in the warehouse. Wale wanted the senior management team in New York, local leaders in North Carolina, warehouse managers, as well as frontline workers to fully understand the Open Hiring concept and the changes it would bring to the company.

> "What if we're working next to a convicted felon?"

Make Time to Discuss Biases at All Levels of the Organization

One key turned out to be letting managers and employees voice their initial concerns when the concept was first introduced. Nick Carney, a manager in the distribution center, recalls:

> In the first rollout, people started asking what does this mean for the team? Each level of the organization was briefed on what Open Hiring was and they had a chance to talk about their initial feelings. What about safety? What if we're working next to a convicted felon who's murdered someone? Are we gonna have more theft?

The company was doing background checks and drug screens at that time, and managers still had to deal with personnel challenges. Theft and substance use in the workplace weren't the norm, but it happened, nonetheless. Slowly, Carney's team started asking, "So what's the difference?" He explains:

> First we just allowed people to talk about their feelings, to put their fears out there. Then, we sense-checked those concerns to see how they were different from the current process. That's how we leveled with ourselves.

Carney also thought back to his previous job in the warehouse of a big box store.

> We used to get complaints that we hired just young people into entry-level positions. We weren't getting anyone with any experience. And I wondered if some of this had to do with the fact that we were screening out people who had lived and learned. They're not even getting a chance. So all we're doing is dealing with inexperienced people who haven't made a mistake and gotten caught yet. I asked our team, "Wouldn't you rather have somebody who's had a little life experience versus people who don't know any better and haven't yet stepped into all the traps life provides?"

Clarify Expectations: Performance Standards Don't Change

Carney initially thought Open Hiring would flood them with lower-quality job candidates. What would that mean for performance and productivity in the warehouse? Was it going to decline?

Wale, the distribution center's HR leader, insisted performance wouldn't falter because of Open Hiring. "None of the performance measures were changing. The only difference is we're giving these open hires a fair shot. They're still obligated to meet our business performance standards. And they're held to the same level of accountability as everyone else on the team."

Wale was proven right—and then some. The Body Shop distribution center set productivity records during a peak rush season when the warehouse routinely got swamped with orders to process. Some of that performance improvement arose from changes to the company's fulfillment process. Equally important were efforts to cross-train new hires to perform more difficult tasks soon after they start working. Carney, now fully on board with Open Hiring, said, "I tell my team all the time, how proud I am of them and what a great job they do."

Confronting assumptions about performance was a key step in introducing Open Hiring. Recruiting previously marginalized job candidates didn't mean the company had to lower its expectations about job performance. Sure, it might mean some changes to training and onboarding. But that would be good for all employees.

Leverage Best Practices: Cooking up Lessons from Greyston Bakery

"Because Open Hiring is such a radical concept," Wale says, "we knew it would be helpful to show our employees firsthand what this program would entail and what success would look like."

The Body Shop benefited greatly by learning from Greyston Bakery, a pioneer in Open Hiring. Based in Yonkers, New York, Greyston produces millions of pounds of baked goods annually for customers like Ben and Jerry's and Whole Foods Market.[23] They have used this approach to staffing for years while building a successful business with 70 Open Hire employees. And, hey, they make all the brownies used in Ben & Jerry's ice cream flavors so you know they're doing something right. Representatives from Greyston visited the distribution center in North Carolina, shared their story, and showed how the Open Hiring process could work, while still maintaining high expectations about performance. "Hearing Greyston's story firsthand helped our employees understand Open Hiring beyond initial biases and the positive effect it could have on expanding our potential talent pool," Wale says.

The Body Shop's leaders knew they couldn't change the organization's culture by simply announcing they were going to start hiring people who previously would have been excluded. Introducing a new staffing approach takes time. Giving managers and employees a chance to express and talk through their feelings was a key step. Reluctance didn't mean "no way." It's just part of the change process.

Learning from other early adopters is a valuable tactic. Businesses that have succeeded at employing marginalized workers have tremendous credibility, so finding companies to learn from should be a top priority. The Body Shop was rolling out Open Hiring across its international operations, so they viewed early initiatives in retail stores and the distribution center as pilot projects.

2. Design an Effective Pilot

Viewing these efforts as learning experiences is important because there's no one-size-fits-all approach to Open Hiring. Factors such as organization size and the number of jobs to be filled impact the rollout of Open Hiring initiatives. The Body Shop did three things to make their pilots successful learning experiences.

Initially, the effort in both the distribution center and retail stores focused on hiring seasonal workers in the late fall to support the holiday rush. Once it proved viable, The Body Shop made Open Hiring its permanent recruitment model for all entry-level hires in retail stores and distribution centers in North America. The program has since expanded to The Body Shop UK and Australia. The success of this program began with the pilot stage, where they received valuable manager feedback, established recruiting partnerships, and were prepared to address mistakes.

Learn What Managers Need to Be Successful

Jennifer Crespo, The Body Shop store manager in Ft. Lauderdale, initially felt ill-equipped to understand the needs of her homeless employee and others facing challenges outside of work. With the influx of Open Hires who were facing barriers to employment that she hadn't confronted before, Crespo and her colleagues told leadership that managers needed additional training. The company used this feedback to create new resources to help leaders manage a more diverse workplace. The pilot also identified additional training needs for new employees, which are described later in this chapter.

Find Strong Partners to Support Targeted Recruiting

The Body Shop's distribution center regularly had to scale operations from 60 full-time employees up to 265 during peak season. To expand the pool of eligible talent, management worked with local nonprofit partners to ensure that people who are frequently overlooked for employment opportunities were aware of job openings at the distribution center.

Wale, the distribution center's HR leader, explains, "To foster greater equity and inclusivity, we're not necessarily focused on a certain 'type' of candidate—but rather any individual who would be disqualified because of their lack of previous experience or inability to pass a background check or drug test."

The warehouse management team worked with a staffing agency and one local nonprofit, Wake Local Reentry Council, which serves formerly incarcerated individuals, to help create a pipeline of ready-to-hire seasonal workers. "Partners like Wake LRC," Wale says, "have the expertise to help us understand what people transitioning back to the community truly need to feel supported in the workplace. Open Hiring gives people an opportunity to work, but support from our key partners helps them get the extra care needed to succeed."

When piloting Open Hiring in its retail stores, management wanted to attract applicants from marginalized communities facing barriers to employment, not just anyone in search of a job. To meet this goal, The Body Shop mandated targeted recruitment for 15 stores in the US. Those stores worked with local nonprofit partners who serve the needs of particularly marginalized populations, such as the formerly incarcerated, immigrants, and those experiencing homelessness. Cindy Alcantara, inclusive hiring manager for the company's retail stores, explains:

> We learned many of the people in these marginalized communities don't know positions exist in our stores because they don't have the resources or means to search for jobs. Working with NGOs, who work with these communities, was vital to connecting with these people.

Expect to Stumble and Learn

In retrospect, The Body Shop management could have done plenty of things differently if they had known what Open Hiring would mean when it was implemented. Commenting on the distribution center's experience, Wale notes:

> As soon as we began the pilots, Open Hiring made us look at everything we thought was the right way to handle human resources and recruitment and pre-employment screenings. The way that we're hiring now is so different from the traditional mindset of how you bring in talent.

So if our leaders weren't fully on board and willing to stumble a bit, then it would have been really difficult to succeed because the implementation can't be perfect.

Knowing what they know now, they might have set up a system to identify the challenges their new hires faced outside of work, such as housing and transportation. They could have equipped line managers and supervisors with tools to better manage the needs of new hires from the get-go. To encourage more individuals from marginalized groups to apply, the company could have targeted its recruiting sooner in some markets. Finally, they could have adapted other human resource practices faster to support Open Hiring. Instead, these changes came later when the company ran into problems and learned to adapt.

3. Decode the Different Needs of Marginalized New Hires

Depending on the business context, Open Hiring is likely to require flexible approaches for training and job design for a more diverse workforce. One part of Nick Carney's continuous improvement efforts in the distribution center was reinventing training processes so the team would be ready to handle the peak rush as the holiday season approached. Some of these changes involved training new hires in more complicated tasks that required scanning an online order, packing the box, and producing a shipping label.

Soon after implementing the new training, Carney met with a new hire who confided that he had a learning disability. Harold boasted about his regular participation in the Special Olympics. He also confessed he was not sure he could process E-commerce orders using a computer, which was his first assignment. "I'll try to learn it. But to be honest," said Harold, "I'm not going to be good at doing this. If you see I'm not doing it right, and there are other positions I might be better at, please give me a chance."

The supervisor quickly recognized this initial job was not the right fit for Harold, but not because Harold wasn't trying. He was always on time and ready to work. So they kept him on and trained him in a role that didn't require the use of a computer. Once Harold knew what to do, he just focused on his job picking products in the warehouse. Carney recalls:

> Talk about somebody who was grateful when we took him off that first job and said, 'Okay, that didn't work. Let's try this.' He was thrilled! Harold got recognized one day during peak season in a meeting. They gave him a VIP T-shirt and he got to choose a motivational button. He picked one that said "Team Player." He wore that button proudly on his vest every day.

Why Psychological Safety Is Essential

Not every new hire is as forthcoming as Harold about what they need to succeed. A new employee may have been formerly incarcerated or have a learning disability—or both. The Body Shop management recognized that, in addition to helping those employees overcome or mitigate their personal challenges, the company had to create enough psychological safety for workers to feel comfortable sharing what they needed to be successful.[24] After all, people were now being hired after answering three simple questions:

- Are you authorized to work in the US?
- Can you lift 25 pounds?
- Can you stand on your feet for eight hours?

This meant The Body Shop managers knew nothing about their new hire's situation outside of work. It is not hard to imagine new employees would feel uncomfortable revealing their needs outside of work. Wale recalls:

At first, we had no idea how to engage in conversations around what support they might need to succeed at work. Do you have a way to get here? Do you have somebody to look after your kids? We weren't asking the questions we thought were uncomfortable. You know, like do you have a home to go to?

We also weren't asking about their criminal background. For instance, if somebody had a court date or they had to see their parole officer, they weren't telling us. They just didn't show up for work. And suddenly we're wondering, 'Where did he go? He was doing so good.' And then the guy just no-showed on Thursday. Because there was no psychological safety to come up and say, 'Jen, I'm going to court.'

Create a Culture to Discover Employee Needs

The Body Shop management did three things to create a culture where employees would feel more comfortable sharing their needs outside of work.

First, leadership made sure managers in the distribution center had a clear understanding of the goals, benefits, and overall impact of Open Hiring. The company made sure supervisors understood *why* it was so important to foster more open communication with their staff. This meant that conversations around attendance, quality of work, etc. became tailored to the individual and their specific situation. "Employees who feel supported and trusted are much more likely to reciprocate and be more open with their supervisor," Wale says. "They understand that their specific needs will be handled fairly and balanced along with the needs of the business."

Second, each new hire orientation in the distribution center began with the manager providing an overview of expectations about workplace conduct to level the playing field for all workers. Wale explains, "Expectations for employees remain the same, whether they came in through the Open Hiring process or not. Everyone is expected to uphold The Body Shop policies while also carrying out their roles and responsibilities properly."

Finally, new hires were told that management can't assist them with their unique needs if they don't share the challenges they may face while working at The Body Shop. Wale adds:

> Sometimes it takes a new employee months to understand that this company actually cares about them. That means you need supervisors open to saying, 'Hey, if you need time off, just tell us.' In fact, it's pretty normal that somebody who's working on reentry is going to have situations come up where they're going to miss work. It's so much better if they can be open with us and tell us so we can plan for them to be off. We didn't know how to communicate and talk about this stuff before. Now people feel safer talking about these things, and it's much more accepted.

Build Processes for Sharing Needs Outside of Work

Despite the above efforts, feedback from the Open Hiring pilot showed the company needed a process to identify obstacles that might undermine new hires' ability to stay on the job. Working with feedback from their line managers, as well as input from Greyston Bakery, Cindy Alcantara, the company's Inclusive Hiring Manager for North America, created what the company calls a "joyful collective" form. (This is a term used in the company's Purpose-Driven Leadership Training which is taken by all store managers.)

This form invites every new hire to share a little bit about themselves, if they want to, so the company can learn more about them as an individual. Part of the form also encourages workers to tell the company about their current needs, whether it is housing, financial literacy training, help with transportation, and so on. This confidential information is forwarded to HR managers, who chat with employees and provide them with employee assistance information to support them. Alcantara explains:

> Developing this form so we can get a heads up on what would support new employees better is super important. We've learned through trial and error that there's another level of support some of our open hires need. The most important thing is that new employees now have someone who is going to contact them one-on-one just to check on them and what they need. But it's been a process. We've had to learn what the full spectrum of employee support looks like.

4. Reinvent Training to Support Diversity

Historically, The Body Shop tried to hire people with retail experience for their stores. But with Open Hiring they've taken on people with zero experience. Management quickly recognized a difference in how new entry-level customer consultants approached their job. New hires who had never worked in a retail environment didn't know how to stock a shelf or what to do when a customer came into the store. To address this, The Body Shop developed new training courses given to all new hires. Store manager Jennifer Crespo explains:

> Now they spend several hours each day learning on the computer or in live conversations with managers until they're ready to go on the floor. The training is presented in different ways to accommodate different learning styles. We make it as fun as possible. They do a quick little

test at the end of each lesson to see where they're at. And then we just build their skill set on the shop floor with everyday practical work.

Now every new consultant in a store goes through this additional training that we didn't have when we started Open Hiring. There used to be a lot more emphasis on hiring for retail experience. But since we've had this program, we've realized experience can come from them just being here with us teaching them.

Develop New Training for Leaders

Training hasn't just changed for employees. It has been enhanced for store managers, too, who may find themselves confronted with novel challenges managing a more diverse workforce. For example, Crespo recalls her first days working with her homeless employee:

> It was a scary situation. I didn't know where he'd be staying each night. And I didn't know if it was appropriate to talk to him about it. I didn't know how to address it. We told management we needed programs to help us as managers understand how to talk to someone like this, living in this kind of situation. That was the biggest challenge.

Learning from its Open Hiring pilot programs, The Body Shop rolled out comprehensive training programs for both management and entry-level employees, developed in collaboration with G3, an innovative workforce consulting company. These courses focus on the mission and purpose of inclusive hiring, as well as managing, and leading without bias. They also help build customer service communication skills through more authentic communication.

One new course on Inclusive Leadership addresses a range of soft skills such as self-awareness about biases, courageous listening, and increasing emotional intelligence. Cindy Alcantara, inclusive hiring manager, explains, "We continue to be challenged with the biases

> **Open Hiring doesn't mean difficult employee problems go away.**

that exist in Open Hiring. So, all these skills are needed to address resistance to change. It's essential these challenges are discussed, so leadership teams understand why Open Hiring can impact them and how they manage in this context."

Leadership training has proved essential because Open Hiring doesn't mean difficult employee problems go away. But now supervisors are better equipped to deal with them. For example, Nick Carney arrived at the distribution center one day and found one of his temporary employees totally disoriented. This guy had performed really well at first. But now he appeared to be using substances on the job, which would require a tough conversation.

Later, Carney realized this problem would not have been avoided, even with a background check, since the employee had no police record. "In reality, these types of things can happen even if you have a background check or drug screen in place," Carney concluded. Proper training, however, prepares managers and leadership to navigate these tough situations.

Ankle Bracelets Come Out of Hiding

The story of Victor, The Body Shop employee experiencing homelessness in Florida, has a happier ending. When his seasonal assignment ended after the holidays, the store manager had no position to offer him. But Victor's experience with The Body Shop allowed him to land a job in another store nearby. He bought a scooter and rented a place, so he no longer had to sleep on the beach. Victor still visits The Body Shop store often. "It was a short-term opportunity for him, but the benefits could last a lifetime," says Crespo.

At the distribution center, things continued to change. Harold learned a second job before moving on and participating in another Special Olympics. And there's been a transition in the culture. Some employees now feel comfortable wearing their ankle monitoring bracelets so they are visible instead of hiding them. Workers sometimes leave to see their parole officer or take a call from them during the day. The company even let someone serve a week-long jail sentence because they told their supervisor what they needed. Nick Carney and his team members weren't equipped to deal with this before, but it's become part of the day-to-day workplace.

Unexpected Benefits of Open Hiring

Open Hiring has taught many of The Body Shop employees lessons they never expected. As head of HR for US distribution, Wale reflects:

> I've learned all employees have a common goal, which is to provide for their family, change the trajectory of their life, and feel like they're a valuable member of the team. Our employees know most employers still require traditional pre-employment screenings like background and drug tests, so the opportunity at The Body Shop is uncommon and one to be taken seriously. Many are very vocal about their excitement and relief to have found a way to start their work lives again.

Store manager Jennifer Crespo has seen firsthand the benefits of hiring traditionally marginalized workers, and they go well beyond business performance:

We often talk about the metrics but, really, a lot of it has to do with just giving people the opportunity to have a job that not only impacts them but their families and the direction of their lives. I've learned you never know what someone is going through, and to break down our biases not only impacts ourselves, but our business and the way we think about the world. It's really eye-opening and humbling to know we had such a big impact on someone's life by simply saying, "Yes, you can work here."

CHAPTER 4

JBM Packaging's Fair Chance Program: "It's not about the alarm clock"

JBM Packaging, a family-owned firm, had proven itself one of Ohio's leaders in second-chance hiring. Since 2016, it has been striving to offer employment to those who were formerly incarcerated. But in 2022, CEO Marcus Sheanshang and his management team realized they had to reinvent their hiring process. Coming out of the COVID-19 pandemic, turnover was at an all-time high, and their overburdened HR staff struggled with the interviewing, training, and coaching processes needed to sustain their commitment to second-chance hiring. This case provides important lessons for building a sustainable program that will support your future talent pipeline.

It's a muggy August morning in Lebanon, Ohio, and another machine operator has just quit. Like most companies dealing with the post-COVID "great resignation," JBM Packaging is losing workers faster than they can be hired and trained. No one feels this stress more than Amanda Hall, the company's head of talent acquisition and training.

Hall is one of the firm's great success stories. After spending two years in prison, JBM hired her as part of their Fair Chance program. By mid-2022, she was responsible for all recruiting and hiring in the company, and now she runs the training program for JBM's envelope-folding machines as well. Although it's not explicitly in her job description, it's Hall's job to make everyone who comes through JBM is a success like her.

The changing labor market, however, has made JBM's second-chance hiring program, dubbed locally as "Fair Chance," far from adequate. With the company constantly hiring and training entry-level operators, the additional costs of running Fair Chance have strained the company financially—and Hall admits to being overwhelmed by the program too. But the central problem remains: without more trained employees, JBM's leaders can't continue to grow the business. Looking back on this challenge, Valerie Plis, director of human capital and culture, explains:

> These are entry-level roles, but it takes a minimum of four weeks to get new hires trained before they're adding to the company's bottom line. It was a multifaceted problem. We had more people leaving and also applying for jobs than Amanda had the capacity to handle, and her role had just been expanded.

Fortunately, JBM didn't have a problem finding talent. In fact, they had a waiting list because of its recruiting efforts in Ohio prisons and some savvy phrasing in its job postings on Indeed, the job search website. But Plis admits getting people to apply for jobs was only half the battle:

JBM's leaders had to rethink their approach to hiring ex-offenders.

> Once they got here, they weren't staying. We had to figure out how to turn the tide to hire more efficiently and improve retention. Every company was experiencing the same workforce turnover issues we were, but we didn't

want to use that as an excuse for not finding a solution. We started brainstorming how we could recruit and assess candidates more effectively and set them up for success on the job.

JBM's leaders had to rethink their approach to hiring ex-offenders coming out of prison. To scale their Fair Chance program, Valerie Plis and her team didn't invent anything new. Instead, they doubled down to expand the impact of their second-chance hiring program. This initiative had seven goals:

- **Create a collaborative interviewing process**
- **Streamline the hiring process with "Talent Tuesdays"**
- **Reinvent community partnerships**
- **Provide ongoing support for non-work challenges**
- **Use scorecards to define success clearly**
- **Train leadership to be sensitive to the diversity of their employees' circumstances**
- **Manage compassion fatigue**

Catching a Break after Prison

After three years in prison and four months in a halfway house, Charles had begun cranking out applications for jobs. So far, no luck. As described in chapter 1, Charles was trying to restart his life and leave behind a drug-driven lifestyle. While searching on Indeed one day, he came across JBM Packaging, which advertised itself as a "felon-friendly" company. Charles applied online.

He was surprised by their quick response. Amanda Hall, JBM's head recruiter at the time, contacted Charles for a phone interview—and then invited him for an in-person meeting. Hall was so impressed with Charles's commitment to change the course of his life that she offered him a position that same day.

Five months after leaving prison, Charles had a job. It felt great. He started as an entry-level operator packing boxes. Within four months, Charles's productivity landed him a promotion.

A year and a half after joining JBM, Charles works as a cutter on the third shift, 11 p.m. to 7 a.m. Working in the early hours of the morning, he cuts paper to size for the machines that produce envelopes. He likes that it's physical work. He moves around a lot and gets into his own rhythm. There's also lots of math involved. That appeals to him.

"It feels good to go to work and do something I like," says Charles. "I'm working for a good company that wants to see you succeed."

Not only has the job allowed Charles to get back into the workforce and show what he can do, but it has also helped him start saving money to buy things he needs. He sounds giddy when he talks about being able to get a car.

Charles likes the availability of "life coaches" who work with employees on personal issues. "It's helped to be able to reach out to somebody to talk about the different things you go through in life when you're trying to change and be successful, and how to deal with different obstacles that come your way. Those coaches have been incredibly helpful."

His job as a machine operator is great, but Charles has other dreams now, too. "Cooking is my passion," he says, confessing that operating a food truck might be in his future. "Everybody has different life changing moments. When I came home from prison, I was determined to do positive things with my life and surround myself with positive people. I didn't want to put myself in a negative environment that would ruin everything I worked so hard for. Since I've been home from prison, things really fell into place for me. Working at JBM has been a big part of that."

1. Create a Collaborative Interviewing Process

One of the first things JBM did was reorganize its hiring process into a more collaborative team effort. Amanda Hall had spent the last few years interviewing second-chance candidates before deciding whether or not to make a job offer. She often evaluated recently released inmates who faced challenges that could undermine their ability to stay employed. Taking a compassionate approach was important to her, but if she hired someone with potential housing, transportation, or childcare issues, for example, her colleagues might have to deal with these problems:

> If I hired somebody, they might tell me they will be getting their driver's license within a certain time frame of when they leave the halfway house so they could get to work. But then their life coach at JBM actually has to help them navigate that process to get their license. That coach had to cover all the details of getting the license and explain it was going to require a lot more work and a lot more steps than the new employee initially thought. It made the coach's job harder.

The two life coaches at JBM play an unusual role, according to the CEO Marcus Sheanshang. Instead of helping with professional development, they are responsible for assisting employees with *personal* growth and development, including all areas of wellness that could be barriers to sustaining successful employment. Coaching tasks include helping employees find solutions for housing, transportation, and child custody problems. Other coaching support focuses on practical and social skills, with coaches helping employees develop productive coping skills, build healthy relationships, manage stress, navigate disappointment and handle feedback. Sheanshang doesn't kid himself. His company's HR budget is much larger than other firms JBM's size. But the CEO knows it is worth the investment.

In fall 2022, the company created a more collaborative interviewing process—one that doesn't depend solely on Hall. Now two life coaches and the supervisors who manage new entry-level hires are involved. So those who work most closely with Fair Chance hires feel a new sense of ownership in helping them be successful, especially if problems arise.

Even though Hall has spent time in prison and experienced the challenges of successfully transitioning back to employment, she can't always judge the potential of a candidate. Explaining the old hiring process she says, "There would be a lot of times when I would interview somebody, and I would be on the fence. But I was the only one interviewing, so I didn't have somebody else to check my assessment of the candidate."

Hall and her colleagues redesigned the process to involve meetings with three people. The supervisor conducts a technical interview, which is like a standard job interview: Why do you want to work here? What aspects of the job look exciting or challenging to you? What are your career goals? And so on.

Next, one of the life coaches leads a "holistic" interview to assess where the individual is on their personal journey. Where are they living? Do they need transportation to get to work? If substance abuse has been a problem in the past, do they have a solid recovery plan? If they have been incarcerated, how did they get there?

[Warning: see "Consult Local Ban the Box Laws" about what's legal in your state (or city) before you start asking these questions.]

Warning: Consult Local "Ban the Box" Laws

Note, more states and municipalities today have "Ban the Box" laws that prohibit employers from asking job candidates about their criminal history. These convictions only become relevant after a job offer has been made. Ban the box laws are designed to ensure that job applicants be evaluated on the basis of their skills and work history and not excluded up front because of past criminal convictions.[25]

In some states, like California, employers must provide a written explanation of why they are withdrawing a job offer due to the results of a background check. In JBM's case, they post the jobs as "felon friendly," so candidates are more likely to bring up their past history because they know criminal convictions are not a barrier to employment. But if the applicant is coming from another source that doesn't indicate past convictions, then the interviewer does not bring the subject up. JBM's life coach Allison Steele explains:

> It's all about how we word it. We're not asking 'Do you have felonies in your background? Or do you have anything in your background?' Instead, as a fair-chance employer, we say up front, 'We provide employment opportunities to people that may have criminal backgrounds. If we decide to extend an offer to a candidate they will undergo a background check and drug screen. Knowing that, is there anything that you would like to discuss in advance?'

Finally, Hall, who was an experienced corporate trainer early in her career, developed a peer assessment process where she takes candidates onto the production floor to shadow a machine operator doing the job they would be hired for. She follows up this shadowing exercise with a short quiz to see whether the applicant can remember instructions, complete the task, show initiative, and ask good questions.

After the three interviews, the team discusses each candidate to arrive at a hiring decision. Life coach Allison Steele has found it very helpful to have multiple "heads and hearts" involved in the decision-making process:

> We were interviewing a candidate and I did the holistic interview. In terms of personal development, she had a good support system and a solid recovery plan. But then the applicant went through the peer assessment interview and Amanda got a completely different version of the person I had interviewed.
>
> In my interview the woman sat up and was very attentive. But in Amanda's interview, her body language changed. She was very laid back. That was one thing we noticed. And she made an off-handed comment to Amanda about always being late at her previous jobs and that she could struggle with having to stand in one place, which was often a requirement of the operator's job. Of course, we didn't hire her.

2. Streamline Hiring Process with "Talent Tuesdays"

One of the problems with JBM's old hiring system was the inefficient interviewing process. As head of talent acquisition, Hall would spread job interviews for entry-level positions throughout the week, never knowing if the candidate would show up. To make the hiring process more efficient, the JBM team created "Talent Tuesdays."

These designated hiring days—in which the entire recruiting and interviewing process is squeezed into two hours one day a week—saved Hall from trying to schedule and conduct interviews throughout the week, and it made the hiring process more collaborative. First, potential applicants RSVP to attend a weekly information session starting every Tuesday at 10 a.m. These sessions start with an information session and a short video to help potential job candidates decide whether working at JBM is something they might want to do. A life coach does a 30-minute presentation on what JBM is all about—its core values, commitment to second-chance hiring, and a description of current job openings.

Interested candidates then move immediately to begin the three-step interview process described above. The team can rotate six people through the interviewing process in 90 minutes, then come together to decide who gets offers. Hall summarizes the value of Talent Tuesdays for hiring:

> The fact that it's a collaborative hiring approach is the best thing. It's no longer just me making the decision. Everybody involved expresses their opinion on each candidate. We make a job offer because we feel that candidate is going to be a good long-term fit for the company. It's a more streamlined, more time-efficient, well-rounded approach to hiring.

3. Reinvent Community Partnerships

Talent Tuesdays have simplified and streamlined the recruiting process, but they surfaced another problem. JBM recruits inside prisons, but they also work very closely with community partners who serve formerly incarcerated individuals, as well as people recovering from substance and alcohol use disorders. Consequently, many of the applicants who showed up on Talent Tuesday were referred to JBM by different agencies and community organizations around the state. The problem: too many of these applicants couldn't meet the basic requirements needed to work at the company.

"It was great all these people were signing up," life coach Allison Steele says, "but we had to make sure we had the right candidates showing up. Too many people couldn't pass the basic math test. Or sometimes people would show up high."

Steele and her colleagues had to rethink their relationships with community partners to make sure they were getting qualified candidates. One agency, for example, repeatedly sent people to interview who lived in another part of the state. JBM knew from experience that it's not practical to ask people taking an entry-level job to relocate to live near the plant. Because of recurring issues like this, JBM needed to vet partners just as much as potential job candidates. The company wants partners who are proud of the candidates they send for interviews.

To refine their talent pipeline, JBM created a "preferred partners" program to build better relationships with talent suppliers. One way of strengthening the relationship, according to Steele, was to give partners a very clear picture of what success looks like:

> Our team sat down and reflected, 'What is it we want to see in a candidate or a team member?' And then we communicated that to our partners, saying, 'Here's who we're looking for.' Developing standard language that we can communicate to everyone helps us hold partners accountable. We can go back to them and ask, 'Can you tell us why you sent us that person? As a reminder, here is what we need to see in your referrals.'

Success with a particular partner often means developing a good relationship with one person working at the agency, instead of trying to educate a whole group. This might be as simple as bringing donuts to the partner to keep JBM top of mind.

4. Provide Ongoing Support for Non-Work Challenges

Success doesn't end with recruiting the right candidate. The real work is in the ongoing support that JBM provides off the production floor. With two full-time life coaches on staff, the company has recognized the need to help Fair Chance hires navigate the never-ending barriers that face those coming out of incarceration.

In response, JBM created the Better Lives Program, which provides weekly coaching sessions while on shift for all new Fair Chance employees for the first six months. In addition to this on-the-job coaching, workers also have access to coaching on parenting, financial literacy, and legal services. In addition, they can work toward independent transportation with an in-house RoadMap2Wheels program, or they can obtain low-interest-rate loans when facing personal hardship.

5. Use Scorecards for Feedback

To further scale its second-chance program, JBM implemented employee "scorecards," rubrics that make explicit the criteria defining an employee's successful performance. Scorecards include categories like reliability and attention to detail, and they spell out the behaviors and outcomes an employee must exhibit to be judged successful in each area. In other words, they specify how you "get a three" (i.e., top score) in "attention to detail" or "quality work."

The secret is in the feedback that they communicate.

To mitigate problems with new hires early on, JBM's managers use these criteria to evaluate each new team member weekly for their first 90 days on the job. This lets workers know how they're doing. A typical scorecard conversation follows the format of, "Here's what we see. Here are the awesome things you're doing. And here's where you're falling short. How can we help you get to a three in that area?"

Scorecards have allowed management to paint a picture of success and have weekly development meetings with supervisors that closely monitor the progress of new hires. Life coach Allison Steele offers an example:

> We had somebody at risk on the production floor. Their score from the supervisor was low in an area that indicated they weren't helping their co-workers. This guy was just sitting idle at his machine. In the past, that might have been let go and then festered and gotten worse over time. But now I'm saying to the supervisor, 'Hey, you need to follow up and make sure you're telling this guy what his scores are and let him know what success looks like.'
>
> We're holding supervisors accountable to have those coaching conversations. And guess what? This guy got all threes on his score card the next time. He killed it this week. He just told me, 'My supervisor came and talked to me and told me I couldn't just hang around. I needed to be busy.' This week he's been busy helping others, and his boss told him he's killing it! When I saw him today, the smile on this guy's face was amazing.

Like almost every innovation, the scorecards have had to evolve to become more useful for managers. Initially, some supervisors thought the categories were too complicated for frequently scoring employees, so the HR team simplified the scoring system. Steele explains:

> It's all about giving feedback to the team members so they know where they're doing well and where they need to improve. Whatever tool that encourages the supervisor to do that works. The secret is in the feedback that they communicate, and if we simplify the tool, they're more likely to use it. So then, the team member sees a path to success.

6. Train Leaders to Be Sensitive to Employees' Life Circumstances

Part of building a sustainable second-chance process is embedding new leadership skills at all levels of the organization. But how do you lead when dealing with individuals who have had severe trauma in their lives?

JBM's managers focus on building healthy relationships with employees. Doing this means workers need to feel safe and secure, both physically and emotionally, but in an environment where they can also address real business problems. To do this, Valerie Plis and her team have adopted a trauma-responsive approach to their management training. This means assuming the widespread impact of trauma on the lives of second-chance employees (and all employees for that matter) and adapting management practices at all levels to deal with this past trauma.

To complicate the challenge, JBM's head of HR recognized that the firm's managers did not truly understand the daily struggles and obstacles their second-chance team members were facing. They also didn't recognize that the path to long-term success for these employees was often not linear but rather a series of ups and downs. As a second-chance hire herself, Hall wholeheartedly supports Elevate, the company's custom-developed trauma-responsive management training:

> I was so glad to see our supervisors go through this training because, from my past experience, I know what new hires are feeling. But for supervisors to get it, that's what really is going to make the difference for the team member. If their supervisor understands what they've been through and has that empathy and can be there to support them, that's what will make people stay and grow and flourish.

Training JBM's leaders to be effective meant, in practice, giving them tools to lead with their head and their heart.[26] A common mantra in the company is "without profit there is no purpose." Make no mistake about it, JBM exists to make money. If it doesn't do that, there can be no second-chance program.

To manage team members effectively, supervisors need skills to set expectations, consistently give feedback, hold people accountable, and have tough conversations that are balanced with empathy and a strong relationship with individual employees to coach them for improved performance.

Plis and her team developed a training program that they started delivering to JBM's production leads and supervisors, gradually working up to higher levels of management, as well as high potentials. The five half-day training sessions include tools built around Gallup's Clifton Strengths Assessment.[27] Managers practice what they have learned by working through problem cases in small groups to develop action plans for handling difficult supervisory situations. Every supervisor also has an individual development plan to ensure they are accountable for applying what they have learned in leading their team. Steele, who as a life coach is a strong proponent of a trauma-responsive approach to management, concluded:

> Being able to support people who have suffered through trauma is a 'must have' if you are going to hire second-chance workers. Of course, there's different levels of people in the company who need a trauma-responsive approach. But, since the COVID pandemic, today's workforce has changed. People want healthy environments, healthy cultures. So this sensitivity to trauma is necessary not just for second-chance hires.

7. Manage Compassion Fatigue

To support staff who work extensively with second-chance employees, JBM's leaders realized they needed to provide resources to overcome "compassion fatigue." This became especially problematic as the Fair Chance program became well known, attracting many more applicants.

Compassion fatigue is a feeling of burnout that occurs from repeatedly taking on the suffering and problems of others who have experienced extreme trauma or stress.[28] It's a common phenomenon in the healthcare sector, where many jobs involve taking care of individuals with complex, intensive needs that often cannot be resolved.

The HR team at JBM confessed to experiencing compassion fatigue while working with a large number of second-chance hires. In general, many employees in entry-level manufacturing jobs quit or are fired after a short time, but experiencing the churn of new hires who have been justice-involved before coming to JBM can feel even more frustrating. Steele illustrates the emotional challenges she and her colleagues face:

> We had an employee who took a lot of her mentor's time and a lot of my time. She was coming off the streets and a life of prostitution. There was a lot of trauma in her story and how she responded to individuals. She had a lot of talent and potential. You could see that in her. But she was used to doing everything on her own and getting her to accept coaching to do things another way was very hard.
>
> Then she reached a tipping point where she lost it, shouting that she felt disrespected, which was triggering to her. Tears are rolling down her face. I'm trying not to cry because your heart breaks for people in these situations. You need tremendous compassion as a coach.

But then, from a business perspective, you say, 'Okay, this is heartbreaking. But, overall, this team member is becoming toxic to her team.' So, we had to make the tough decision to let her go. When you lose people, you start questioning your value and worth as a professional. You begin to get jaded. You're putting all this time and effort into somebody and sometimes the outcome isn't what you had hoped for. It's disappointing. Then you start asking, 'Why am I doing this?'

Hall, the head of talent acquisition and training, started to feel compassion fatigue in even more acute ways. Since she was a second-chance hire herself, she attracted a lot of attention from other new hires.

I don't know how our coaches do the work they do

At first, I was a lot more invested in new employees and their personal journeys. As their recruiter, I was their first point of contact with JBM. So Fair Chance hires used me as their go-to person for everything. I felt responsible to help people with whatever they needed. I'd put a lot of time and energy into them as a peer mentor. You see them find success, but then something derails them, and it's hard not to take it personally.

Director of human capital Valerie Plis started to see the emotional toll on her staff:

I don't know how our coaches do the work they do. It's so hard to walk alongside someone going through heavy stuff that no human should ever have to deal with. Whether it's sex trafficking or reuniting with children you've not seen in years. Or hearing how someone was sexually molested by their stepfather. The list goes on. These are scenarios that nobody should have to deal with. It gets really hard emotionally.

Plis and her team identified five tactics that help manage the impacts of compassion fatigue on veteran JBM employees.

Set Boundaries

Boundaries are important because they help keep you from feeling overly responsible for others' choices. Earlier in her career, Steele didn't have good boundaries with those she helped. "That led to a lot of suffering," she says. Sometimes depression sets in if you don't protect yourself. Steele reflects:

> If they choose to use drugs, I have to be able to sleep at night knowing I gave them everything I could in the time they were here. But they made that choice. I have to release myself from that. It's unfortunate, but it's their life. It's their journey, knowing that it might set them up for a comeback. If I didn't put in good boundaries for myself I wouldn't survive as a coach.

Encourage Self-Care

Every job requires taking care of yourself to recharge your batteries. But continually managing other people's emotional trauma to help them remain productive employees can take a huge emotional toll.

Avoiding compassion fatigue requires recognizing when you have nothing left to give your colleagues and having a boss who understands these situations. "I make sure I take care of myself," says Steele. "Having a flexible schedule is a huge part of that, along with a manager who understands when you are struggling and asks, 'What are you doing to help yourself?' and encourages and holds you accountable to do that. That's key."

Embrace the Gray

Coping effectively with compassion fatigue at JBM means accepting the complexity of the problems second-chance employees face. Steele remembers when a new hire was late for work. "Just buy him an alarm clock," one executive colleague suggested. In the manufacturing environment, broken machines often become the implicit metaphor for fixing human problems. But people—and their problems—are much more complicated than machines, as Steele explains:

> A lot of times people in business want to make it black and white. Either you show up for work on time or you don't. It's not a black-and-white thing. Everybody's got different problems, but it's never one thing. It's a million things. I just met with someone who after being incarcerated for years is learning to be a parent again. In one moment, a single woman became a mom of three boys all under the age of six. She must get two to daycare and another to school in another district every morning. All of a sudden, she is relying on strangers to meet a very tight timeline, so she can be at work on time to start her 7 a.m. shift. Establishing good routines, appropriate discipline, and healthy relationships, while dealing with shame and guilt for all the years she was absent, doesn't resolve overnight with an alarm clock. Where do you start?
>
> Our managers have to lean into the tension, instead of running away from it, because that can be really uncomfortable. Sometimes, we've had to challenge our managers, and say, 'I appreciate that you were able to get to work on time today, but is it possible that there may be more contributing to your employee's performance problem?' It's asking the question, 'Is it possible?' We have to lean into the tension created by the complexity of our team members' lives and learn to live with the gray. Responding to the trauma in their lives is messy and takes time, but it works.

View Setbacks through a Different Lens

Compassion fatigue can also be reduced by resetting expectations about workforce development. In traditional business environments, we think of employee development and personal growth as moving in a steady upward trend. That is the norm. But when these expectations are consistently not met, frustration can aggravate compassion fatigue.

The JBM team recruiting and training second-chance hires views development and personal setbacks through a different lens. Plis, head of HR, says, "Their journey to success comes with ups and downs. It's a zig zag route. And it comes with setbacks. So, for us, that's been a part of managing the emotional tension, recognizing that a setback doesn't mean this person was a bad hire. A setback doesn't mean this person should be terminated."

As a life coach, Steele sees this situation often:

> An employee was arrested for domestic violence the other day, and they ended up going back to jail until they were bailed out. But I met with that person, and they're actually doing great. They are contesting the charge and there's no evidence to support it. He's moved out of what was a very toxic situation. It was a setback. But he's already back at work. And he's actually much further ahead than he was a year ago. From setback to come back is the story.

The company sticks with an employee as long as they are willing to listen to a manager's feedback and try to change. But when a worker isn't responding to repeated feedback, then JBM knows they have to let the employee go.

Teamwork Is Key

As head of recruiting and training for all second-chance hires, Amanda Hall learned through experience the importance of teamwork in coping with the emotional ups and downs of her work:

> I now make sure that I send employees to the appropriate person for their problems. That's because we now have specific people assigned for certain things. So I send them to their supervisor instead of trying to save the world and take everything on my shoulders. Otherwise, you'll just burn out and quit.

Steele offers a similar account:

> You have to do this with a group. There's just no way we could do this second-chance work by ourselves. On days that I'm struggling, Amanda will help me, and days that she's struggling I help her. We have a lot of grace and understanding for each other because it's a hard job. I call Valerie up after a difficult meeting, thinking I should work somewhere else, and she talks me off the ledge. We give each other a lot of understanding and encouragement on those hard days. We truly make each other better. That's what's great about the Fair Chance process we've built.

Plis, Steele's boss, knows to instill the importance of teamwork: "There's not a single one of us that's a superhero, and we had to stop pretending like we are."

Fair Chance Pays Off

CEO Marcus Sheanshang is clear that JBM started Fair Chance hiring to address its shortage of talent, which was a big problem for the company. But, at the peak of the COVID pandemic, annual turnover was 68 percent even with Fair Chance. The unstable workforce, combined with the Great Resignation as the pandemic ended, forced JBM to find innovative solutions within its Fair Chance hiring program. It worked. By late 2023, Fair Chance hires made up over 50 percent of the company's production workforce and turnover was down to 31 percent.

Still, Sheanshang is realistic about the impact JBM's commitment to hiring the justice-involved will have on its workforce needs. He concludes:

> We know every Fair Chance hire won't result in a long-tenured employee. But we want to provide them with stable employment while they get their life back on track through employer-sponsored resources for parenting, financial literacy, and transportation, for starters. In the end, we measure success based on their ability to continue making progress when they leave JBM.

This CEO wants to see his company's Fair Chance program continue to grow. He also hopes to see more of these team members promoted into leadership roles. And he wants to help other companies start their own programs to broaden the positive impacts on those coming out of prison. Finally, Sheanshang sees some unexpected benefits from his company's investments in Fair Chance hiring.

> We make everyday products, but trying to help those coming out of prison and being part of their journey has been very gratifying. I didn't fully appreciate how much our other employees would become invested in the program. We're a more purpose-driven business today, which was not our intention at the start. But it makes coming to work each day more fun.

CHAPTER 5

Lessons Learned from Second-Chance Companies

Hiring those who have been formerly incarcerated is seldom simple. But it can yield hardworking, loyal employees that make the extra effort well worth it. Companies profiled in the previous three chapters—Precisely, The Body Shop, and JBM Packaging—have learned critical lessons that can help you accelerate new initiatives to tap this under used talent market. This chapter shows how to address the common challenges all businesses face in hiring those who were formerly justice-involved, such as building effective partnerships, gaining support of existing employees, and supplementing HR resources. If this sounds overwhelming, given your tight budget, see the box in chapter 15: "Investing In Marginalized Workers When You Have Limited Time and Resources."

Companies committed to second-chance hiring operate in a wide range of industries and business settings. In the previous three chapters, we looked at three businesses doing just that:

- **Precisely** hires highly trained business development reps who can compete in a regular employment market and sell complex technology products to high-level executives.
- **The Body Shop** rolled out an Open Hiring program company-wide for entry-level positions.

- **JBM Packaging** has committed to hiring 240 justice-involved employees by 2030. The firm already has a mature second-chance hiring program that must adapt to meet the needs of the staff and this promising talent pool.

Although these companies are pioneers in second-chance hiring, it's tricky to generalize about tactics and lessons learned from early adopters tapping this underused talent pipeline. Every company is different, and it's important to begin by assessing your goals in adopting second-chance hiring.

In *Untapped Talent*, Jeffrey Korzenik identifies three ways employers can approach hiring ex-offenders. The first is a kind of churn and burn approach: hiring the formerly incarcerated at minimum wage and providing them with no support. Think fast food restaurants. The assumption is a few will stick.

Korzenik calls this approach the "Disposable Employee Model."[29] It takes advantage of marginalized groups to keep labor costs as low as possible. It is often motivated by the availability of a Work Opportunity Tax Credit, which reimburses businesses 25 to 40 percent of the employee's first-year wages.[30] Except as very brief transition employment, these types of jobs do almost nothing to help people going through reentry succeed in life after prison. If this is your employment strategy, I have no recommendations.

Another approach is to treat justice-involved applicants like everyone else you hire. This is what Korzenik calls the "Undifferentiated Model." Unfortunately, too many companies have tried this method, not understanding the complex needs of those who have been formerly incarcerated. If you have tried this path and it hasn't worked out, this chapter can help you succeed if you are willing to try again.

The goal is to learn from those who have tried to apply a more customized approach to hiring and employment. Companies like The

Body Shop, Precisely, JBM Packaging and dozens of others recognize the tremendous challenges facing justice-involved candidates. They also see a unique and profitable opportunity to meet their company's needs for productive, loyal employees. Through the dozens of interviews I conducted with employees and experts, I found six critical success factors that every leader must consider when tapping into the market of second-chance talent. Think of this approach as learning from positive deviance[31]—that is, learning from unexpected success stories. Here's what they teach us.

1. Find Your "Why"—An Emotional Connection to Second-Chance Hiring

Employing people with a criminal history can be incredibly uplifting. It is also frustrating and heartbreaking at times. Nearly every leader I talked to who committed to hiring justice-involved applicants had emotional skin in the game. Jacquie Gallo, EVP of operations at Pursuit Aerospace, and Pete Leonard, founder of I Have a Bean coffee roasters, both have family members who have been in prison. They have witnessed firsthand the incredible systemic obstacles ex-offenders face when transitioning back into daily life, things most of us take for granted.

Brenda Kay at Precisely developed strong relationships with women in the Televerde program at Arizona's Perryville prison. Over many visits to the facility, she was inspired by the efforts of women who wanted to change their lives. The more time she spent with them, the more she became committed to helping former inmates succeed at work after prison.

"This experience changed my life forever," said Alan Lazowski, CEO of LAZ Parking, the second largest parking company in the US. This rabbi's son visited Connecticut's Cheshire Correctional Facility and was inspired by a prison reform program that prepares young inmates who want to turn their lives around. LAZ Parking already practiced second-chance hiring around the country, but Lazowski's prison visit inspired him to commit his company to hiring more justice-involved individuals. Today they have over 300 formerly incarcerated employees in the state of Connecticut alone.[32]

For Marcus Sheanshang, CEO of JBM Packaging, investing in second-chance hiring is a spiritual calling. "I believe it's obedience to God. This was nothing I meant to do or had any interest in doing. I've gotten to run this great business and, boy, we should do some great stuff with it!"

Resources to Jump-Start Your "Why" for Second-Chance Hiring

Want to increase your motivation to tackle the challenges of second-chance hiring? These resources can supply inspiration (see endnotes for URLs):

- *I Have a Bean* is a video about the experiences of second-chance hires at this tiny coffee roaster.[33]
- *Outside In* (2017) is a movie about a man who struggles to readjust to life after prison in his small town and forms an intense bond with his former high school teacher.
- *The Second-Chance Club: Hardship and Hope After Prison* by Jason Hardy (2020) offers an inside look at the painfully inadequate resources available to a New Orleans parole officer trying to help those recently released from prison.
- *Untapped Talent: How Second-Chance Hiring Works for Your Business and the Community* by Jeffrey Korzenik (2021) is a terrific book that should be read by any leader looking to invest in a second-chance hiring program.
- *Dave's Killer Bread Story* is a short YouTube video about Dave Dahl's journey from prison to being a hugely success-

ful entrepreneur who is committed to opening doors for ex-felons.[34]
- ***The Many Lives of Mama Love: A Memoir of Lying, Stealing, Writing, and Healing* by Lara Love Hardin (2023)** portrays one woman's odyssey from suburban mother to drug addict to inmate, as well as her struggles to overcome shame and the obstacles to building a career in the wake of prison.
- ***UTEC: Trading Violence and Poverty for Social and Economic Success.*** This short video shows the challenges justice-involved young adults face when they try to break out of the system of poverty and gangs that traps so many.[35]

If you have read the stories from the previous chapters, you probably already have some sympathy for those burdened by a criminal record. Maybe you know someone personally or have met formerly incarcerated individuals who you feel deserve another chance. It helps to be emotionally committed to supporting second-chance applicants. That's because you will run into obstacles and disappointments. Being passionate about making a difference in the lives of the justice-involved will help you keep going when times get tough. But make no mistake about it, you are still hiring these marginalized workers because it is good for your business in the long term.

Who Is Our Partner? Workforce Development Nonprofits vs. Staffing Agencies

Warning: this sidebar could put you to sleep. There is a lot of talk in this book about partners and partnerships. The talent supply ecosystem can be very confusing. Here is what you need to know when you hear the word "partners" in the context of recruiting marginalized workers.

The many different types of nonprofits and for-profit employment and staffing agencies go by different names that often mean the same thing. Don't beat yourself up for being confused. The terms used to describe agencies vary a lot. The key is to ask questions about any potential partner so you understand their mission and business model.

- **Workforce development nonprofits**—much like Televerde, they provide skills training and opportunities for job placement, usually in specific industry sectors or regions. They may also provide a wide variety of resources, such as childcare or language training.[36]

- **Employment (or staffing) agencies**—may be generalists providing candidates for a variety of positions. Or they may specialize in proposing applicants for particular types of jobs.

- **Temp agencies**—also serve as a bridge between companies and job applicants but they focus on providing temporary, seasonal, or part-time workers. Sometimes, employees will have a contract for a "temp-to-hire" role that gives an employer the option to hire a temporary worker full time at the end of the contract. A lot of marginalized workers end up getting hired this way.[37]

- **Publicly funded agencies**—such as American Job Centers, provide publicly funded services under different mandates, most commonly career centers under something called WIOA. Don't ask. Look it up if you aren't confused enough yet. They use public funding (state, federal, local) to serve different populations of job seekers, such as the formerly incarcerated. These centers may have a mix of governmental and nonprofit employees.

Your partnerships may include some combination of workforce development nonprofits and a staffing agency that actually handles the employment paperwork. Who you partner with depends on your industry and the geographic location of the positions you are filling. Who are the nonprofits and agencies in your region? Do they have experienced, knowledgeable staff with good connections with the nontraditional talent pools you want to tap? Ask hard questions about this. Be skeptical.

2. Don't Try This Alone—Find Trusted Partners

Just because your company decides it is open to second-chance hiring doesn't mean ex-offenders will begin flocking to your door. Most businesses need partners to pave the way, steering traditionally marginalized candidates to them for consideration. In reality, people coming out of prison probably have no idea employment opportunities exist in your company. Unless your organization has a direct connection to a prison, you need a partner to connect you with viable candidates with criminal records. (See sidebar "Who is Our Partner?") For example:

- Precisely works with Televerde, a workforce nonprofit that trains inmates with sales and marketing skills, to identify promising candidates for business development sales positions.
- JBM Packaging partners with CityLink, a Cincinnati-based coordination center, to address transportation and housing needs for new employees adjusting to the challenges of re-entry.
- The Body Shop with its Open Hiring model worked locally with the Wake Local Reentry Council to identify candidates for its distribution center in North Carolina. Its retail stores used local staffing agencies around the country.

Chances are, wherever your business is located, you can make similar connections. In Bridgeport, Connecticut, for instance, local employers can connect with Career Resources, Inc., a nonprofit workforce development agency that provides work readiness programs for those recently released from prison. Career Resources also has a staffing agency that helps formerly incarcerated individuals find jobs with local employers. On a larger scale, the South Dallas Employment Project is a regional coalition of businesses, government agencies, schools, workforce agencies, and nonprofit social organizations. This diverse group collaborates to address the staffing and training needs of employers, as well as the wraparound services ex-offenders need to perform effectively on the job.

Finding the right trusted partners to supply justice-involved job candidates depends on you deciding what you are looking for. Does the company need skilled workers or people you can train on the job? Are you looking for a couple of employees or a steady talent pipeline? Your specific staffing needs will dictate the type of partners needed to successfully employ second-chance hires. Most of the time companies connect with outside partners to identify ex-offenders looking for work. Sometimes, employers will refer new hires to these partners to provide essential wraparound services, such as help with transportation, housing, and child care.

The Body Shop worked with its partners both ways. With the help of Wake Local Reentry Council, their distribution center found job candidates going through reentry, and if HR identified an employee's special needs for things like housing, transportation, or financial literacy, they referred new hires to other partner organizations for those services.

Reentry Checklist: Critical Support Activities

Among the common tasks returning citizens need to sustain employment:

- Procure a driver's license, Social Security card, and/or birth certificate needed to complete an I-9 employment form
- Obtain stable housing
- Address transportation needs
- Meet childcare and other family service needs

- Access health, wellness, and substance abuse recovery services
- Acquire workforce-readiness and job-specific skills training and certifications
- Secure legal assistance to meet parole requirements
- Access digital & financial literacy training
- Obtain reliable cell phone and email services

Assess Partner's Workforce-Readiness Training

Not everyone who comes out of prison is ready or capable of being employed in a full-time job. Just ask those who have been behind bars. They'll tell you not everyone they did time with is a viable job candidate.

One of my favorite resources for this book was Ed Hennings, an indefatigable entrepreneur who spent 20 years in prison. Since being released he has opened a series of successful businesses. (See "From Inmate to Boss" sidebar.) Hennings regularly interviews and hires those who were formerly incarcerated. He says, "I know from hiring people myself that you have to be on your judgment game. There are some people that come home that are not ready to change."

The best partners provide preliminary screening to identify promising second-chance hires. In practice, however, nonprofit workforce development organizations and employment agencies have different levels of commitment to those they serve. Some, like Televerde, are deeply invested in the long-term success of former inmates. Their second-chance candidates are extensively trained when they leave prison. Some staffing agencies, on the other hand, may have little or no investment in understanding the work readiness of their clients.

JBM Packaging had to re-educate some agencies it works with that were sending unqualified second-chance candidates for interviews. Some lived too far away from the plant. Others lacked even basic math skills needed for the job. Some individuals weren't sober when they interviewed!

Staffing agencies usually have different agendas and talent pools they are serving. They may be working with the formerly incarcerated who can be emotionally fragile and lacking in work experience. These candidates may also be struggling with recovery from a substance use disorder, and be stuck in an unstable living situation. The agencies want as many of their clients to be hired as possible. Indeed, many applicants have great potential and just need a break. But the likely success of others is much more uncertain. Smart employers will recognize the competing objectives workforce agencies have and temper their expectations accordingly.

Are You Clearly Communicating the Skills Candidates Need?

Workforce development nonprofits and staffing agencies need clear direction about your criteria for successful job candidates. This is something employers often fail to provide.

Wes Jurey is head of the South Dallas Employment Project (SDEP). This is a mega-coalition of more than 180 businesses, government entities, schools, workforce agencies, and nonprofit social entities. SDEP's purpose is to get justice-involved individuals trained and placed in thousands of unfilled jobs paying a sustainable wage. Everything in Texas seems to occur on a grand scale. One in three working-age Texans has a criminal record.[38] Some 30,000 individuals are released from prison *every year* in Dallas County alone. At the same time, thousands of well-paying jobs in sectors like logistics, manufacturing, and construction go unfilled. SDEP does important work addressing a wide variety of reentry needs.

One of SDEP's biggest challenges is getting employers to explicitly spell out the skills and qualifications they need in job candidates. Jurey insists that many of the capabilities businesses need can be met by nationally recognized certifications, such as logistics technician or forklift driver. These can be acquired with a few weeks of training and can save employers time and money in getting new hires productive. But SDEP has spent considerable time educating employers about certifications. These certifications provide a common language between employers and talent suppliers to specify the training companies need in qualified job candidates. Make sure you are aware of training certifications that line up with the jobs you need to fill.[39]

Hold Partners Accountable

JBM Packaging has learned to hold partners accountable for the talent they are providing. One way they do this is by providing their preferred partners with a rubric specifically defining what JBM wants to see in a job candidate. Communicating their specific needs allows JBM to go back to a partner and ask them why they sent an unsuitable candidate to interview. If there is any confusion, JBM reminds agencies what they expect in referrals. This direct feedback strengthens relationships with workforce partners over time.

3. Build Support of Management and Employees

Another success factor when tapping the second chance talent pool is gaining the support of your current team. Every company I studied that tries to hire ex-offenders had to gain the support of senior executives, supervisors, and employees. Gaining buy-in doesn't always go smoothly, however, and the process can vary considerably depending on management style. Whoever leads this effort must pay explicit attention to what others in the company are thinking if they want new hires to get the support they need. This means listening to objections, giving colleagues time to process their fears, and educating key stakeholders about the pros and cons of second-chance hiring.

To create a sustainable second-chance program, you need support from four different constituencies:

(1) Top management

(2) Line managers and supervisors

(3) Human resources, and

(4) Employees who will be working with second-chance hires.

Unless you're the CEO or GM, you need your boss's active support to overcome the obstacles you are likely to face. Brenda Kay enlisted Precisely's CEO Josh Rogers before pursuing second-chance hiring. Nicolas Debray, former president of The Body Shop Americas, was a strong supporter when the retailer began rolling out Open Hiring in 2019.

Supervisors and line managers who will be overseeing new hires also need to be on board. Oftentimes, this group's work is most directly impacted when tapping this new source of talent.

Your human resource department will have to deal with changes in how the company handles background checks. HR staffers may also be called on to provide more employee assistance for addressing challenges second-chance hires face outside of work. You need HR managers who believe in your plan to access the justice-involved talent pool. They also need to be experienced and compassionate enough to deal with the challenges this initiative will bring on.

Finally, most employees on the front line who will be working closely with second-chance hires must also be on board. This may be the most challenging group to enlist at first.

The dynamics of your organization will, in part, determine how difficult it is to gain buy-in from the above groups. The strategies below have proven effective for other organizations and may aid your efforts.

Communicate Your Plan and Invite Responses

When you propose a program like second-chance hiring, expect negative responses initially. People need time to process this unconventional staffing change. Let them vent their concerns, then begin a dialogue. Store manager Jen Crespo at The Body Shop recalled introducing Open Hiring to her staff:

> There were a lot of questions. What if they have a criminal history? What if they're going to hurt us? What if they don't show up? We had to confront these biases. We talked their concerns through. I told them this was a learning experience for all of us. We had to keep an open mind and not be afraid to ask questions.

In a smaller family-owned company, the CEO took a different approach. He worked hard to convince current employees about the value of hiring those with a criminal record in a labor-starved market. The company has an anonymous feedback box and employees didn't hold back.

- "I don't want to work with these people."
- "I liked this company better when your father ran it."

The CEO faithfully read all these comments aloud in all-employee meetings. He made sure people felt heard. He didn't want to spring second-chance hiring on his staff, and this gave him clear direction on which pain points to address.

Build Credibility with Proposed Partnerships and Early Adopters

Getting support from key constituencies is much easier if you show you have done your homework. Communicate that you are developing relationships with potential partners to provide candidates and essential wraparound services. Most importantly, point to other companies who have successfully employed second-chance hires.

Brenda Kay had tremendous credibility because of her longtime connection to Televerde and its training programs for inmates. She could speak passionately about the skills these applicants would have and their commitment to turn their lives around. Also, Televerde has a long track record as a successful partner working with employers.

Leaders at The Body Shop used their connections with Greyston Bakery to educate employees and supervisors about the benefits of Open Hiring practices. Greyston has pioneered Open Hiring for years. And having managers from Greyston share their stories at a Body Shop meeting added a lot of credibility. Marcus Sheanshang at JBM Packaging took notes from nearby Nehemiah Manufacturing because of their long track record of success with second-chance hiring.[40]

"Sense Check" Employees' Concerns about Hiring the Justice-Involved

When bringing Open Hiring to The Body Shop's warehouse in North Carolina, management invited distribution center employees to share their concerns. Jennifer Wale, head of HR, heard multiple concerns about a possible increase in theft but pushed back: Do you not have those issues already? Yes. So it's not a situation where the background check and the drug screen will make these things go away? Wale says,

> We were able to give them a reality check that shows we live with biases, and Open Hiring is a way to help others. Some employees, after the meeting, came forward and said, 'This will be great because I know somebody who can't find a warehouse job. They're having to work outdoors or get money some other way. They could really benefit from this.'

It's healthy to encourage employees and managers to process their feelings about hiring nontraditional candidates in this way, but that emotional processing takes time. One manager at The Body Shop pointed out, "You have to budget time to help employees get comfortable with Open Hiring. You can't say, 'I'm gonna roll this out to my team in a week, and we're gonna start recruiting and hiring immediately. It's not going to happen.'"

As much as you wish to help those with a criminal record, you still must empathize with your current team. Sense-checking does both by bringing all parties closer to the facts and providing space for employees' initial feelings to be processed.

4. Don't Reduce Performance Standards

One of the unspoken concerns about second-chance hires is that they will be held to a lower performance standard or that overall expectations must be reduced. Nick Carney, a distribution center manager, initially believed if The Body Shop reduced barriers to hiring, he would get lower quality job candidates who would negatively impact performance. He was wrong. Here are three steps to sustaining quality performance when hiring ex-offenders:

Be Explicit about Performance Expectations

In companies hiring from this talent pool, justice-involved employees are held to the same performance standards as other employees. It's important to mention this when enlisting the support of your colleagues. Jennifer Wale, head of HR for distribution at The Body Shop, was clear that all Open Hiring does is give marginalized candidates a "fair shot." Performance measures don't change. All employees are expected to meet the same business standards.

In practice, outputs sometimes actually improve with second-chance hires. This was the case at both Precisely and The Body Shop.

Brenda Kay is particularly proud that two of her top-performing business development representatives (out of 40 BDRs) were previously incarcerated.

When piloting Open Hiring, The Body Shop's distribution center set productivity records during the peak rush season when the warehouse was routinely swamped with orders to process. Manager Nick Carney was surprised at how quickly new hires were able to perform difficult tasks soon after they came on board.

Keep Managers on the Hook for Performance Improvement

Having skilled supervisors and managers is always essential to employee development and retention. But these capabilities are especially important when managing second-chance hires. To maintain performance standards, supervisors must give frequent and clear feedback to workers on what they need to do differently. Holding supervisors accountable for this is an important step.

JBM ultimately created scorecards for supervisors to use when giving detailed, specific feedback. These rubrics help evaluate each team member weekly during their first 90 days on the job. The goal is to mitigate problems early on with employees burdened by the many challenges of reentry and their experiences in prison.

When an operator was spending too much time sitting idle at his machine, he got feedback that he was scoring low in the category of "helping co-workers." This new second-chance hire needed to know he was expected to stay busy helping his colleagues. He couldn't waste time on the job. A week later his behavior had completely changed and the supervisor let him know the improved performance was recognized and appreciated.

Beyond improving management feedback, both JBM Packaging and The Body Shop enhanced training programs over time to help supervisors address more complex employee needs of marginalized workers.

Store managers at The Body Shop learned they needed additional training to manage a more diverse staff. For example, how do you support an employee who confides that they don't have stable housing? In response, the company rolled out an "Inclusive Leadership" course that addressed soft skills such as self-awareness about biases, courageous listening, and increasing emotional intelligence.

> We're continually challenged with biases that become evident with Open Hiring.

Cindy Alcantara, inclusive hiring manager for The Body Shop North America, explains, "These skills are needed because we're continually challenged with biases that become evident with Open Hiring. It's essential these biases are discussed, so leadership teams understand their impact on how they manage."

Unspoken in this discussion of maintaining performance standards is the issue of privacy when it comes to revealing that a new employee is a second-chance hire. At Precisely, this information is kept confidential. It is up to the individual to disclose it or to keep their personal story private. At JBM Packaging, on the other hand, they are so proactively involved in "fair chance" hiring that no effort is made to disguise an individual's past. Decisions about revealing an individual's justice involvement will invariably depend on company context, HR policies, and the new employee's desire to keep their story private. No matter what, you should be thinking about these decisions when you first consider hiring the justice-involved.

Maintaining Performance May Require Extra Support

In the world of second-chance hiring, there are some businesses, particularly very small ones, committed to almost exclusively employing ex-offenders who need little support with other aspects of their lives. At I Have a Bean, a tiny high-end coffee roaster, owner

Pete Leonard says, "I just want somebody who's just going to show up at work and do what they're supposed to do. Being such a small business, I don't have the bandwidth or money to keep training people." Leonard is completely committed to second-chance hiring, but only for those who need limited support. He says, "Sometimes we've paid rent for people, fixed their cars, bought clothing, picked them up, or dropped them off. It's not 'wraparound services' by any means, but it is lending a helping hand where we can."

In the world of second-chance hires, resolving performance problems isn't always a simple fix. At JBM Packaging, when one employee started being chronically late for work, a JBM executive declared, "Just buy him an alarm clock!"

But Allison Steele, a life coach at JBM, says,

> Is it possible there are more complex issues related to this performance problem? Instead of prescribing an easy fix, you need to embrace the tension around complex performance problems. Often an employee needs support in addressing multiple issues. Maybe this employee has undependable childcare or transportation issues out of their control.

You need to decide whether your business can address or outsource some of that much-needed support. Sometimes, frankly, external complications are just too overwhelming. One painful challenge is knowing when to let second-chance hires go. JBM Packaging sticks with an employee as long as they listen to a manager's feedback and try to change. CEO Marcus Sheanshang says,

> It's hard to find the balance between being kind and recognizing if they're not ready to change, they're not ready for us. You have to balance your heart and your mind. We're here to help people. But we have to run a business, too. There's a delicate line you walk saying, 'Hey, you might not

be ready to work here now. We're here when you're ready.' It's not black and white. Sometimes you see people who are so fragile. You talk with them and see they're putting on a brave face. But you know they're going home to some crappy place where a family member is using drugs or they're in some other bad situation.

Gregg Croteau is CEO of UTEC, a nonprofit agency that works intensively providing work training and wraparound services to gang and justice-involved young adults in Lowell, Massachusetts. He says, "The individuals you hire shouldn't be seen as different. But the coaching and support can be different. The attitude should be, 'We're going to give you more of what you need to be successful in the workplace. But we aren't going to treat you differently on the job.'"

From Inmate to Boss:
Lessons from an Employer Who Did Time

Ed Hennings doesn't need a job. He's too busy building his own businesses. Hennings spent 20 years in prison for reckless homicide when he intervened in a fight to protect a family member. Since his release, he's opened and run a beauty salon, a box trucking business, and now a cool men's shoe business.

Coming out of prison after 20 years, Hennings was nervous, fearing life and technological change had passed him by. But he found people walking around the streets of Milwaukee with their eyes focused on cell phones were the ones who weren't productive. While they were busy scrolling, Hennings was taking action. With an eye on the future, Hennings had taken a cosmetology course while in prison. He knew that if he didn't have some skill, he would likely return to his old gang lifestyle.

He landed his first job with a cold call to a barber shop. Within a year Hennings had opened up his own salon. One day, a client getting his hair cut told him about the box trucking business. Soon

Hennings was running up to five trucks delivering furniture and Amazon packages locally. Recently, he launched a new line of stylish men's work shoes—Ed Hennings Quality Footwear.

This guy is the real deal. He is a convicted felon who knows what it takes to do second-chance hiring. Hennings sounds like every other 50-year-old manager when talking about the impatience of the "younger generation" and their allergy to hard work. He is totally open to hiring people who will work hard for him, no matter what their background is. And he still can't find drivers for his trucks!

His approach, though unorthodox, provides lessons useful for managers looking to tap into the talent pool of second-chance candidates. Here are five things he's learned:

1. Look for the Applicant's Plan

When it comes to hiring the justice-involved, Hennings wants to know if you have a plan or realistic dreams for your future. He says:

> When I talk to somebody about driving a truck, or whatever the job, I always ask 'What are your goals? What's your plan?' If somebody doesn't have any goals, I'm not going to bring them on. What I've learned over the last seven years as an entrepreneur is that if it's only for the money, people are going to try to fleece the business for everything they can get. But people who have a goal or a plan have an incentive to be at work on time. They need the money, maybe to start a business or buy a house. These people have extra incentive to be at work because they have a bigger plan than just coming to work every day.

2. Paradox: Don't Assume Second-Chance Hires Will Stay, But Encouraging Growth Creates Loyalty

Hennings is clear. He treats all employees the same. "Be professional, keep coming to work and pursue your dreams," he preaches, adding:

> 'Don't let this job be your last stop. Make it your stepping stone to bigger and better things.' That's what I want to see from people, whether they've been incarcerated or not. We have

to give them the incentive. 'I know you want to own your own business. This is how you get there.' I'm saying, 'You can do it. You got to do it!' I don't vibe well with defeated people. I'm not gonna let you stay around long with a defeated mentality.

The irony is that encouraging people to grow and dream is more likely to create loyal, hard-working employees who stay longer than you might expect.

3. Use Recruiters That Candidates Relate To
Hennings is frank about the challenges of engaging with second-chance candidates. If you can't communicate and connect with this demographic, he insists, then bring in somebody they can relate to. He explains:

> I may have some Harvard people on my team, but I don't send them out to do this type of hiring. I'm gonna go in there, sit down with these guys and say, 'Hey, man, we got to get this shit together, man.' And they listen, as opposed to somebody else where they're thinking, 'Come on, man. You don't know what it's like to be in my shoes. You don't know what it's like to come from where I come from.'

4. Balancing the Head and Heart: Business Is Always the Priority
Hennings is all about second chances, but as a business owner, he's ruthlessly clear about his priorities. If there is any doubt about an employee's performance or honesty, the person is gone. He's very upfront with individuals he knows have come from incarceration. If they want to drive for Go Time Trucking and learn the trucking business, he tells them:

> I served time like you. I put my heart and soul into this business and I'm not risking it for you. I'm going to help you if you want it. But I can't let you jeopardize what I worked so hard for. If you put me in a situation where something is missing, remember, I'm choosing my business and everything I worked for. I want to see you succeed. But you got to want to see me succeed, too.

5. Finding "Diamonds in the Rough" Is a Process That's Worth It!

Hennings is realistic about the search he goes through to find productive employees from those who were recently incarcerated. He will hire several people before finding one really ready to change, and who brings the loyalty evident in gang life. Reflecting on his experience, he says:

> When you find that person, they make you so proud. They bring that same drive, loyalty, and the same fight they have on the wrong side over to the right side. But to discover them, you have to go through a process of finding people ready to do that.

Hennings concludes, "It takes a little more work to try to decipher all of that, but I know from hiring people myself you just have to be on your judgment game. There are some people that come home that are just not ready to change—true enough—but there's a large portion that are ready to change, given the opportunity."[41]

5. Upgrade HR Resources to Support Second-Chance Hires

When hiring justice-involved applicants, you will almost certainly have to enhance your human resource capabilities if you're committed to helping new hires reach performance standards despite outside circumstances. Here are three changes to plan for.

Create a Process to Identify Extra Support Needed

Thanks to its Open Hiring pilot, The Body Shop learned they needed a way to identify all new hires' needs outside of work in order to stay on the job. Cindy Alcantara, the company's inclusive hiring manager for North America, created a form that invites every new hire to share their personal preferences and interests, if they want to. This helped the company learn more about them as individuals.

The form also encouraged workers to tell the company about their immediate needs such as housing, financial literacy training, help with transportation, etc. This confidential information was forwarded to HR managers who sent it to the right employee assistance person.

JBM Packaging has a different process for discovering what support employees need. The company's two "life coaches" meet weekly with justice-involved employees to figure out what, if any, services individuals need. Needs vary from legal assistance or counseling for substance abuse recovery to help with housing and purchasing a car.

Your approach to second-chance hiring dictates the type of process you need to discover what support individuals need. Are you recruiting directly from prisons or halfway houses like JBM Packaging? Is an employee's past justice involvement widely accepted by other employees? Or are your workers' stories of incarceration private and theirs to share if they choose to, as they are at Precisely? No matter what, to make second-chance candidates a successful source of talent for your company, plan to develop some process for learning about the supplemental assistance individuals need.

Develop Extra Coaching Capabilities

Hiring workers going through reentry also means upgrading your coaching game. This extra training or guidance may come from inside or outside the company. Here are three examples of coaching resources:

On-the-job coaching. You may be surprised by the skills new hires are missing. Precisely found too many of its new business development representatives, who were second-chance hires, didn't know how to work a trade show effectively. Dressing appropriately, showing up on time for their shift, and proactively engaging with people walking by the company's booth were all behaviors that had to be taught in a brief training program. Skills and behaviors needed on the job are usually best taught by immediate supervisors and managers.

Specialized employee assistance coaching. For non-work problems, Brenda Kay, Precisely's SVP of business development, is clear about the limitations of her own coaching abilities when employees need help with personal challenges outside of work. Kay insists she has her company's employee assistance program staffers on speed dial when business development reps need extra support. Of course, the availability of employee assistance program expertise will depend on the size of your organization. Companies with inexperienced or limited HR resources are at a disadvantage here. Second-chance hiring is very difficult for HR novices.

JBM Packaging has two "life coaches" on staff to work with second-chance hires on their personal growth and development. CEO Marcus Sheanshang believes this is a costly but essential investment for his company, which is deeply committed to helping second-chance hires succeed. Describing the coaches, he says, "I call them 'Switzerland' because they deal confidentially with so many different issues to help employees."

In another example of intensive coaching, Nancy Lambert was a psychiatric rehabilitation counselor at US Rubber Recycling. This company invested heavily in second-chance hiring with its Bounce Back program. As a veteran coach for justice-involved job candidates, Lambert's motto is: "My job is to help you keep your job." Lambert, a former federal parole officer, is a type of specialized counselor or coach that more organizations may need to hire to increase the retention of second-chance employees.

Outsource coaching to nonprofits. In its North Carolina distribution center, The Body Shop outsources some coaching to Wake LRC, a local nonprofit that serves formerly incarcerated individuals. The retailer recognizes this nonprofit partner is well-suited to give its second-chance hires the extra help they need to stay on the job. In some cases, The Body Shop's retail stores also work with local nonprofit partners who are skilled at coaching particular marginalized populations, such as immigrants, those experiencing homelessness, and individuals with a criminal record.

Improve Hiring and Onboarding Processes

How do you get better at identifying "diamonds in the rough" from the talent pool of ex-offenders? Part of doing your homework is being clear about how the organization will handle background checks for candidates with a criminal record. Your HR department will need a process for responding when second-chance candidates are flagged as having a "felony conviction." Companies set different boundaries on what kinds of criminal records make an applicant unacceptable.

For example, there still is widespread resistance to hiring those convicted of sex-related crimes. JBM Packaging has a policy of not hiring people who have committed crimes against women and children. One thing employers don't understand is they have to set their own criteria about what kinds of convictions are acceptable in new hires. But those with experience in second chance hiring know it is important to view each applicant as an individual and to consider their crime in context. A 35-year-old who committed a crime of passion 15 years ago may be a much better bet than a 23-year-old who was just released for multiple offenses selling heroin. The three companies profiled in the previous chapters discovered that hiring justice-involved candidates is a journey requiring continuous improvement.

One option for better hiring is to expand the interview into a more collaborative process. Instead of one recruiter doing all the interviewing, JBM redesigned the hiring process so it requires meetings with three people. A standard job interview is now done by a supervisor, then one of the life coaches does a "holistic interview" to assess a candidate's readiness for work (e.g., Do they need transportation to get to work? If substance abuse has been a problem in the past, do they have a solid recovery plan?) Remember to review the sidebar in chapter 4, "Consult Local Ban the Box Laws," so you know to check city and state legal restrictions before asking questions related to incarceration.

> ... many people in marginalized communities are unaware positions exist in their retail stores.

Finally, at JBM a third interviewer takes candidates to shadow a machine operator who is doing the job they would be hired for. This brief exercise includes a short quiz to see how well an applicant can remember and follow instructions. By considering insights from the three interviews, JBM's hiring decisions are now a more collaborative and effective process.

Before interviewing, however, comes recruiting the right candidates. The Body Shop learned quickly that many people in marginalized communities were totally unaware that positions exist in their retail stores or warehouse. So they proactively pursued partnerships with local workforce nonprofits who serve overlooked populations like the formally incarcerated or those experiencing homelessness.

Once The Body Shop launched Open Hiring, the HR staff collected detailed feedback from store managers to determine how the program needed to be improved. This led to a series of new training programs for managers. The pilot also showed that open hires were more likely to lack skills needed to work in a retail setting, so training programs were introduced to fill these skills gaps. Recruiting, hiring, and onboarding processes will continually evolve as companies gain experience employing those who were formerly incarcerated.

6. Be Willing to Stumble and Learn from Mistakes

When exploring the market of second-chance talent, there is one more critical success factor. The decision to hire people with a criminal record or other underserved groups inevitably means there will be bumps in the road. Once The Body Shop had committed to Open Hiring, Jennifer Wale said,

> The way we're hiring now is so different from the traditional mindset of how you bring in talent. If our leaders weren't fully on board and willing to stumble a bit, then it would have been really difficult to succeed because the implementation can't be perfect.

Accepting the inevitable "mistakes" that come with hiring marginalized workers means acknowledging three things.

Expect to Cope with More Uncertainty

When Brenda Kay convinced her company to let those with a criminal record apply for jobs as business development representatives, she didn't know whether the women trained by Televerde would be able to succeed in the competitive hiring process. But eventually nine women made the cut.

The Body Shop implemented its Open Hiring pilot program, and store managers and warehouse supervisors quickly discovered they didn't know how to talk to employees about their needs outside of work, such as how to get time off to see a parole officer or what to do about housing.

Experiencing this sense of not knowing the next step or likely outcome is an unavoidable part of tapping into the second-chance talent pool.

Plan to Address Unanticipated Needs

It took a while for the need to become evident, but management at JBM Packaging discovered its supervisors didn't understand the lived experience of the ex-offenders the company was hiring. This made it difficult for those supervisors to coach second-chance hires with the empathy they needed to succeed. This overlooked gap in lived experience ultimately had to be addressed with a new training program for supervisors.

The Body Shop was surprised to find marginalized workers usually had no way of knowing about job opportunities with the retailer. Simply launching an Open Hiring program provided no assurance that candidates the company was targeting would actually apply. Solving this problem required a new effort to find qualified nonprofit partners in the local community who were already serving the needs of marginalized groups. "It's been a process. We're still learning what the full spectrum of employee support looks like," said Jennifer Wale, head of HR for the distribution center.

Uncover Biases and Learn from Mistakes

Precisely's Brenda Kay went into an Arizona women's prison seriously questioning the competency and capabilities of the inmates in Televerde's sales and marketing training program. She now freely admits how wrong she was in making assumptions about the skills and determination of the women she would eventually hire at Precisely. Engaging with formerly incarcerated job candidates consistently reveals untested biases that prevent companies from exploring the vast second-chance talent pool.

But even if a company commits to second-chance hiring, seeking to overcome biases, one of the biggest challenges in hiring any marginalized worker is deciding when to keep an employee and when to let them go. Often, inadequate performance is directly related to non-work issues employees face. This head and heart dilemma is a fine line to walk, according to Marcus Sheanshang, CEO of JBM Packaging. He confessed to mistakenly sometimes letting his heart rule, retaining an employee who just wasn't emotionally ready to work, when they really needed to be let go for the good of the business. Mistakes are part of all hiring processes and second chance hiring is no exception.

The Next Step Is Yours

Second-chance hiring isn't for every organization. But the demographic deck is stacked against businesses when it comes to finding skilled and even unskilled workers, and the talent pool of working-age adults in the US with a felony conviction is much too big to write off.

Your emotional commitment and business context will go a long way to determining the risks you are willing to take when hiring the formerly incarcerated. But even if you believe wholeheartedly in second chances, your business context may determine the practicality of hiring ex-offenders. Running a nuclear power plant or a children's preschool raises different concerns than ensuring a warehouse, manufacturing plant, or call center operates at peak efficiency. Your setting and tolerance for risk also influence your hiring practices and vetting process.

While The Body Shop is committed to hiring marginalized workers without a formal interview, resume, or drug test, JBM Packaging uses a much more rigorous interviewing process. Precisely, which sells sophisticated marketing software, hires only highly trained and vetted sales reps. I Have a Bean, a tiny high-end coffee roaster, is committed to only hiring the "cream of the crop" second-chance applicants who need little support before becoming productive. Each business has to assess its own willingness to take on risk.

Could your business benefit from second-chance hiring? Answering these questions can help you decide:

1. **What are the entry-level or lower-skilled jobs that are very difficult to fill in our company?**
2. **Can we find a partner in the region who prepares justice-involved individuals for the workplace? Does that potential partner have good references from other employers?**
3. **Why do we care about giving the formerly incarcerated a second chance?**
4. **Are we prepared to convince others in our company that it's worth a try?**
5. **Are we willing to make mistakes and suffer disappointments along the way?(Unlike your other hiring decisions, which *never* produce mistakes or disappointments, right?)**

If you have jobs you can't fill and can answer "yes" to the questions above, then second-chance hiring may be worth a shot. You have little to lose and, hey, you might change a life or two in the process.

SECTION 2

Recruiting and Employing Refugees

This section includes the stories of three organizations that are committed to recruiting, employing and retaining foreign-born workers, who may be refugees, asylum seekers, or immigrants. (See "What Should I Call You?" on pages 11-14.)

These stories show the incredible emotional and practical challenges refugees face when trying to find good jobs in the US. All three cases focus on employers hiring foreign-born workers into entry-level jobs. In reality, even refugees who are educated and reasonably proficient in English struggle with underemployment when they come to this country.[42] Foreign-born workers usually lack professional networks, as well as familiarity with the job search process, the workplace culture and career pathways in US companies. So it is hard to find stories of companies who are regularly hiring professionally-trained foreign-born workers. No doubt some employers have cracked the code for accessing this skilled talent, but most opportunities for new arrivals are in entry-level roles.

The experiences of Boston Children's Hospital, Clampco Products, HDF Painting and Main Street Gourmet show how, with the right leadership, partnerships and training, foreign-born workers can be a great resource for hard-to-fill jobs. Finally, these stories teach us how initiatives to employ foreign-born workers evolve over time. Refugees aren't the only ones on a journey. Chapter 9 summarizes the lessons learned across these different settings and provides insights from additional research.

The United States has a long history of integrating immigrants and refugees into society and the workplace. And the demographic trends are immutable: the structural labor shortage will, for the foreseeable future, continue to worsen in the US. Even amid shifting political environments, encouraging legal immigration and the employment of foreign-born workers will be increasingly essential for business growth.

CHAPTER 6

Boston Children's Hospital: How Partners Build a Talent Pipeline of Foreign-Born Workers

Like all healthcare organizations, Boston Children's Hospital faces major challenges in recruiting, training, and employing qualified staff for many positions in its complex operation. This chapter captures the lessons from their highly successful program, developed in partnership with Jewish Vocational Service of Boston. It shows how they recruit and train immigrants for hard-to-fill jobs critical to the institution's success in groundbreaking medical research. Rethinking the positions and how they could be filled by immigrants with limited English skills has created a tremendous opportunity to tap an underused, loyal, and hardworking talent pool.

Research and new discoveries are a big deal at Boston Children's Hospital (BCH), the top-funded pediatric research center in the US. Researchers and the staff who support scientists are critical to Boston Children's mission.

In August 2018, the hospital's research operations team was struggling to recruit and retain the research operations technicians needed to maintain and move forward with research studies. New hires would sometimes show up for their first day of work, but then not return on day two. The job paid $16 an hour. In a competitive labor market, people could find easier, less challenging jobs for the same pay.

Being 20 percent short-staffed on technicians posed a threat to the progress of certain projects at the hospital. Without enough technicians, BCH couldn't take on new research initiatives. Susan Schafer, director of research operations, explains:

> Being short-staffed with technicians impacts the leadership team because they must fill in, since research is our number one priority. And that creates a domino effect where the department's leaders are less available to provide customer service or special services to the researchers. Supervisors and technicians must work a lot of overtime preparing and cleaning. People get really tired and there's a lot of burnout when we're short-staffed.

Why Recruiting Wasn't Working

The way the hospital was recruiting technicians clearly wasn't effective. Anxious to find a solution, research operations leaders asked the hospital's HR department to review the entire recruiting, hiring, and retention process, including sourcing, interviewing, and assessment, as well as compensation, to see where the problems were.

Working with the research department's HR lead and the head of talent acquisition, Kristin Driscoll, director of workforce development at Boston Children's, identified key reasons for the staffing problems. Driscoll's team conducted focus groups with research operations employees. They soon realized BCH clearly needed to look at training and retention activities.

In practice, the hospital's language and literacy assessment tended to screen out potential candidates, and those who made it through had trouble communicating with one another due to a variety of cultures and accents.

The training new hires received was also inconsistent, presenting a major problem given the range of tasks involved in the technician's job. Work in the labs is very physical and fast-paced. Typical responsibilities include cleaning and running sanitation machines and checking other critical supplies. In addition, technicians need proficiency in English to be able to communicate with colleagues and researchers, read and respond to written prompts, and follow department standard operating procedures.

In the end, it became clear that potential applicants did not understand the entry-level research operations role. "It's not a common position," says Dr. Karen Krueger, senior director of research operations at Boston Children's. "People don't know what the job is. So it's hard to advertise a difficult, labor-intensive position that presents a lot of opportunity for career growth both inside the hospital and in the broader medical research industry."

Rethinking the Language Requirement

Searching for a solution, Driscoll's team began talking with Jewish Vocational Service of Boston (JVS), a longtime training partner for other jobs in the hospital. Mandy Townsend, senior VP of employer engagement at JVS Boston, worked with her team to further diagnose the hospital's staffing challenges. JVS helped to create a better approach by reviewing job descriptions, shadowing technicians on the job, studying the tasks, understanding standard procedures, and gathering information about the environment technicians worked in.

JVS also reviewed existing training materials. With this detailed analysis, Townsend provided frank feedback saying, "You're asking for a high level of English and a high school diploma and you're paying less than other jobs that require fewer work duties." Something had to change.

The hospital agreed. But because of other constraints, the education level and compensation couldn't change (although salaries have increased considerably since then). Research operations had no latitude in those areas. Boston Children's Kristin Driscoll, head of workforce development, explains, "That's when we started to ask what we could do differently to engage a group of people who have a high school diploma, but don't have the exact English skills we need. Could they get there with some support? That's how the new training program began."

> We know from working with a lot of refugees…a job like this can be ideal for individuals when English isn't their first language.

JVS suggested recruiting candidates with some English fluency, but who didn't yet have enough context-specific English to be successful in the technician's job. The hospital's training partner also proposed building a program that would give qualified participants the English training they needed to succeed in this hard-to-fill role. Devi Shiwnath, training program director at JVS, says:

> To do this job, a degree isn't required, and a successful technician can have an intermediate level of English skills because the job doesn't require a lot of verbal communication. They use a lot of standard operating procedures that can be taught.
>
> For example, in our research, we identified the types of candidates who have been successful in the job. We met a technician from Vietnam whose English skills were not very strong, but he had been in the job 17 years. He was thriving and felt very comfortable. At JVS, we know from working with a lot of refugees and immigrants, a job like this that offers a decent wage, parent-friendly hours, and

doesn't require a lot of writing and reading of new things can be ideal for individuals when English isn't their first language.

Designing a Prototype Program

With input from focus groups and after talking with JVS, Driscoll's HR team provided recommendations to the research operations leadership group. The hospital would partner with JVS to create a training program that produced a dependable pipeline of talent:

- JVS would recruit, assess, and select candidates for a 12-week training program that included six weeks of job-specific English language training.
- The hospital would interview the candidates and select six for each training cohort.
- BCH would hire a full-time training coordinator for the program to ensure consistent training.
- In addition to English language training, participants, who were being paid while in the program, would receive four hours of on-the-job training daily.
- After 12 weeks, the hospital would make job offers to some or all of the trainees in a cohort, and they would start work the following week as research operations technicians.
- JVS would provide regular coaching for program participants before, during, and after the training to address special needs that could undermine effectiveness of the training and ongoing retention.
- Driscoll and her team at Boston Children's would meet weekly with JVS to discuss any problems, concerns, or changes with the current cohort and technicians who had recently started on the job.

Winning Support for the Pilot

Driscoll's team took several key steps before launching the new training program. Initially, they had to get backing from the research department to make sure management was comfortable with this approach. But getting agreement on how to solve the staffing challenge was not simple. Krueger, senior director of research operations resources, recalls:

> Getting buy-in wasn't an easy process. We had to be convinced it was a good idea, and that took a lot of discussion. In our limited space, how many trainees could come on board at once without overwhelming our staff's ability to train them? There was a lot we had to figure out before going forward.
>
> Another hurdle was getting the budget approved. Boston Children's is a nonprofit, so anytime you're asking for money, you have to explain over and over the benefits and why It's needed. How is this investment going to save us money in the long run?

Driscoll's team also had to make sure there was consensus about the new training program among HR colleagues in specialized areas. Certain details had to be researched and approved. This required input from the hospital's experts in compensation and employee relations, as well as the legal department.

If You Build It, They Might Come

Before Boston Children's could launch the new program, they worked with Jewish Vocational Service, their recruiting and training partner. They had to design marketing materials to recruit viable candidates. This included website pages, as well as fliers and customized emails that mentioned English-as-Second-Language training and support. Both the hospital and JVS built in extra time for outreach and recruiting because they had no idea how long it would take to fill the first cohort.

To spread the word about the training program at the hospital, JVS wrote copy and launched ads on Facebook, Instagram, Google Ads, LinkedIn, Indeed, Craigslist, and their own website. They also reached out to community-based organizations serving different immigrant populations. When potential applicants provided their contact information, JVS invited them to an information session to tell people about the research operations training program.

JVS had been training immigrants in other programs in the Boston area for years, so they could also email information to existing community partners who would refer candidates to them. For example, the state's department of transitional assistance, which supplies food stamps and childcare vouchers, would spread the word about the training by sharing fliers with clients.

Refugee or Immigrant? Why Does It Matter?

It is easy to be confused by the different classifications of foreign-born job candidates who are not US citizens. Yaron Schwartz, director for the US at the Tent Partnership for Refugees, explains important differences this way:

> We use 'refugee' as a catch all phrase for all forcibly displaced migrants in the United States, because people fleeing violence and persecution come to the US under a variety of different legal immigration statuses. 'Refugee' is just one of those legal statuses, but others include 'special immigrant visa holder,' an 'asylum seeker,' 'humanitarian parolee,' and a few other categories. We focus on all of those people who are forcibly displaced, due to persecution or violence, using 'refugee' as a catch all phrase for all of them.

> From an employer's perspective, refugees in the US don't need to be sponsored by an employer. In contrast, an 'immigrant,' who chooses to move to the US for economic, education or family reasons, needs an H-1B visa, or another type of visa to work legally. But refugees receive their work authorization documents directly from the US government. That's a game changer for many companies who don't have the bandwidth to be able to sponsor an employee.

No Brag, Just Fact: Designing a Realistic Information Session

Devi Shiwnath designed the pilot program on the JVS side. She knew selecting applicants who would be successful in the training required being very forthright in describing the realities of the job and asking the right questions:

> It's a tricky thing to market. This is a full-time training program that leads to a full-time, benefited job at a prestigious hospital. But our goal was not to sell it as 'the best possible training program you could ever do, and you'd be so lucky to get into it.'
>
> The goal was to show them the hard parts of the job, while still helping applicants understand how they fit into the mission of Boston Children's Hospital. We didn't want to say, 'You should do this because you get paid well and we're giving you training.' We said, 'Are you okay wearing a mask all day? Can you stand for eight hours?' Then we showed them pictures of the facility so they could understand the actual context of the job.

Needle in a Haystack: Finding Qualified Trainees

To recruit 8-12 candidates to be considered for each cohort in the program, JVS sorts through hundreds of applicants and conducts scores of interviews to weed out those who don't want to work in the specific setting—for example, those who are planning to go back to school and can't commit to at least a year. Many obstacles come up in qualifying people for the job, and JVS tries to redirect those candidates to other opportunities.

Finding applicants who understood what it's like to work in research labs was key to the program's success. Lab technicians at Boston Children's have to be at work by 7:00 a.m., so commuting time and early-morning childcare needed to be on the applicants' radar. Devi Shiwnath, one of the program's designers at JVS, adds:

> Another thing that comes up is health problems. A lot of the immigrants or refugees we're serving are the caregiver for their families. So we've had clients who've had family members get sick, and they've had to drop out of the interview process.
>
> We've also had people who had to go back to their home country because something came up, or they're having to move further away from the city of Boston because who can afford to live here anymore? The city is driving people further and further out and that's not something we can fix. I have clients who are commuting well over an hour, but they're willing to do it because they now have a great, stable job.

In addition to attracting applicants, JVS developed assessments to qualify candidates who could be successful in the research operations job. No math assessment is necessary, since there is little requirement for that in the job. Nor do they need to assess computer skills. As long as candidates can comprehend and reply to basic information in an email, they have enough computer knowledge for this role.

But in screening applicants, JVS needed to check reading comprehension to make sure trainees can understand and respond to basic text. The job requires some basic reading, completing forms, and following written standard operating procedures—all of which is sometimes a struggle for people who speak a language other than English or who are new to the field.

Preparing for an Interview at BCH

Once Jewish Vocational Service accepts a candidate to be interviewed by the hospital for the research operations tech program, Shiwnath's team helps them prepare an updated resume and practice for the interview. Shiwnath says:

> We have a full-on interview prep day with them. We discuss common interview questions, and we review the job again, and how their skills fit. That's because in the immigrant community, talking about yourself is not done as often. So we help them understand, for example, that the job they had in Haiti is relevant. A lot of immigrants have been made to feel their past work isn't important. We fight through that and remind them, 'Yes, your past employment is very relevant.'

Each new set of candidates from JVS gets tours of the facility from research operations managers so they can see where they would be working. At the same time, back-to-back interviews are scheduled with hospital staff for the candidates that JVS is proposing. After the tour and the interviews, but before the hospital chooses six trainees for its next cohort, there comes an important interim step, as Shiwnath explains:

We let the candidates cool down a little bit and ask, 'Hey, what did you think of that tour, honestly?' And there will almost always be one or two people who say, 'Oh, no, absolutely not. I don't want to work in this environment.' And we'll say, 'That's fine.'

We train our coaches so that if someone realizes they don't want the job to make them feel really good about their decision. We let them know how grateful we are that they didn't just push through to do the training, that they actually said 'no.' That's because it can be hard to say 'no' to an opportunity sitting in front of you.

Identifying Who Will Succeed

Since its inception, the hospital has graduated more than 40 technicians from their training program. This experience has taught Boston Children's which candidates are more likely to thrive in the job. From the JVS perspective, Shiwnath says:

> It's a culture shock to come into this research facility if it's your first or second job. It's better for someone who has had some professional work experience. We're looking for people who are extremely reliable, willing to take feedback, and interested in learning. Somebody who is okay with repetition day to day is going to thrive here.
>
> We have a technician who was a police officer in Haiti for 18 years. He is all about discipline, accountability, reliability. He's really comfortable with the fact that every procedure is the same over and over every day. He's from the very first cohort and he's still here. But someone who wants something different and new every day is going to have a hard time.

Sometimes too much previous experience in healthcare can be counterproductive, as Kristin Driscoll explains:

> When you come to the US as a doctor from another country, many job seekers have to start over. So, we've had people using the program as a stepping stone to get into another job at the hospital. But those professionals are often better suited for other roles and we have programs in place to help them achieve the best job fit.
>
> Now we tend to guide foreign-trained health professionals to other opportunities since the research operations tech role is entry-level. We want to make sure the trainees are open to making a commitment to the department.

Show Time: Training Solution Goes Live

After building support and gaining approvals, the pilot program launched in April 2019. The first cohort had six people with intermediate level English skills. They received 12 weeks of training for which they were paid about $16 an hour. The decision to pay trainees was critical to attracting candidates who couldn't afford to give up the income from a job. But one complication Driscoll's team had to resolve was how much trainees should be paid relative to people who were already working the job and other new hires who didn't need language training.

The pilot led to an ongoing program that provides six weeks of job-specific English training. Participants come to the hospital under a temporary job code as "trainees" to avoid certain HR complications, and they start their day learning the job's regular tasks. After lunch, four days a week, participants receive two hours of English instruction, which is all contextualized to the job.

People hired as trainees have some proficiency in English, but they lack the vocabulary needed to work in the technician's role.

The afternoon classes reinforce the language they're learning during on-the-job training in the morning. Language training also teaches people how to communicate with others on the job. Driscoll explains:

> Technicians don't normally interact with scientists, but sometimes a researcher will come in and ask, 'What are you doing?' So the language training teaches employees how to respond in this situation.

After the six weeks of language training, trainees continue with on-the-job training. When they complete the 12-week program, most trainees are offered a full-time position and they start work the following week with an increase in pay.

Bajra's Story: From Bangladesh to Boston Children's

Bajra, as you saw in chapter 1, is an immigrant from Bangladesh whose husband left her shortly after resettling in Boston. She worked two jobs to pay rent and put food on the table for her two children. After five years of this grueling schedule, Bajra began squeezing in English language classes at Boston's Jewish Vocational Service (JVS).

One day at JVS she heard about a job at Boston Children's Hospital. She applied for the research operations training program and was one of the first people to be hired as a technician after completing the 12-week program. It wasn't easy. She remembers when she first came to the hospital's lab being very scared of the elevators and the machinery she worked with. "Maybe I can't work here," she thought.

But Bajra is an eager student and before long she mastered the technician's job and was teaching others. She recently applied for a supervisory position at the hospital that takes advantage of her leadership and training skills.

Bajra is proud of what she has achieved. Last year she bought a house in a Boston suburb.

She still takes classes at JVS. Someday she hopes to go back to school. Her daughter recently finished college and works as a video editor. Her son enlisted in the US Army, which will help pay for college. These days she loves to garden, cook, and teach others things she has learned. 'I am settled now in my mind and my life,' she says with a smile. 'The technician's job is much better than the other jobs I had. I'm proud to be supporting the scientists who are discovering new medicines for children. I can learn a lot about science. I love this job.'

Challenges of Running the Pilot Program

Of course, the pilot faced its share of obstacles. Driscoll recalls the HR team's concerns:

> There's always anxiety about will the program work? We're spending a lot of money to try this. Is the research department going to be happy? But, in the case of JVS, because we've worked with them on other programs, that anxiety was less.

Because of the time required to run the new program consistently, the HR team recommended the creation of a dedicated training coordinator position. Resources in research operations were already stretched very thin, but the department found a staff member who had worked as a technician at Boston Children's and who had originally learned English through programs at JVS. Driscoll was pleased to have this new coordinator in the role, but she says the scope of the program remained daunting:

> There were definitely moments where we're thinking, 'Okay, how exactly are we teaching these standard oper-

ating procedures for the department? How will this work? And how are we working together with JVS to build the training?' That first time around the team had to create everything from scratch around the assessment process and the English curriculum for the job. What's the department teaching these people? How are we doing that? What's the order of everything?

Living with Things Out of Your Control

While curriculum design could be managed, Driscoll quickly learned there were many things out of her control:

When it comes time to hire trainees full-time, there are always frustrating moments. You might have the greatest group of people, but then there's a family member sick, or somebody gets another job offer. So many different things can happen. Somebody's references didn't come back. Or we can't get a copy of their high school diploma or other barriers to employment. Sometimes that's a big problem. And sometimes the participants themselves aren't always up front about their readiness to work, or the feasibility of being in the program. Things come out of nowhere. Those can be pretty disappointing. Sometimes you can salvage it and sometimes you can't.

Creating a Sustainable Program

The rollout of the pilot program revealed another crucial detail: little details really matter. For example, whether a trainee starts with the rest of their group or not makes a big difference. Some of the small HR-related steps have to happen at certain times. Driscoll elaborates:

There are so many different steps to get cleared. It's such a detailed process. And, if you're someone who's entering the workforce in the US for the first time or reentering, or you've never worked in healthcare, it's like 'Why are they asking me for all my immunizations? Why are they asking for all these different things?'

It's easy for people to drop out, but I think because of the experience on the JVS side, they're asking all those questions upfront. This way no detail is left unaddressed. It's a matter of good project management.

Course Corrections: The Weekly Team Meeting

One key attribute of this training program is a weekly meeting with members of the core team at the hospital and at JVS to discuss any problems, concerns, or changes needed with the current cohort in training, as well as with technicians who have recently started on the job. Meeting participants also provide updates about the progress of the English class and the job training. When there's an issue, the team creates a plan to address it. Driscoll observes:

> I think this is the special sauce for all these initiatives we do. It's the communication and the problem-solving. It's the early and often communication if one of the trainees is having a hard time or facing a challenge. It's the program operations and the coaching. Also, we're constantly planning for the next group. It's a very collaborative effort to cover all of those details.

Coaching for Success

To minimize the impact of surprises, trainees and new hires receive ongoing coaching to deal with specific problems. Coaches routinely help participants address childcare issues, family illness, proper communication with their manager, and more. Driscoll adds:

> This is the type of thing that wouldn't happen if you were a regular hire. If they hired me, and all of a sudden I had a sick family member and I didn't call in and say, 'I'm not coming in today. There's been an emergency,' then I'd probably lose my job.
>
> **If somebody built this program, but they didn't provide any coaching, it wouldn't work.**
>
> But having that coaching support, where if I make that mistake, the JVS team is going to say, 'Hey, we understand why that happened and why you did that. But we need you to think bigger picture from the employer's standpoint. They need to know where you are. They're relying on you.'
>
> Sometimes a person says, 'I don't want to do this job anymore.' Participants can get overwhelmed by the volume of work and what we're asking them to learn. We really lean on coaches to provide a lot of that support. Some of it is helping the person cope with feeling overwhelmed in a new job.

Having JVS as a partner makes this extra support possible, and as Devi Shiwnath at JVS notes, it's key to the program's success:

> If somebody else built this program, but they didn't provide any coaching, it wouldn't work. They're navigating all these things in addition to starting a professional job in a new work environment. And for many of the people we serve this is the first job they've had of this sort. In coaching people new to working in the United States, we sometimes have to help them navigate how to have hard conversations, how to speak up if they don't understand something, and how to ask better questions.

A lot of candidates are single parents who don't know how to navigate public health systems or find important knowledge they may need to do the job. Maybe they really want this job. But they have to pick up their kids at two o'clock. The coaching is like, 'Can I help you find after school care? Then can you work until 4:30?' That's key. Sometimes it's as simple as saying they need help with something. We navigate a lot of that in this program because of the backgrounds of candidates we work with.

Workforce Training Pays Off

The key objectives of the research operations tech training are to effectively staff research operations and to bring new employees into the hospital who will stay at Boston Children's. There is normal attrition, of course, but given the costs of training and onboarding, the research department needs new technicians to stay at least a year for the program to pay off. As Susan Schafer, director of research operations, notes:

> The payoff is huge. People coming in through the training program are very grateful. They're hardworking. They have to work because there's no one else they can depend on. And, whether it's the people or the program, we're having new technicians promoted faster than in the past and becoming trainers for the new cohorts. It's working really well.

By end of 2022, the hospital had run seven cohorts over three years. They've had 42 trainees. Some 73 percent completed the program and were hired, and 56 percent have been retained in the department. Several have been promoted to level 2 technicians or trainer positions, and two now work in other parts of the hospital. Quite the turnaround for a frontline position that was once so hard to fill.

To build on this progress, the research operations department created a formal career ladder so staff can anticipate and pursue career advancement. In addition, the HR team has an internal education and career coach to help new technicians plan their careers in the hospital. Kristin Driscoll, the hospital's director of workforce development, explains:

> We tell people, 'This is what we're offering right now. These are the opportunities, the scholarships, computer classes.' Everything under the sun. Research operations is one of the biggest departments participating in the programs because the staff's schedule remains the same. They don't have varying hours, and most of our classes are offered in the afternoon or early evening hours. So it's accessible for our new trainees. And then our coach can work with people to build out a plan after thinking about what they want to do.

When the hospital's research department was hiring technicians one or two at a time, it seemed as though they were constantly training new hires. With the cohort model, however, the number of job requisitions the department needs to post has substantially decreased.

> ...research operations now onboards three to six people at a time, ...and the department has a reliable pipeline of trained technicians to help plan for growth

With the new program, research operations now onboards three to six people at a time, and even if one or two participants don't work out, the department has a reliable pipeline of trained technicians to help plan the growth of future research activities.

From a monetary standpoint, the training costs JVS $9,800 per seat to run for a cohort of six people, with BCH's research department paying about $6,400 per trainee. JVS has been subsidizing the uncovered costs through external grants.

The investment is worth it given the costs avoided due to turnover, extra overtime, third-party agency staff placements, the disruption of research operations, and potential burnout of remaining staff.

In developing its partnership with JVS to train immigrants, Boston Children's has shifted from the train-and-pray model to a talent pipeline model where the hospital knows it will be hiring qualified candidates who will support critical research efforts for years to come. As Driscoll notes, the program's value extends beyond the research team:

> From the HR workforce development standpoint, we're taking this model and copying it to other areas like behavioral health and patient access, and other entry-level positions that don't require a specific credential. It makes those jobs accessible for people who don't have the funding for training. And this helps them get their foot in the door at the hospital. Then, we can help grow and develop that person within the hospital. This approach pays people to learn jobs that we critically need at Boston Children's.

Five Lessons for Training Foreign-Born Workers

Having trained and onboarded more than six cohorts in training and onboarding research operations technicians, the team at Boston Children's Hospital and Jewish Vocational Service have learned important lessons in supporting workforce initiatives designed to train and employ immigrants more effectively.

1. Old Solutions Won't Cut It Anymore—Think Creatively

For example, Boston Children's examined how hard it was for non-native English speakers to apply for jobs in the hospital. Not surprisingly, as head of workforce development, Kristin Driscoll's HR team found if you've never filled out a job application in the US, it's a complicated, multi-level process that is hard to navigate.

Traditionally, candidates would apply for a variety of entry-level jobs at the hospital and get no feedback if they were turned down. To improve the hiring process, Driscoll's team now conducts introductory calls with job applicants, sort of like an informational interview. Driscoll explains:

> We learn about the candidate, so we can advocate for them beyond their application. We know that for workers who've recently arrived to the US, it's very hard to get that first job. Many end up in very entry-level positions, because they're limited by their resume, or maybe their English skills, or both. Navigating the US job system is really difficult for foreign-born workers.
>
> Required English level proficiency varies by the job in a healthcare setting. But for people who have been working on their English, we can at least provide coaching and feedback around what might be a good starting job for them. And we can also show them how to interview more effectively, or what types of questions they're going to be asked, so they can prepare a little bit.

2. Collaborate With a Trusted Partner to Build Your Pipeline Over Time

To fill the research operations technician roles, Driscoll and her team realized they needed an experienced partner organization that had demonstrated the ability to find, assess, and prepare immigrants for training. JVS Boston fit this bill, given their long experience in training foreign-born workers. Boston Children's knew they had to be cautious about potential partners who might promise more than they could deliver. They looked at the agency's track record in producing qualified candidates over time. One question to consider: where will your coaches come from? Mandy Townsend, the senior VP of employer engagement at JVS, agrees:

> Find a training provider with a business mentality. They will understand the finances of the project, the delicacy of running an excellent pilot, and how results should be quantified to deliver.

3. Help Candidates Picture Working for You

Reflecting on lessons learned, Karen Krueger, senior director of research operations resources, explains:

Planning is everything. A big part of success is the planning and working through exactly what the candidate needs to know to make them want to work here. Try to anticipate what it's like for a person to walk in the door who knows nothing about your program. Even before they're hired, we bring them in and show them what the place looks like. We make sure that they understand the realities of the job, even though it's been explained to them.

They walk into the facility and get a sense of where they would work. And we're able to help them picture themselves working for us. And all the training we do is to encourage them to keep going. We continually remind them, 'You're going to learn more. This is going to get more interesting.' And, again, ultimately it's providing them opportunities for growth. So it's not a dead-end job by any means.

4. Use Coaching to Address Barriers to Employment

According to Susan Schafer, head of research operations, one of the things the team had to expect was that problems arise. Coaching for program participants and graduates is key to success and helps to remove barriers. Making use of hospital resources like Employee Assistance Programs, financial well-being benefits, and others can be helpful for training program graduates and other staff within the hospital.

5. Plan to Pay People in Training

Driscoll realized the hospital had to think differently about compensating research operations technicians if it was going to attract more promising candidates. "Entry-level workers often can't afford to train or work for free to learn a new skill. We had to approach this non-credentialed job in a different way. We are going to pay people for the time they invest with us." said Driscoll, who added, "If we're going to build a new staff of technicians, we have to compensate people for their time."

CHAPTER 7

Clampco Products: Betting on Refugees to Build a Sustainable Business

Like most small manufacturers, Clampco Products has struggled to recruit and retain productive entry-level workers. This Ohio-based, family-owned manufacturer took a big gamble when it began hiring refugees. Taking on foreign-born workers with little or no English skills was a bet that has paid off big time. Clampco's story shows how one company navigated numerous challenges, such as cluster hiring when new employees spoke no English, finding jobs that were the best fit for refugees, and overcoming transportation trials. In the end, it is all about helping new employees cope with the inevitable—and sometimes funny—surprises that come when people from different countries and cultures try to find common ground in the workplace.

"What have I done?" thought Jason Venner when nine Congolese refugees arrived at his family-owned manufacturing plant outside of Akron, Ohio on a warm summer day in 2017. Venner, vice president of Clampco, still remembers that moment.

> We brought them into our conference room and showed the refugees some required OSHA and sexual harassment videos in English, of course. They had no idea what they

were watching. But our safety program requires us to show these to all new employees. I could tell they were more concerned about what they were going to be doing. Is this going to be a nice place to work? Several of them had literally just gotten off a plane from Africa. They were probably jet-lagged. We tried to have them fill out paperwork, but some couldn't use a pencil. That was the level we started at.

Clampco Products is a family-owned business with 275 employees that makes customized stainless-steel clamps and fasteners for customers in aerospace, construction, marine, medical, and a variety of other industries. They were desperate for entry-level talent to manually assemble smaller orders of clamps. They also needed operators to run automated equipment that produced thousands of clamps a day.

Venner had been to numerous forums listening to employers in northeast Ohio complain about the shortage of good employees. He had tried all the usual solutions—job fairs, job posts on social media, and networking through government employment agencies. Clampco had also used a lot of temp agencies and headhunters without much success. They even tried organizing a local manufacturing partnership to create a pool of job candidates. Nothing worked.

Venner knew that when workers were not available, increased overtime was needed to get jobs done. This could lead to quality issues and scheduling problems, both of which hurt the company's profitability. An important part of Clampco's competitive advantage was its ability to deliver with short lead times. But being short-staffed required those delivery schedules to be pushed out, which didn't make customers happy. Continual turnover in the workforce also meant experienced employees were constantly being pulled off jobs to train new hires. Workforce shortages were costing the business significantly.

Deciding to Tap Refugee Resources

One day Venner was airing the usual complaints about the ongoing labor shortage. The head of the local economic development group listened thoughtfully before speaking. "There is a solution," she said. "It just depends on how open-minded you're going to be."

The director suggested contacting a local resettlement agency about hiring refugees who had recently moved to the area. Venner knew refugees were relocating to the region, but he had no idea how to tap into this group. Getting the suggestion to connect with the agency was a serendipitous moment that would change the workforce at Clampco in ways Venner never imagined.

He contacted the Ohio Resettlement Bureau* and gave their director of employment services a tour of the plant. The bureau invited Venner to try an experiment. They had nine Congolese refugees coming to the Akron area within a month and would Clampco be willing to take a chance employing them? The refugees spoke only rudimentary, if any, English. Venner took the chance.

> **We were so hungry for available workers it didn't matter what part of the world they came from.**

The Democratic Republic of Congo has suffered through decades of violent conflict, forcing millions of people to leave their homes. After years in refugee camps, thousands of these victims legally find their way to other countries. In the last two decades, the US has been one of the leading recipients of Congolese refugees hoping to start a new life.

Clampco's vice president recalls their decision to invest in foreign-born workers:

---

* This agency's name has been disguised at their request.

We were so hungry for available workers it didn't matter what part of the world they came from. I was willing to give it a try because of the way my parents had built the business. They started it in my grandma's garage and were open-minded right off the bat. Anybody willing to help is a resource. I believed our staff would work past the initial language barrier.

But having an idealized view of working with refugees can only get you so far. Clampco had to confront several challenges to successfully tap into this market of foreign-born workers.

Cluster Hiring Helps Language Training Pay Off

Language was the most obvious obstacle the company had to overcome to turn these foreign-born workers into productive employees. Clampco, however, had an important advantage from the start: instead of hiring just one or two Congolese workers, they effectively hired a cluster of them. This meant any investment in translation capabilities or language training benefited several employees, not just one. If one or two left, the investment was still worth it. And, perhaps more importantly, this cluster of workers were often members of the same family. They shared common social bonds and language, which made staying at Clampco more comfortable and compelling. Venner observes:

> Individuals coming from a foreign country are probably very frightened at first. To show up on the job with your dad and mom in tow is probably very reassuring. It wasn't an intentional strategy at the outset, but clustering is effective because it supports a sense of community and doesn't split families up. Also, one member of that first group of individuals we hired was a former teacher who

spoke a little English. He was integral in helping us do a lot of translating.

Clampco supervisors initially trained their new employees from the Congo to work in the manual assembly area. Through a lot of pointing, smiling, and nodding, veteran employees demonstrated the process and then watched the new hires practice. Fortunately, the second shift included several women—often referred to as "den mothers." They took a special interest in teaching the refugees, which also meant the women learned basic Swahili words—please, thank you, bathroom, smoke break, and so on.

But this experience was a wake-up call for Venner and his team. They recognized the limits of the refugees' English language skills and made English language training a priority. Venner's team set up a small computer lab where workers would come two days a week for an hour before their shift to go through an online English module. They were paid to be in class, and Clampco provided food, which seemed to help.

Management also found free or low-cost resources providing English-as-a-second-language training on software platforms the company could use as beta testers. This allowed Clampco to tap into training software that would otherwise cost $3,500 a head. Venner explains:

> The language barrier was the biggest challenge. These individuals were smart, and they wanted to work hard. But literally, we didn't know how to tell them, "Break time is at noon." So it slowed things down. It took a year for that first group we hired to get their feet underneath them so they were autonomous. That meant they could sign into their jobs and do paperwork on their own and sign their names.

When there is training material that everyone needs, such as a safety module, the company draws on Congolese employees who are strong English speakers and has them translate for small groups to make sure the lessons are communicated.

As the company hired more Congolese refugees, they found younger workers were often more proficient in English. In small groups, these newer employees would tutor fellow refugees who lacked English skills. Eventually, Clampco converted the language lab into a fully operational training room with computers set up for all kinds of training. They also started offering GED classes to US-born employees who hadn't finished high school. The need for new training benefited more employees than expected.

Missing the Bus at 2:30 a.m.

Clampco is located in a small city 25 minutes outside of Akron, where there is no viable public transportation. One of the first problems the company had to solve was getting the refugees to and from work. None of them had driver's licenses, much less cars, and they were living almost half an hour from the plant. Congolese workers were staffing the company's hard-to-fill second shift, which ended at 2:30 a.m. This seriously limited commuting options.

Venner got creative and found a temp hiring agency that promised to provide bus service to get employees to and from work. This transportation solution meant that instead of hiring the refugees directly, Clampco initially hired them through the staffing agency so they could get to the plant. The busing solution worked temporarily, but it didn't prove dependable. Sometimes, the agency's bus failed to show up at 2:30 a.m. to take the refugees home from their second-shift jobs. That would leave workers milling about outside the plant in the middle of the night waiting for a ride. Supervisors had to stay with them until everyone was eventually picked up. No one was happy about that.

When Clampco converted its initial cohort of foreign-born workers from temporary to permanent employees, the bus service was no longer an option. The company encouraged workers who had secured a driver's license to begin carpooling. They found family and friends were the best predictor of where ride-sharing would work. Soon, it was not unusual for three cars to arrive at once crammed with refugees ready to start their shift. Busing proved a good way to get the program started, but encouraging employees to find their own transportation was key to making it sustainable.

Strong Partnerships Address Resettlement Challenges

Venner's serendipitous connection to the Ohio Resettlement Bureau (ORB), a refugee resettlement organization, provided the company its first wave of new employees. But Clampco wanted partners who could help them transition successfully long term. They also needed experts to handle legal documentation that proved foreign-born candidates were qualified to work, as well as providing initial work readiness and language training.

Soon after refugees first arrived, Venner and his HR and IT managers met with the ORB's leaders and staff attorneys. They quickly affirmed this nonprofit organization was skilled at dealing with complex immigration issues and the process of getting refugees resettled. Venner and his colleagues also learned more about the US workplace orientation training given to ORB's clients.

Venner was strategic in building relationships with partners who could help him employ foreign-born workers. By building a relationship with ORB early on in Clampco's efforts to hire foreign-born workers, he wanted to ensure it would be easier to work out problems that inevitably would arise later. He explained:

I let the bureau know I've got to run a business. So, if one of these individuals doesn't work out, I want them to have met me and realize I'm not just some guy making decisions based on a balance sheet. There are good reasons behind our decisions. And there was another reason we went to meet with ORB. If things worked out well, I wanted Clampco to be their number one client. I don't want these workers going somewhere else.

Overcome Staff Resistance to Doing Difficult Things

Venner came away from his visit to the bureau thinking this could be a goldmine of future talent. Building a strong partnership also gave him legitimacy with his managers to say, "This is me taking care of the business." Venner also found a temp agency that was used to working with immigrant populations to fill staffing needs at bigger companies. Once the agency understood what Clampco wanted in hiring refugees, they completed employee intake and verified the I-9 employment eligibility paperwork to get the new arrivals ready. Clampco's vice president insists,

> This is not charity. It's a serious investment in our future. I thought we could solve our short-term labor shortages by creating long-term partnerships and pathways with a group that was willing to work hard so we could continue to grow and serve our customers.

Still, when he first decided to hire the refugees, Venner had expected some pushback from his current employees. He got what he describes as "typical responses":

- "Jason's going to bring in these folks who will take our jobs." (Of course, that was never the case, he says.)

- "If they're coming to this country, they should speak English."

Clampco's leaders acknowledged these feelings. But the company needed workers badly, especially on the night shift. When the individuals they hired got past the initial training stage and started showing their value, experienced employees became much more supportive and welcomed the revival of that shift. It meant veterans didn't have to work as much overtime.

> **The most important lesson out of this experience is you keep learning about things you need to improve on.**

Line managers faced the biggest challenges, particularly as refugees started to take on more complex work. Handling more difficult tasks required more attention from supervisors. Venner recalls:

> The plant manager and I had a couple of meetings talking the supervisors through their frustrations and reinforcing to them that I've asked them to do this very difficult thing, but that I know they can do it.

For example, there was a touchy time when US-born workers complained about the body odor of some refugees they were working with. Venner is philosophical about this experience, saying:

> Hiring these individuals has taught all of us, myself included, an element of grace. Together, we're all part of this thing called "humanity." I may show up to work one day having forgotten to put on deodorant. Things happen. So, there was some gentle education for the Congolese. And also for the supervisors. We realized that there were soft skills supervisors needed to talk to their employees and explain these situations and work through them.

Eventually, the plant manager started meeting with Clampco's supervisors from both shifts every day at three o'clock. These meetings allow supervisors to share information about personnel issues and to make decisions about production process problems. Venner says:

> It's helpful for our supervisors to feel supported because they have a hard job. But the most important lesson out of this experience is you keep learning about things you need to improve on. The challenges are never going to end, especially if you have cultural and socioeconomic differences. You're always reaching across the aisle so to speak to get everybody moving in the same direction.

Finding a Fit: What Jobs Can Refugees Do Best?

Even with Clampco's investment in English language training, one unexpected challenge was figuring out what jobs new employees with limited English could and couldn't do. Initially, the Congolese workers were trained in the manual assembly area. This made sense because despite having almost no English, new hires could be successfully taught through demonstrations and by seeing blueprints. But finding other jobs that fit wasn't as simple as it first appeared, and management hadn't yet thought about pathways to career advancement for its foreign-born workers.

The first Congolese workers Clampco hired were assigned to do manual work, assembling clamps by hand. Although these tasks seemed simple on the manual assembly side, they required more knowledge of English than management realized. Orders are small, but several components in manual assembly require some reading. Even today, only a few refugees at Clampco who speak and read English fairly well work in this area.

The company discovered over time that the high-volume, high-repeatability work suited those with rudimentary English language skills much better. Most Congolese refugees hired after that first wave went directly to Clampco's highly automated work cells. Those with very limited English could quickly begin using high-volume machines that involve only a couple of parts and might produce 500,000 clamps a year. Once taught to run the machine, new hires could be producing parts within a matter of hours. Some refugees progressed more rapidly than others, of course. Two of the original group began operating 300-ton punch presses, two-story-tall machines that require considerable training to set up. These operators must pay close attention to detail because one mistake can produce thousands of unusable parts.

Clampco's reputation as a good employer for refugees spread in the Akron area, and more and more recent arrivals from the Congo began applying for jobs. They came with varying levels of English language skills. Venner said:

> We had to figure out what type of work naturally fits them. Today, on the production floor, we have workers who are Congolese in every area. Do you like working with your hands, pressing a foot pedal over and over, or working with robots? We try them out in different areas. And we've found the older Congolese employees worked as well in all areas as younger ones.

Your understanding of what jobs foreign-born workers can best perform will probably evolve and so will your training that supports them. That's the lesson from Clampco's experience. A few jobs are better suited to those with limited English skills, and they won't always be obvious. Some employees will progress faster than others when it comes to acquiring new language skills, and they may be eager to move to more complex jobs. But Venner has found a surprising number of Congolese are not anxious to take on more complex positions, even though they may be capable of a promotion. He has even noticed some seem to downplay their increased proficiency in English as an excuse for staying in their current job. This has been a surprise. Don't assume everyone wants a promotion.

From Congo to Clampco: Papa Is Not a Rolling Stone

> Lusata was 34 when he left his homeland. The civil war in the Democratic Republic of Congo meant he and his family lived in constant fear of being killed by soldiers. They fled to neighboring Zambia, where they lived a marginalized existence as refugees with thousands of other Congolese fleeing violence in their country.
>
> Lusata and his wife spent 17 years in limbo in Zambia, never knowing when they could leave. Their oldest child secured papers and resettled in Finland; such is the unpredictable diaspora of Congolese refugees. Lusata studied agriculture but worked as a community health worker, a job he liked. In 2016, everything changed when his family was allowed to emigrate to the US. They ended up in Akron, which must have seemed like a very foreign place.
>
> Lusata speaks six languages, including multiple dialects of Swahili and some French. Initially, he dreamed of continuing his work as a community health worker. But with limited English, the job market had different plans for him. His first job was as a cultural liaison in an Akron school, helping Congolese parents and students communicate with teachers. A local resettlement agency found him the role, and they insisted he sign a contract committing to stay for a year. "That job was great. But, if there was no school, I wasn't paid," recalls Lusata, who had to support his family, which grew to include seven children. "Sometimes you had a job. Sometimes not. During vacation, no job, no money. I wasn't happy about that."
>
> One day Lusata was asked to visit Clampco to act as a translator during orientation for some newly hired Congolese employees. He

liked what he saw of the company, which already included a small community of workers from his home country. He asked if he could work there, but the resettlement agency insisted he had signed a contract and could not leave his part-time job at the school for another six months. He returned to the school and honored his commitment.

Lusata applied to Clampco six months later and was hired immediately. He liked assembling clamps. But it took him a long time to understand the assembly process, although he did it well once he was trained. The hardest part was when new products were introduced. He couldn't decipher the blueprints. He needed help from his co-workers.

When Lusata first came to Clampco, some people couldn't pronounce his name and simply called him "Papa." He wasn't sold on the name at first, but with a face weathered by years of struggle, his new nickname stuck. Two of Lusata's older children later worked at Clampco and they used it regularly in addressing their father. "Now I am proud to be called Papa," he says with a warm smile that subtly reveals a missing front tooth.

Lusata has some chronic health problems. The stress and strain of the war and years as a refugee in Zambia have caused his back to hurt and his legs to swell, producing constant pain if he stands too long. He's found a way to change positions on the plant floor every thirty minutes. Now he works around these physical challenges. In the meantime, his perspective has shifted in his seven years at the company.

> My dream when I came to America was to continue training as a community health worker. I don't dream that anymore. I focus on what I am doing here. Maintaining my job as a technician is what I am working on now. I'm very happy here. We have a lot of Congolese working at Clampco, and they like it very much. We are given a job we can do well, and the collaboration between the workers and managers is good. We work as one team.

Culture Divides—Humor Heals

Foreign-born workers bring with them the norms and behaviors of their home country. Sometimes this causes confusion in the workplace. Other times it leads to experiences that are humorous in retrospect.

For instance, the culture of workers from the Congo is very communal. If the plant manager had an issue with one refugee, the whole group would show up in the manager's office, even though most of them didn't know why they were there. This created more than a few awkward moments in resolving problems. Addressing issues collectively was something Venner and his team had to learn to expect.

When refugees were converted from temp hires to full-time employees, they lost bus transportation provided by the staffing agency. In finding creative ways to get to work, one employee drove a sporty Mustang he somehow secured without even having a driver's license. Local police were not amused when they saw this new arrival driving down the middle of the road. But they were more understanding when Venner explained the agitated refugee's only motivation was to get to work on time.

Engaging with employees who have not yet been socialized into the US culture surfaces different priorities, needs, ways of communicating, and problem-solving. Learning to respond constructively to these surprises is critical for success. But, in Venner's experience, the lack of predictability is more than worth it. "For every difficulty we ran into there was a feel-good story that came with it," he says.

> **Repairing communication breakdowns can sometimes lead to authentic, heartwarming connections.**

For example, a young refugee approached Venner the day after all the Congolese employees had shown up when he was expecting to speak to just one of them. She said, "I want to apologize for the group. We were all embarrassed. We thought you were upset with us." Venner smiled and explained that he wasn't upset. He was just trying to work through the language barrier to understand what one employee's problem was so they could fix it. Repairing communication breakdowns can sometimes lead to authentic, heartwarming connections.

Ongoing Challenges Are Not Lost in Translation

Clampco hired anybody the agency sent when they took on their first group of refugees. Now, they have set stricter guidelines about who they hire. The company requires foreign-born applicants to have at least some conversational English abilities before taking them on. It has proved too taxing to employ people with no language skills.

No one learns English overnight. The challenges of communication and language are ongoing when hiring foreign-born workers. Upon discovering potential hires spoke one of four different dialects of Swahili, Clampco had to set boundaries on how much it would invest in translation for its employees.

Venner had experience in the human resources department. He knew how much paper the company threw at a new employee related to rules, policies, regulations, and so forth. He realized the cost of translating all this into four dialects alone would be exorbitant. So management began thinking about how to make Clampco a more visual factory with colored scoreboards (green and red lights) and roman numerals, instead of written signs around the factory. Now, operators can look up and see visual cues that tell them when they need to pick up the pace.

The company has also set new standards for its software vendors, choosing suppliers whose user interfaces can accommodate different languages. Recently, Venner made the difficult decision to change payroll providers. Clampco needs software that will allow employees to read pay statements in their own language. Venner admits:

> We can't translate everything. We're just choosing the most critical things we can provide employees. And we've become wiser. We want to be welcoming, but the operating language of the business is English. We have to trust that the Congolese themselves will figure it out and will learn basic conversational English.

Career paths present another evolving challenge when managing foreign-born workers, as they must benefit both the employees and the company. Venner believes career paths can shrink turnover:

> The quality of our products and our profitability increases the longer employees are here. We want to reduce turnover to the point where people should only be leaving for a career change. It shouldn't be because there is no opportunity for them here.
>
> We offer the same career improvement paths to Congolese employees as we do to anyone. Language may be more of an issue, of course. So, it has to be done on a case-by-case basis. For example, if we are working with a welder who wants to become a technician, we have to invest in more training. They will have to learn decent English, but we'll pay for a tutor if it encourages them to stick around for two more years.

Benefits of Hiring Refugees

Clampco has hired about 15 Congolese refugees annually over the last five years. Of course, not all stayed. But foreign-born workers now make up 25 percent of the company's total direct labor workforce. Seven of the original nine hired were still with the company six years later.

Hiring refugees has produced at least three benefits for the company. The first is filling major staffing gaps in the plant's second shift. Clampco now has a waitlist of refugees who want work there. How many manufacturing companies can say that today? Venner says:

> If we hadn't explored this route, we'd still be facing the worker shortage a lot of other employers have. But once we turned on that faucet—brothers, uncles, cousins, nephews, nieces, grandmas—they were all waiting in line to work for Clampco. They just happen to be from the Congo. We wanted a group interested in a factory job and willing to get their hands dirty. If they were from Burma or Nepal, it wouldn't have mattered. We would have found a way to work with them.

With new technologies that can measure output of the automated machines in real-time, Venner's team has also found the foreign-born workers are outproducing their US-born counterparts: "They've reinvigorated our second shift production staff, and they work their US-born counterparts under the table. It's made us realize we can be more efficient than we thought."

Finally, hiring refugees brings unexpected challenges, but those issues are often less concerning than many standard workforce problems. With more foreign-born employees, transportation, visa, and communication challenges replace normal HR issues such as employees with substance use disorders and poor attendance. Venner finds the new surprises a worthwhile tradeoff:

As Americans, we take a lot for granted. But the people we've hired come in the door and feel the need to prove themselves. They have to have a job. To have a job, they have to have a home, and in order to keep those things, they have to work hard. As a result, the number of personnel issues we deal with are next to none. We're a different workforce now.

It's Good Business, Not Altruism

Venner knows hiring Congolese refugees has changed his company. And he is adamant that the decision to invest heavily in foreign-born workers is not an act of charity.

This is me trying to staff the company so that we don't lose business, so we can keep paying people. and so my parents can retire comfortably. If this group of employees coming from the Congo are willing to help, then we'll bring them along too.

Outside of overcoming the language barrier, the biggest challenge for me has been patiently reminding people in the business community that I didn't do this because it looks good on my resume. Our business was struggling and we found a solution. These are great workers. And the rest of our workforce suddenly has new standards to hit.

When Clampco's front door opened six years ago, and Venner saw nine Congolese refugees nervously walk in, he remembered thinking, "Oh, man, this is either going to be really awesome or just really bad." Today he knows the answer.

From Haiti to High Gloss: How a Small Company Tapped Refugee Talent to Help Build a Future

Like almost every business owner looking for staff, Dan Frost has struggled for years trying to find dependable, hardworking painters who can complete high-end residential jobs in the Boston suburbs. Recently, he decided to do something about this ongoing problem. A local Best Western hotel in his Concord, Massachusetts, hometown had been transformed into a shelter for newly arrived migrants, many of whom were seeking asylum from Haiti. Frost emailed the shelter's manager and said his company was looking for one or two apprentice painters and asked if they had anyone he could interview?

The manager emailed Frost back immediately, saying she had several people he could talk to. The next day, the veteran painting contractor arrived at the old hotel, where the shelter manager had two men ready to be interviewed. Working with a translator provided by the shelter, Frost interviewed each man, who only spoke Haitian French, asking them about their past work experience. They each seemed to have some basic painting experience, but Frost was unsure how that would translate into the high-end residential work his company did.

Their motivation to work was clear, however. One of the men later confessed he had spent four months looking for a job. "They just wanted to know when can I start," says Frost.

Two days later, Frost returned with his son Harrison, co-owner of the business, along with one of their foremen to meet the two refugees, as they would when considering any new hires. Again, working through a translator, the younger Frost and the foreman came away impressed.

Dan Frost says he was looking for three things in his interviews: people who work hard, who will be on time, and who are receptive to instructions. "If you do those things, we can train you," says Frost. He saw that potential in the two men. He explained through the translator that all new employees had to pass a three-month trial. After that, they'd get the benefits of paid holidays, and the business offers health insurance. "We have an employee handbook that we have done in English, and we've done it in Spanish, and even Portuguese. Now we have to do it in French," Frost says with a smile.

Since the two Haitian refugees already had work visas, they started work the following Monday. Frost was amazed at how easy it was working with the shelter and having new employees on the job within a week. "I thought it would be a longer process," he says.

One of the keys to making this venture work was the willingness of the company's supervisors to deal with the challenges of translation. Frost saw that the two Haitians were very good with their phones. "All of our foremen have bought into using a translation app," he says.

Harrison, the younger Frost, runs the business day to day and is very comfortable using translation apps on his phone. He and his foremen dictate to their phones in English and their newest employees immediately hear—and see—the translation in Haitian French from the phone. Of course, their replies are instantly translated back into English. The communication is pretty seamless.

Transportation was the other challenge the Frosts had to deal with. When he interviewed the men, they said getting to the job sites would be no problem. They would take an Uber. All the work sites were in Concord or nearby towns, so sometimes a shift manager could even give them a lift home. One of the men has a Massachusetts driver's license, but no car. Dan Frost is already thinking about eventually getting a company van that they could use to commute.

Two months since they first visited the Best Western shelter, the Frosts can't say enough good things about their new employees. They have never missed a day or been late for work. They work hard and pay attention to detail. "They would probably work 12 hours a day if we let them, but we don't," says Harrison Frost.[43]

Dan Frost has been surprised by how well the process worked, and he's already thinking about tapping the refugee talent pool again. In the meantime, he's been promoting the idea of hiring foreign-born workers to other small business owners in the region. This won't work for every small company, of course, but Frost has some advice for those who want to give it a try.

1. Be Open-Minded

Frost is too smart and polite to say it any other way. My interpretation of his point: *don't be racist.* Be open to people from different cultures and backgrounds. "Once you get these guys working," says Frost, "and see how positive it can be for the business, you realize they're not different from us. They all want to provide for their families."

He points out that his approach comes back to his philosophy of doing business. Hesitating for a moment to gather his thoughts, Frost says, "We operate our business like a family. You can't approach it like 'I just want to use these guys to make as much money as possible.' I want to see my guys succeed just as much as I do. If you set your business up that way, then this thing can really work."

2. Be Patient

When employing a refugee who doesn't share a language with their team members, Frost's advice is to always have someone like a foreman with them to bridge communication gaps and ensure they know what to do. Over the years, he has seen so many painting contractors take a new hire and just throw them onto a job and let them go. "But, in this case, you have to be able to handhold for a bit. That's where the patience comes in."

3. Be Organized and Hands-On with Training

Having patience segues into the need for a thorough training program. Frost spent a day with his two new hires showing them how to set up a job. "It's not as simple as opening up a paint can and cleaning your brush. There are so many nuances and little skills you have to learn to be a competent painter," says Frost, whose company routinely works for demanding clients in multi-million-dollar homes.

The detailed training has paid off. Frost said his son texted him the other day, amazed at the quality of work being done by their new house painters from Haiti. Normally, Frost said, you start inexperienced employees working on the exterior of homes. But Harrison had them working on an interior job doing very detailed sanding that day. "He was blown away by their prep work," says Frost. "That's a much harder, more sophisticated thing to be doing."

Future Opportunities

Frost is encouraged by his experience hiring foreign-born workers. With some of his employees approaching retirement age and young people not coming into the business, he is already imagining the possibility of his newest employees becoming foremen, so he can hire more recent arrivals. "The talent pool is there," he says. "Companies just have to be set up to bring them on."

Frost hasn't forgotten his first visit to the converted Best Western. The shelter manager took him aside and said, "Look, if you need more than two, let me know, I have plenty of people looking for work." This is the situation at most shelters housing refugees. They present an opportunity for leaders like Frost to grow their businesses while making a difference.

CHAPTER 8

Main Street Gourmet: A United Nations of Food That Says "Eat Dessert First!"

Foreign-born workers became the saving grace of Main Street Gourmet, an Ohio-based bakery manufacturer that previously dealt with chronic workforce shortages. With over a decade of experience hiring refugees from very different cultures, such as Nepal, Afghanistan, and Myanmar, Main Street Gourmet demonstrates the importance of continually adapting their staffing processes and practices when hiring significant numbers of foreign-born workers. This case shows how to think about hiring foreign-born workers as a long-term practice for solving chronic staffing shortages. One essential lesson is learning how to respect and accommodate the needs of employees from different cultures.

Main Street Gourmet (MSG) is a leading provider of customized bakery products for national and regional restaurants and grocery stores. Who wouldn't want to work in a place where "Eat dessert first!" is one of the core values?

But finding workers for this plant just north of Akron, Ohio, had been a challenge for years.

In 2021, the COVID-19 pandemic made the workforce picture even bleaker. This disruption had critical implications for the business.

If MSG didn't find people to fill key production roles, the company couldn't complete orders for their major customers on time. MSG had been dubbed one of the best places to work in Ohio as recently as 2019, but that didn't mean people were storming the gates to apply.

For years, Main Street had found creative solutions to meet its workforce needs. Notably, they relied on hiring foreign-born refugees who arrived in Akron looking for a new start. This practice began in 2008 when they hired a refugee from Myanmar who spoke no English. Employing workers born outside the US introduced new challenges, of course, but the initiative proved successful. Over the years, dozens of Nepalese workers and refugees from other countries found work with Main Street. But once the world became mired in the COVID pandemic, this commercial bakery's staffing problems became more pressing than ever.

Main Street needed to find new sources of talent, and it seemed natural to deepen their commitment to hiring refugees. Kelly Loebick-Frascella, MSG's director of human resources, and her colleagues were well ahead of the curve when it came to successfully hiring refugees. They had spent the past decade learning three key lessons.

1. Success Requires a Lot of Up-Front Work

In 2008, MSG took a chance on Mu Soe, a 23-year-old refugee who had recently moved to the area and was looking for work. Mu Soe was not a typical MSG hire. Yes, she was married and had two young children, but she spoke no English and had lived in a refugee camp for ten years to escape persecution in Myanmar. Loebick-Frascella recalls the decision to hire her:

> We took a chance on her and just committed to the process at that point. The resettlement agency occasionally sent us someone, but they always had good English and some

skills. This was different because with Mu Soe we were committing to a refugee who had no English skills or work experience. Honestly, it took a lot of up-front work. We had to help her understand the language and train her on a lot of basic concepts. But it was worth it. She is still with our organization after 16 years and was just promoted again.

Mu Soe's Story: A Resilient Refugee

A friend had helped her get the job. Mu Soe spoke no English. She used sign language to learn how to work as a maid in a rundown hotel in Akron, Ohio. Even with her husband working and two children at home, she quickly realized $6.75 an hour was not enough to pay the bills. The family had no car. Her job options were limited.

But this challenge seemed easy compared to what Mu Soe had been through in her first 23 years. She doesn't talk much about her childhood because she didn't really have one.

As a little girl, Mu Soe and her family fled their home and hid in the jungle when Burmese soldiers threatened to kill them. Part of the Karen minority, long persecuted by the Burmese military, Mu Soe's mother eventually moved her family to a refugee camp in Thailand. For ten years, Mu Soe lived in a hut in that camp taking care of her younger sisters. They were alive, but there was never enough food.

Mu Soe met her husband in the camp, and they had their first child when Mu Soe was 19. Her second child came at 21. Finally, with the help of international aid organizations, Mu Soe's family got permission to move to the US in 2007. Her aging parents stayed behind.

Living in Akron, Mu Soe quit her $6.75-an-hour hotel job. It didn't pay enough to live on. A friend who worked at Main Street Gourmet told her that MSG was hiring, so Mu Soe asked a local resettlement agency to help her navigate the employment process. She was nervous when she started on the packing line, but Mu Soe got a lot of help learning the job. Her English was non-existent. When she tried to tell them "Thank you," they thought she was using the F-word. Her co-workers politely corrected her.

After three years on the packaging line, Mu Soe moved to the bakery where she worked with a team that mixed dough and baked a variety of sweets, such as muffins, brownies, and granola. Mu Soe worked from 6 a.m. to 6 p.m. three days a week. Some weeks, she would work six or seven days to pile up the overtime. She and her husband wanted to buy a house. And she always sends money back to her parents in Thailand.

After 16 years, Mu Soe has worked as a line leader in every part of the company's operations. Recently, she was promoted to company trainer. She loves learning and has a lot of empathy for new refugees trying to learn the ropes. "Honestly, the job is not hard," she says. "English is hard. But I am learning. I speak every day. If they don't understand me, I ask them to correct me."

Eventually, the family bought a house. Her son graduated from high school and now works at Main Street as a mixer on the production line.

I asked Mu Soe what the job meant to her. "I love my job," she said. "I like to make money, and I like working with people. In the future, maybe I'd like to learn the supervisor's job. I don't have the best English, but I am not scared. I've had a lot of chances to grow."

"Grit" is the word most often used by her colleagues to describe Mu Soe. She recognizes what has made her successful in her role: "I don't give up on people. I believe in them, and we work together to get success."

MSG has never had a formal program to train supervisors or line leaders in working with refugees. But from the beginning it has been about slowing down the training process and being willing to train, train, and train again. Loebick-Frascella promised her supervisors that these efforts would pay off eventually. "Once we got a few refugees onboard who were really hardworking," says the HR director, "supervisors saw the value of the extra up-front work. It became much easier to sell it."

2. Clustering and Referrals Provide Extra Advantages

Hiring a young woman from Myanmar was the start of a new era for Main Street. Loebick-Frascella recalls, "Our first experience gave us the ability to say, 'Yes, we can do this.' It allowed us to get a feel for our ability. Things developed organically from there."

Next, MSG hired a recent arrival from Nepal. In 2008, Akron had become a magnet for refugees from Nepal who were drawn to strong social support systems that often included members of their extended family. As more Nepalese settled around Akron, they contacted family members elsewhere in the US and encouraged them to relocate there. Loebick-Frascella says:

> That opened up our ability to hire additional workers from Nepal. Especially if one person spoke English pretty well, we found we could partner them with someone who didn't know the language. After a few years, Nepalis became the largest part of our foreign-born workforce. This was both organic and intentional.
>
> We made connections and marketed ourselves to resettlement bureaus, such as Asia Services in Action and other nonprofits in the area. When we realized it was working, we would just ask, 'Hey, do you have any family members who need a job?' We were getting a lot of interest from the Nepali community.

3. Adapt to the Nuances of Employees' Cultures

When developing a sizable group of Nepalese workers, Main Street's leaders listened to learn what Nepalis valued in the workplace. "It sounds obvious, but understanding the nuances of their culture has been extremely helpful," Loebick-Frascella says. "It's imperative to recognize what motivates the group overall, what is super important to them, and what things are not important."

For example, Nepali workers at MSG value consistency and equality across the board. MSG needed to understand this when making decisions about pay or differentiators like mandatory overtime. Main Street's management discovered that, unlike the individual-focused aspects of American culture, Nepalese employees embody a "we're-all-in-this-together" attitude. Company decisions need to respect that value.

Another difference dealt with a critical health-safety issue. Many Nepalese have such a simple diet that food allergies are largely unheard of in their country. MSG's managers had to teach Nepalese workers that certain foods could actually make some people sick. No peanut pieces in sugar cookies, for example. When cross-contamination is a major concern, closing this gap in cultural knowledge is key to keeping MSG operating safely.

Five Tips for Onboarding Non-English-Speaking Employees

Depending on the context of your business, there are many ways to onboard and train a new employee who speak limited English. The following five tactics have helped Main Street succeed over time.

Identify New Hires Who Need Extra Care

MSG's human resources coordinator Miranda Rosado handles recruiting for the business. When interviewing foreign-born applicants or during orientation, she informally evaluates their soft skills and English-language competence, noting applicants who may need extra support. (Bringing a translator, usually a relative, to the interview is kind of a giveaway.)

Rosado then introduces the new hire to the company's trainer, Mu Soe, who knows what it's like to come to work with little English. "It means a lot to Mu Soe to work with people like this because it always reminds her of when she first started here," Rosado says.

Mu Soe takes the new hire onto the production floor and teams them up with a partner who will help train them. Usually, this is a veteran employee who speaks the new worker's native language.

Identify Natural Trainers

Some staff are gifted at working with refugees, while others see it as a burden. At Main Street, a supervisor on the night shift is a natural developer. "She will work with someone over and over and over," says Rosado. "She gets a ton of joy out of seeing a new employee make just small incremental improvements."

Not everyone is as enthusiastic about this slower pace of training. Sometimes supervisors become frustrated. Rosado and her colleagues have to challenge those responsible for training, asking, "What have you tried? Is there another way you could teach this?"

Recalibrate Expectations about Training Time and Pitfalls

Training takes longer for employees just learning English. Expect to show new employees how to do a task several times. One of the dilemmas at Main Street is their refugees are so eager to be seen as good employees that they will nod their head as an indication of respect, not necessarily to signal comprehension. "We have to find other ways to teach," Rosado says. "We can't rely on the head nodding. So we ask, 'Can you show me what I just told you?' We get creative in training."

Know When to Use a Translator

Using translations or a translator has become a regular practice at MSG. When doing new hire orientations, Main Street will bring in a translator to make sure new employees understand key lessons. They have also translated critical training documents to make sure foreign-born workers understand them. Finally, Main Street works with an outside organization to develop English-as-a-second-language programs that teach words commonly used on the production floor. For example, how do you communicate to the team leader that a machine has broken down and needs maintenance? "When in doubt, bring in a translator. It will always create more value," says Rosado.

Lunch with Leaders

One of Main Street's signature programs is "Lunch with Leaders," where their most recent hires join their direct supervisors, HR staff, the director of operations, and the general manager for lunch once a month. Loebick-Frascella, head of HR, sees this regular practice as essential to maintaining support for hiring foreign-born workers.

During the lunch, leaders talk a little bit about their own background, where they started at Main Street, their responsibilities today, and why they like working at the company. Then, they ask the new hires to share a little, as they are comfortable, about where they are from, about where they have worked, and about their family. The impact of refugees' stories is powerful. Loebick-Frascella notes:

> It creates compassion. You realize this person who's talking has spent their life in a refugee camp with food rations and violence around them. I think it bakes in empathy. And we have new leaders here who weren't around when we started the refugee program. So allowing them to get more of a firsthand experience is important.

Doubling Down during COVID

MSG had become well known for welcoming foreign-born workers. At least a dozen languages are spoken on the production floor as employees diligently produce batter for blueberry muffins, chocolate chip cookies, and granola. The lunchroom displays flags representing where employees migrated from.

Unlike many companies, MSG has not made automation part of the solution for ongoing staffing challenges. Main Street's critical advantage is its ability to customize jobs for customers. A production team may use several different machines in a day, starting a shift by making muffins and finishing by making cookies. It's a labor-intensive business.

In the wake of the COVID pandemic, disruptions in refugee resettlement hampered Main Street's ability to even find temporary workers to fill jobs. Even the six staffing agencies MSG worked with could do little to help them find workers. Referrals from current employees, especially foreign-born workers, proved to be an unexpected lifesaver. Regardless of ads posted or agencies used, referrals from current employees were the company's number one source of new hires.

Kabul Comes Calling

The flow of the world's refugees is continually changing, driven by wars, the climate crisis, and food shortages. Over the years, people have been displaced from Nepal, Democratic Republic of the Congo, Syria, Somalia, and Haiti, to name just a few countries. In 2021, Afghanistan was collapsing as the US pulled its troops out of what had become a 20-year war. Overnight, the US was faced with a wave of desperate Afghan refugees hoping to avoid the Taliban's iron rule.

> **Main Street's management team knew the importance of educating themselves about the culture of potential refugee hires**

Because of its reputation for diversity, Main Street caught a break when one local staffing agency reached out to them with a challenging offer. The agency had teamed up with the Ohio Resettlement Bureau* to find work for a dozen Afghan refugees about to arrive in Akron. They asked MSG if they wanted to hire these men, some of whom had been on the last US plane out of Kabul when the country fell to the Taliban. Having worked with the US military, they were desperate to get out, even without their families, who would come later.

---

* Name disguised at agency's request. That's how busy they are!

Thanks to their experience hiring Nepalis, Main Street's management team knew the importance of taking time to educate themselves about the culture of potential refugee hires. MSG's human resources coordinator Miranda Rosado recalls:

> Before the Afghan refugees started, I reached out to the resettlement bureau, since they'd been working with the Afghans for some time. I asked what were some things we needed to know or change to cater to their needs and make sure they're successful here.

How to Adapt to Other Cultures: Prayer, Paperwork, and Policies

In hiring Afghan refugees, MSG quickly had to adapt to the religious requirements of their new employees. Many of them were Muslims and needed to take five prayer breaks during the day. Initially, the company was not sure how to accommodate this religious requirement. Designating one meeting room as a prayer room proved workable, but an even more viable solution came from the Afghan employees themselves. They asked to move to the night shift, which meant they would only have two prayer breaks during working hours.

Some veteran Main Street employees, including some Nepalis, grumbled about the accommodations being made for the Afghans, asking why they were given more breaks. Rosado and her colleagues had to educate these workers about the Islamic culture and the importance of providing religious accommodations for practicing Muslims.

Recognizing cultural differences is one thing. Bridging language and transportation barriers proved another challenge, but one MSG was more prepared to tackle. Rosado knew the extra effort involved in onboarding a group of newly arrived refugees: "They had no transportation, so sometimes I had to drive them to take their mandatory pre-employment drug tests. Or I had to get them a translator to help with paperwork in the hiring process or to go over policies and procedures."

Main Street also had to discover when new employees needed additional education on US workplace norms. Just as food allergies were a new phenomenon for Nepali workers, contacting Main Street if they could not come to work or would be late were unfamiliar practices that Afghan refugees had to learn. When Afghan employees missed work, they didn't communicate that they weren't coming. They just didn't show up. Rosado said, "I had to sit down with a translator for the refugees, and explain our attendance policy, and how to call off. A lot of people weren't familiar with these practices because in Afghanistan they don't have these policies in place."

Expect different resettlement patterns for refugees from different countries

Many Nepalis stayed in Akron and built a community that continued to supply Main Street with new employees over the years. But this didn't happen for the Afghan men who landed in Akron without their wives and children. In many cases, their relatives resettled elsewhere in the US. So many of the original wave of Afghan employees left Main Street to reunite with family in another state. Although new Afghan refugees have continued to arrive in Akron, MSG now has only a handful of employees from that country. The lesson is to expect different resettlement patterns for refugees from different countries.

The Future Is Diverse

Today Main Street's workers speak at least one of ten different native languages: Nepali, Karen, Spanish, Dari, Pashto, Hmong, Laos, Hindi, Arabic, and English. Those numbers go up and down as its staff continues to change. About 35 percent of the company's workforce is foreign-born, helping MSG create a company culture well positioned to absorb refugees from countries experiencing a new or evolving humanitarian crisis.

No matter where Main Street's foreign-born employees come from, the company has learned what is needed to successfully recruit, hire, train, and retain refugees. For its hiring strategy to succeed, MSG's systems are driven by what works for its employees, not what is most efficient for the company. For example, in many organizations today, the entire hiring process happens online. But that is not the case at Main Street, as Loebick-Frascella notes:

> There have been times when we think 'Why don't we just put all our hiring process online?' And the answer is because our employees won't be able to get through an application or certain training. Or they won't be able to do it on their own. And that's not okay.

Whether integrating Nepali or Afghan refugees, MSG has learned how to build and support a more diverse workforce. The bakery business continues to grow as the company becomes more adaptive to the changing flow of foreign-born workers. Loebick-Frascella, director of HR, sees great benefits in being such an ethnically diverse company:

> Some of our employee's stories are really inspiring. You witness these people rising above really terrible challenges they've had. Their overall outlook on life is still so positive and hopeful. It makes us want to keep creating opportunities for people who have really suffered.

CHAPTER 9

How to Translate Lessons Learned from Employing Refugees

The Congressional Budget Office projects that immigration will be the nation's only source of population increases and, hence, workforce growth within 20 years.[44] *To survive and grow in the future, most organizations must become more effective at hiring, training, and employing foreign-born workers. But, if it was easy, everyone would already be doing it. Overall, the experiences of Boston Children's Hospital, Clampco Products, HDF Painting, and Main Street Gourmet suggest important lessons every business should consider when trying to meet workforce needs with immigrants or refugees. If this sounds like too much work, see the box "Investing in Marginalized Workers When You Have Limited Time and Resources" in chapter 15.*

Chapter 9 expands on lessons learned from the case studies in the previous chapters. It also includes insights from a dozen other interviews with leaders in companies hiring foreign-born workers and their partner agencies. This chapter provides a framework of critical success factors for those who are serious about employing immigrants and refugees. The previous chapters have centered on hiring workers for entry-level positions, but job candidates with greater English-language proficiency also can be great finds for higher-level, more complex jobs.

Their journeys hiring immigrants and refugees started very differently. Boston Children's Hospital (BCH), which has been hiring immigrants for years, decided to launch a carefully planned training program that would become a major pipeline for training dozens of foreign-born research operations technicians. Clampco Products, a traditional manufacturer, dove in head first taking on nine recently arrived Congolese refugees. Main Street Gourmet (MSG) started smaller, hiring a young mother from Myanmar. This initiative grew organically over time to include dozens of refugees from different countries. HDF Painting, a small suburban business, recently hired two refugees from Haiti living in a local shelter.

> **The misconception that refugees are unskilled labor is not the case at all**

Many people starting a new life in the US have previous work experience and professional careers. In reality, however, a lack of English proficiency is a major obstacle for workers seeking jobs that align with their skills. At least initially, many foreign-born workers must take jobs below their skill level. This can be an unexpected benefit for employers. "The misconception that refugees are unskilled labor is not the case at all," says Matthew Bray, human resources director at Amcor, a packaging manufacturer in Oshkosh, Wisconsin. Amcor has hired more than 70 refugees in recent years. "I don't think anyone recognized the level of talent the refugees would provide. On our production floor we have a dentist, a journalist, small business owners, soldiers, mechanics. The skills and experience these refugees provide run the gamut," says Bray.[45]

Large companies like Pfizer, Accenture, and The Body Shop have recently pledged to hire significant numbers of refugees, in part to support their commitment to diversity, equity, and inclusion initiatives. There can be a significant distinction, however, between job opportunities available to professionally trained refugees who are proficient in English and those still trying to learn the language.

With the flood of new arrivals in recent years from countries like Afghanistan, Syria, Ukraine, the Democratic Republic of the Congo, Venezuela, and Haiti, there is a growing talent pool of professionally trained workers reasonably fluent in English who are anxious to restart their careers. Nonprofits like Upwardly Global focus on helping these immigrant and refugee professionals find jobs aligned with their skills and education.

First, Specify Your Staffing Needs

To study where most refugee hiring takes place, however, my research has focused on entry-level initiatives. The experiences of the employers in the previous chapters show hiring refugees for entry-level jobs can really pay off in different contexts. The nature of the job and the investment in training and onboarding new hires will determine how selective you can be when considering foreign-born candidates.

Boston Children's Hospital took a measured, structured approach, piloting a carefully designed program with a reliable partner, Jewish Vocational Service of Boston (JVS). BCH only considered candidates for its training program who had been rigorously screened and prepared for interviews by its local partner JVS Boston. Despite their critical staffing shortage in the research department, the hospital needed to carefully vet new hires to ensure they could perform under the job's demanding working conditions and remain in the job long enough for the hospital to recoup its substantial investment in training.

Clampco and Main Street Gourmet could afford to be less selective in their hiring than Boston Children's Hospital. Clampco was simply looking for candidates who were willing to "get their hands dirty" in a manufacturing job. MSG had similar criteria but in an industrial baking environment. Clampco and MSG, as a result, followed a more experimental, organic path that led both companies to become reliant on refugees as a major source of talent.

For these two Ohio companies, success, in large part, arose from their focus on "cluster hiring"—simultaneously employing a group of workers who spoke the same language, or related dialects. This meant they could leverage some individuals who spoke basic English as translators for other employees whose ability to communicate was very limited. Cluster hiring also later produced referrals to other refugees from the same country.

No matter what specific staffing needs influence your decisions about possibly hiring refugees, some factors are universal among companies hiring foreign-born workers. Here are five critical success factors to enhance your chances of success when looking for productive employees who have come to the US from other countries.

1. Develop Effective Partnerships with Resettlement and Workforce Development Agencies

To recruit, employ, and retain foreign-born workers you need a good partner whose primary mission is helping new arrivals settle in the US. You will probably end up working in an ecosystem of organizations supporting refugee resettlement. This means collaborating with nonprofits who may provide housing, legal, and transportation support, as well as basic language training. One word of warning: these agencies tend to be overloaded and short-staffed because of the tidal wave of new refugees and asylum seekers in recent years. Be both patient and persistent in collaborating with them.

Other potential partners include workforce development and staffing agencies that specialize in placing foreign-born workers.

Some will be wonderful. Others will be too willing to send candidates who are not job-ready. Be careful. Ask for references from other employers the agencies have worked with.

Boston Children's Hospital already had a strong partnership with JVS Boston, but Clampco didn't have this type of relationship. As soon as Clampco agreed to hire refugees, Vice President Jason Venner began exploring and developing a relationship with the Ohio Resettlement Bureau. Venner needed to make sure they would be a credible and effective partner in supporting his new Congolese employees. Dan Frost at HDF Painting, on the other hand, simply emailed the manager of his local shelter and asked if there was anyone he could interview for a job as a painter. He was not looking for a longer-term partnership.

Regardless of whomever you partner with, don't assume they will understand your specific needs and limitations as an employer. If you're lucky, you will connect with a savvy, experienced employment services director. If unlucky, you will be talking to a young, well-intentioned career coach or recruiter in their second job out of college. As an employer, it is important to quickly recognize the difference and ask for someone more experienced.

Also, remember that resettlement agencies have other priorities and concerns, such as housing and health care, when serving their many clients, who are a combination of refugees, immigrants, or asylum seekers with different legal status, support needs, and language and work skills. They may be your hiring lifeline, but to them, you're but one of many balls to juggle.

> **Good agencies can identify refugees who are better suited to the work environment of your business**

As you clarify your hiring needs for an agency, ask hard questions about the level of job-readiness training the agency can provide. Is it minimal or extensive? Can they provide ongoing coaching, or will that be up to you? What is the experience level of their coaches? Good coaching will be essential when foreign-born hires run into obstacles or feel overwhelmed by all the changes they have to cope with.

Good agencies can also identify refugees who are better suited to the work environment of your business. In Boston, JVS knows the hospital research setting, so it focuses on presenting job candidates who are suited to the rigors of a warm, windowless research environment. This workplace contrasts with a Massachusetts fruit farm that partnered with the International Institute of New England (IINE) to identify Cambodian and Burmese refugees with a farming background.

Unable to find US-born workers willing to spend long hours picking and pruning, Parlee Farms has relied on IINE to connect with more than a dozen recent arrivals with farming experience who want to become part of its full-time, well-paid field crew. "We hire 100 people to do seasonal work in the farm's retail store," says Ellen Parlee, co-owner of the farm with husband Mark. "Every summer I remind the staff if it wasn't for our field crew the rest of us wouldn't be working."

Strong partnerships are key to building a sustainable foreign-born workforce.

2. Find Job Fit for Refugees

Be thoughtful about the jobs where you place foreign-born workers. How much English is *actually* needed to do a job safely and effectively? Where will foreign-born workers add the most value with the least training and disruption for other employees? Don't assume the answer is obvious or that you'll get it right the first time.

BCH couldn't keep their research technician's job filled. They did a careful analysis of the position, including specific skills needed and actual English required. For example, a certain amount of skill reading and writing English for basic reports was important. After looking carefully at the actual work environment, their analysis showed that those with limited English skills could be viable candidates for the role.

Clampco, on the other hand, was desperate for workers, particularly on the second shift. So they simply took on refugees without much analysis of how and where they would work. The new Congolese workers were placed in jobs that seemed simplest—manual clamp assembly. Only later did management figure out that foreign-born workers were better suited to working in automated cells, which requires less English and less training to be productive.

Workers with limited English skills also can adapt to technology-related jobs. At Clampco, Venner noticed the younger Congolese refugees were incredibly facile on their iPhones, so he moved them into more technical roles where their limited English was not a significant problem.

The design of current jobs in your organization may not be a good match for the capabilities of refugees with limited English skills. But with minor revisions, you can create viable positions. Remember, if things don't work out at first, refugees who have recently come to work in your business are likely to be flexible, particularly in lower-skilled jobs. They're usually less status conscious about being moved to another role than their American-born counterparts.

3. Find Different Ways to Invest in Language Training

Most refugees arrive in the US with limited or no English skills. Indeed, language barriers are the number one challenge in effectively employing foreign-born workers. It's a mistake to think you can hire immigrants or refugees without helping develop their language skills. You can do language training inside the company, as Clampco did, setting up a small language lab internally so workers could learn basic English. Alternatively, you could follow Boston Children's lead, and outsource language training from the beginning. See the sidebar on "Seven Ways to Address Language Barriers" for different approaches to overcoming limited English skills.

Seven Ways to Address Language Barriers

1. Use an outside agency for pre-employment screening (and training) applicants. The Ohio Resettlement Bureau prepares refugees for the US workplace by providing fundamental language and job-readiness training. JVS Boston actively screens potential employees for English proficiency before encouraging them to apply for jobs. They also have extensive language training programs. Staffing agencies will sometimes carefully assess language skills, but be wary of their conflicting motivation to sometimes simply place candidates.

For very practical ideas about bridging language barriers, download the guide "Bridging Language and Work: Solutions to Invest in Immigrant and Refugee Talent,"[46] produced by The Tent Partnership for Refugees.

2. Use veteran employees to teach/translate for new hires. Main Street Gourmet and Clampco both rely on experienced employees to work through language obstacles in the workplace. Of course, this works best with clusters of employees from the same country that include someone who can act as a translator.

3. Outsource on-the-job language training to a nonprofit agency. Boston Children's Hospital collaborated with JVS to develop and deliver an English training program customized for the research technician's job.

4. Use specialized translation resources for difficult and important situations. Main Street Gourmet needed translators to help refugees fill out hiring papers and to explain the company's policy for missing work. Invest in translation services in cases where the cost of miscommunication is high.

5. Develop internal language training resources. Clampco, for example, created an on-site language lab. Main Street worked with an outside company to develop customized language training programs designed to teach words most commonly used on the production floor.

6. Switch to technologies that support languages spoken by your employees. Clampco changed to a payroll company whose technology was flexible enough that it allowed Congolese workers to read their pay stubs.

7. Create a more visual workplace using symbols and colors to communicate. Clampco uses scoreboards with green and red lights, along with Roman numerals, instead of written signs around the factory. This tells operators when they need to adjust their pace.

Companies that initially hire refugees with no comprehension of English, as Main Street and Clampco did, often realize this is too big an obstacle. Both companies now require at least a fundamental understanding of English to be hired, but they still plan extra time to train and retrain. Don't underestimate the time it takes new hires with limited language skills to work autonomously. It took a year for the first wave of Congolese employees at Clampco to operate independently. Training can require lots of repetition to make sure instructions are understood. Beware of head nodding where a new hire means to convey respect instead of real understanding.

4. Think Creatively about Coaching

Onboarding, training, and employing foreign-born workers is almost impossible without extra formal or informal coaching resources. Regular employee coaching by JVS team members at

Boston Children's Hospital is an essential part of the program for research operations technicians. But at Clampco supervisors and fellow employees who are refugees themselves provide virtually all coaching for the organization.

Coaches at JVS help with problems on the job, such as how to communicate effectively with a supervisor, or how to help a new technician speak up when they don't understand something. They also address personal issues, such as working through an unexpected childcare or transportation problem. In a complex, intense work environment like Boston Children's Hospital, coaches are essential to keep foreign-born technicians on the job.

Clampco and Main Street Gourmet, on the other hand, rely on fellow employees, sometimes from the same family, as well as supervisors to help refugees. But these smaller businesses still collaborate with local resettlement partners to counsel refugees about challenges outside of work.

When English-language skills are limited, issues of housing, healthcare, childcare, and transportation can be especially difficult. As an employer, think ahead about how to address coaching needs. Do local agencies actually have the capabilities, assets, and time to effectively meet the needs of your foreign-born workers? Will you have to rely on experienced employees and supervisors to provide all on-the-job coaching? Is your human resources department expected to play a role? Does your staff have enough experience, motivation, and patience to take on this coaching task?

In practice, some of your experienced staff will be great at mentoring new hires, such as the "den mothers" at Clampco and Mu Soe at Main Street Gourmet. Others will need training and encouragement about how to help refugees succeed in their new jobs. Consider how you will make sure your foreign-born workers feel welcome and anxious to stay at the company. What will you do over time to help them feel like they belong in the organization? How will your US-born staff learn about their culture? Through some cross-cultural mentoring or maybe potluck dinners?

> **Bringing more refugees into your organization provides counterintuitive benefits**

Developing that sense of belonging is important.

Bringing more refugees into your organization actually provides counterintuitive benefits. It will slow things down temporarily, requiring more training for workers who can't learn as fast in their new language. But it can also increase productivity in the long term by building a more loyal and more productive workforce. This means less training is needed to accommodate turnover.

Don't make untested assumptions about how refugees will have their resettlement and training needs met. Every community and corporation must address these transition challenges in their own way. To be successful at tapping the talent pool of foreign-born workers, you must be innovative, flexible, and patient. Long term, however, hiring these workers will be one of the few truly effective ways to deal with critical skill and workforce shortages in the years ahead.

5. Consider Practical Transportation Solutions Up Front

Plenty of initiatives to hire foreign-born workers fizzle out because managers don't consider how employees will get to and from work. Indeed, some leaders told me they wish they had thought about transportation more before they started hiring. Your difficulties and solutions in this area depend on geography. Where is your company located? Where do employees live? Is public transportation an option?

Boston Children's Hospital is in a city with an elaborate (if shaky) public transportation system, allowing the hospital to cede commuting responsibilities to employees. If you want to work here, you must figure out the commute yourself with some coaching.

Clampco, on the other hand, is half an hour outside of Akron with no dependable public transportation from areas where refugees can afford to live. To hire a cluster of Congolese refugees, the company's management initially had to work out transportation for the group. They hired their new employees through a staffing agency that promised to provide bus transportation for the group. It all sounded great on paper. That is until the bus didn't show up to pick up workers late at night, leaving employees stranded for several hours.

Eventually, a couple of the Congolese refugees got their driver's licenses and bought cars. These workers started carpooling and the transportation problems slowly sorted themselves out. It helped that the Congolese workers were often related or good friends. In another rural scenario, however, a cohort of Afghan men were not friends and felt no motivation to coordinate rides to work. People won't automatically collaborate just because they are from the same country.

As with coaching, transportation solutions must be contextual. Some companies decide to run vans when some of their employees live in the same area. Others commit to funding employee transportation to work for a limited time, such as a month or three. By then employees must figure out alternative solutions, such as getting a license and purchasing a car or carpooling with other employees.[47] Sometimes, the solution will involve nontraditional transit modes. In Lowell, Massachusetts, the nonprofit Bike Connector provides free bikes to immigrants looking for affordable, practical ways to commute to jobs nearby.

If you are employing refugees, your business will suffer if you do not consider the transportation limitations and the needs of your workers.

6. Expect Surprises

Workforce staffing is often an uncertain game of chance these days. Your employees constantly face unexpected changes: new job offers, illness, aging parents, childcare issues, transportation disruptions, and more. Hiring immigrants or refugees makes the game even more uncertain (e.g., language barriers and unexpected disruptions). Paradoxically, this staffing strategy can provide much-needed stability once initial problems are worked out. But you must learn to cope with the unexpected in the meantime.

Boston Children's Hospital has learned to live with surprises like visa problems, the inability to acquire papers needed for employment, and sick family members requiring a trip back home. Proactive coaching has proven critical to limiting cross-cultural miscommunication and setting expectations that help resolve problems, such as being absent unexpectedly, before they become serious.

Resettlement and training agencies can also help you foresee potential disruptions, such as paperwork problems or mental health counseling needed to help employees process trauma.

In the end, the positive benefits of hiring refugees can far outweigh the new challenges they bring. Jason Venner, Clampco's vice president, points out that overall, the company's foreign-born workers present significantly fewer traditional human resource problems than their American-born counterparts. Although you can never eliminate the uncertainties of hiring, providing foreign-born workers jobs and much-needed support can help develop a hardworking, loyal workforce.

How to Get Started

Hiring refugees or immigrants may not be practical for your business. But it could be great! Before you say, "No way," answer these questions to see if your organization could benefit:

1. Do we have entry-level or lower-skilled jobs impossible to fill with dependable workers? Do we have jobs with ridiculously high levels of costly turnover? Have we failed miserably in finding productive employees through traditional sources (e.g., online recruiting, staffing agencies, referrals from current employees)?

2. Do we have higher-skilled professional jobs where we might be overlooking refugees who are proficient enough in English to fill the role with some accommodations and mentoring?

3. Can we find a partner who helps refugees or immigrants resettle in the region? Or is there a staffing agency dedicated to serving the employment needs of refugees? Do these potential partners have very good references from other employers?

4. Do we have the patience for longer onboarding and training needed for new hires with limited English skills? Do we have experienced employees who might mentor them?

5. Have we carefully analyzed the activities required for hard-to-fill entry-level jobs? Do we understand precisely the amount of English needed to perform specific tasks safely and effectively?

6. Are we willing to put up with new surprises and disruptions along the way (e.g., visa or transportation snafus) in exchange for highly productive and loyal employees?

If you answer yes to most of these questions, then maybe you should give more foreign-born workers a shot. You're likely to find some valuable employees who can make a difference in your business. Most importantly, you will be helping some really determined people fulfill their dreams of a new life.

SECTION 3
How to Employ People with Disabilities

The next three chapters focus on organizations that have benefited significantly from hiring people with developmental disabilities, which is an umbrella term for a wide range of physical, cognitive, and intellectual impairments. By examining the case studies that follow, you'll discover ways to tap into this pool of talented workers, learn the obstacles that may impede success, and be surprised at the sometimes unexpected benefits of these innovative staffing solutions.

Minnesota Diversified Industries is a social enterprise that has produced products in a manufacturing environment for decades by employing those with a wide variety of disabilities. Classic Wire Cut is a medical products company that discovered a goldmine of young CNC machinists diagnosed with autism spectrum disorder (ASD). Heartland Systems Corporation (disguised) is a large company that has found critical tasks in its data-intensive business where individuals with autism have distinct advantages in providing high-quality outputs.

Chapter 13 looks across the experiences of multiple organizations and goes even deeper, identifying the key motivations and critical success factors needed to benefit from this group of traditionally marginalized workers.

Of course, this section shows just a tiny sample of the employment possibilities for people in this underused talent pool. But it also offers a glimpse into the challenges that those with disabilities, their advocates, and their employers face. **My primary purpose is to encourage busy managers to actively explore new ways people with disabilities can help address chronic labor and skill shortages in tomorrow's workforce.**

This section was perhaps the most difficult to write in a way that accurately reflects the experiences and potential of a wide range of workers with disabilities. It focuses heavily on people diagnosed with autism spectrum disorder, who are often described as "neurodiverse." I want to recognize the heated debate in the disability community about whether to identify people on the spectrum as "individuals with autism" or simply "autistic." An increasingly common way to describe those with ASD is as level 1, 2, or 3. I use a combination of terms out of respect for the different perspectives on this issue of labeling.

CHAPTER 10

Minnesota Diversified Industries: How a Mission Makes Money When Hiring Workers with Disabilities

Minnesota Diversified Industries (MDI) is a social enterprise that employs people with a wide range of disabilities. Products and services include mass production of plastic totes and trays, as well as an array of custom packaging solutions and medical device assembly. Chances are your company will never employ this many marginalized workers, but MDI has learned valuable lessons in recruiting, onboarding, and sustaining the employment of people with disabilities that can help companies looking to augment their workforce.

Operations Manager Jeff Gervais had seen this problem before. A major customer asks his company to dramatically increase its production volume for six months. Minnesota Diversified Industries (MDI) manufactures totes, which are containers used in logistics and retail settings to transport everything from envelopes to retail products. They had planned to make a million totes, but now a government agency wants eight million in just a few months.

Addressing this uptick in work would be no simple matter. MDI is committed to employing people with disabilities, so Gervais couldn't just hire a bunch of people to beef up the company's production lines. In this unconventional setting, the hiring process is more complicated.

MDI has continued to grow over its 60 years, adding three facilities in northern Minnesota. As a social enterprise, CEO Eric Black says, "Our mission is to provide inclusive employment opportunities for people with disabilities." But he quickly adds, "No profit, no mission."

Employment numbers have ranged from 200 to 600 depending on customer demand. Out of MDI's current workforce of 450 employees, about 45 percent have a documented disability, such as physical impairments or intellectual or mental health disabilities. About 25 percent of the staff works part time because of constraints caused by transportation or housing needs. Living in a group home can prevent employees from working on night shifts. Sometimes there are income limits needed to retain government benefits.

When Gervais and his colleagues must scale manufacturing operations quickly, they balance four critical success factors to recruit, train, and support workers with disabilities:

- **Customize recruiting and onboarding practices**
- **Develop more skilled supervisors**
- **Solve scheduling jigsaw puzzles**
- **Balance demands of competing objectives: profit vs. mission**

1. Customize Recruiting and Onboarding Practices

Most organizations will tell you that finding employees who "fit" is the key to successful hiring and sustained employment. This is especially true when recruiting those with disabilities. Hiring and training requires three practices that are different but not particularly difficult to implement.

Touring and Talking

MDI's employee services department is responsible for supporting the company's workers, which includes figuring out accommodations needed for those with disabilities. Jeanne Eglinton, vice president of employment services, said providing potential employees a tour of the plant is essential to assess fit.

A company tour becomes a kind of informal interview with each candidate, allowing the hiring manager to learn about them and their other work experiences. Eglinton explains:

> I try to find out about their dream job. If somebody's dream job is to work in retail, why are you here? They shouldn't come to us if that's really what they want to do. The tour is also a way of giving them information about us, like what type of schedule they would have, how many days a week they need to work. We get all that information out there. And, most importantly, part of the tour is going out on the floor and actually seeing the work. That's key for both sides.

Over time, MDI's hiring process has evolved to help the company assess the best fit for all potential employees. Eglinton recalls a job candidate with autism who realized he could not work with the kind of lighting the plant used. In another instance, she gave a tour to a woman who was highly motivated to work but she had serious balance issues. The production floor would not have been a safe place for her.

Even though operations didn't think he would be a good fit for the job, they still gave him a chance

Like other employees, workers with disabilities have a variety of career objectives, and they often become apparent during the tours. For example, some younger employees view MDI as a steppingstone in their career. Often, the company helps them get into the workforce, gain confidence, and develop skills so they can move on to other job opportunities.

Another employee wasn't born with a disability but suffered a traumatic brain injury as an adult. He's older and only works part time to keep his government benefits, which he needs for health reasons.

Finding an employee who is the right fit for a job sometimes means looking inside the company. MDI's CEO Eric Black has encouraged his staff to give employees new opportunities, even when they may not meet all the qualifications for a job. "We want to make sure we're always asking the question 'Do we have somebody else already here who could fill that role?'" said Eglinton.

One of the many labor-intensive services MDI provides is third-party validation of product performance. When operations needed to fill a job to test roofing shingles, employment services suggested a recently hired employee who would normally not have been considered for the position. Employment services had gotten to know this individual during the onboarding process. They recognized he could handle the specific steps involved in shingle testing. Even though operations didn't think he would be a good fit for the job overall, they still gave him a chance. "He's like a rock star back there now," Eglinton said proudly.

Lynn's Story:
When Showing up is More than 80 Percent of Success

There is an old saying that 80 percent of success in life is just showing up. Well, showing up is what Lynn does best. She's still not sure how she graduated from high school. It definitely wasn't fun. With thick-rimmed glasses and halting speech, she says it was hard to make friends. A learning disability and an intermittent stutter meant Lynn struggled in class. Reading and videos weren't helpful when it came to learning. High school is a frustrating place for hands-on learners.

"I still don't know how I graduated," she says. "I just showed up and never missed a class. I did my best."

But five years ago, after showing up on the production floor at MDI for 30 years, Lynn was promoted to the front office. Today, she works 40 hours a week as the production and office services specialist. She answers phones, does time-keeping used for payroll and billing customers, and greets customers when they come into MDI.

Lynn still remembers the last job she had before being hired by MDI. She worked on a production line at a company for one day, but she wasn't fast enough. They told her not to come back. Then she got a job at MDI where she drove a forklift, and worked on a pack and ship line, scanning items to go in boxes and printing packing slips. She was pulling orders for big companies like 3M and Novartis. She did that for 30 years until she was promoted to the front office.

Asked about her biggest challenges at work, she turns to her colleague and, in a stage whisper, asks if it's okay to talk about when the company almost closed in 2007. Lynn confesses she was afraid that she would lose her job. She didn't know where she would go. "I would have been really nervous. I don't know what I would've done to find a job. I plan on staying here until I retire," she says.

What she likes most about MDI is the people. They're nice to her. "I feel comfortable working here," she says. "I don't have to worry about not being accepted because of my glasses and my stutter. I don't have anybody here that I have confrontations with. I don't even know how to be mean to anybody."

On her way to lunch, Lynn still goes out to the production area and the warehouse to see her friends. She was nervous when she moved to the front office after 30 years. She thought people on the production floor wouldn't talk to her anymore. She still makes a point of going by on her way to the lunch room. Her co-workers can count on it. Because one thing about Lynn, she always shows up.

Use Partnerships to Find Potential Staff

Finding partners who can qualify and refer candidates with disabilities is key to hiring at MDI. The company does three things that are essential to increasing the flow of qualified candidates.

Expands its community of nonprofit partners. MDI casts a wide net when hiring. All employees on the production floor are hired as contractors through nonprofit organizations and staffing agencies that support individuals with disabilities. Of course, different nonprofits support people with different types of disabilities or life situations. MDI has developed relationships with many of them. They also often ask traditional staffing agencies if they know of individuals who have disclosed a disability who might be a good fit.

Increases transparency around temporary jobs. MDI doesn't have the human resources infrastructure needed to rapidly increase hiring, so it processes new hires through temp agencies. This approach communicates more explicitly that the employee's job is only expected to be temporary. Contractors are now referred to as "seasonal employees" to further emphasize the transitory nature of the relationship. But when MDI finds particularly productive contract employees, they will often convert them to permanent status. This has become important in recent years as more local companies have begun hiring workers with disabilities, creating a more competitive market for this talent.

MDI learned the hard way that layoffs are more painful for employees with disabilities. After two high-volume years due to unusually big contracts, customer demand dropped off dramatically, and MDI had to let a lot of people go. It was very hard, notes Eglinton:

> I'm not going to say our approach is totally successful because it's really hard when you've developed relation-

ships with people and then they're not here anymore. But we have a bias towards keeping people with disabilities as long as we can. We look at who's going to have a more difficult time getting a new job after they leave MDI. Most of us can find a job. It may not be the ideal job, but we can find one. For a person with a disability, it's probably going to be much harder. So we do everything we can to keep employees identified as having a disability as long as we can.

To best support its workers during tough times, MDI prioritizes being transparent and giving individuals as much notice as possible about cutbacks in production.

Insists on good job coaches. In some cases, a nonprofit will bring a team of workers with disabilities into an MDI facility. The agency provides its own job coach so these employees can operate as a small unit. This sounds great in theory but sometimes proves problematic. Job coaches are often underpaid by their agencies, which leads to turnover. MDI has had to constantly train new coaches who don't have experience with what employees on their team need and what the company expects. Setting expectations for coaches is key, one operations manager explains:

> For the team approach to be successful, we need very good job coaches to come with the workers. Coaches need to be effectively engaged with their employees so they understand the job and expectations for performance. I've told our nonprofit partners we don't pay people to come in here, sit down, and do nothing. We expect everyone to work up to their ability and everyone has different abilities in what they can do.

Anticipate a Longer Onboarding Process

The customized onboarding process at MDI takes longer and can be more unpredictable when integrating workers with disabilities. Rather than let this be a deterrent, the business has fine-tuned its onboarding process by proactively addressing and anticipating potential complications. Here are three ways they do that.

Plan on a longer learning curve. Eglinton emphasizes the importance of setting realistic expectations about how fast new employees will become productive:

> It may take a new person with a learning disability longer to understand the full job. Instead of trying to teach a new hire the whole assembly process in one day, we give them time to learn one piece of the job before moving to the next step in that assembly process. They're going to have more success if we help them master one step of the whole process, so they become competent before moving on to a different task.

Spend time developing relationships. MDI's longer onboarding process provides new hires more time to build relationships with their supervisors and coworkers. "Sometimes people with disabilities are not the most outgoing in developing new relationships," Eglinton says. "Supervisors also need time to understand what support an individual needs and where they can best fit in on the production line. Once you develop a relationship with someone, you tend to be more interested in their success. This step is really important."

Provide the right supports to promote communication. Having workers with disabilities on the production floor can require simple—but profound—changes that impact communication. MDI gives extra attention to signs and symbols used to communicate in the workplace. Two plants used to have large analog clocks on the wall, but some employees couldn't read a clock face. They replaced those clocks with digital ones and phased in color-coded signs to replace written instructions and signs. Some employees are unable to read, or they read at a very basic level. So if they are doing some type of sorting job, color coding items makes the work much easier.

Eglinton notes that since making their workplace more accommodating, MDI has broadened opportunities for people with disabilities by rethinking the prerequisites for some jobs:

> In some cases, we have asked does the job really need a four-year degree? Do we have the right expectations for candidates? What are we willing to be flexible on so that we can take somebody and train them, instead of looking for someone who already has the skill set? And anytime you're doing that, you've got to ask whether your supervisors understand how to support and help somebody be successful.

2. Developing More Skilled Supervisors

To increase production capacity, MDI needs supervisors (known as "line leads") who can think creatively about solving production problems, given the widely varying skill levels of their team. Operations Manager Kyle Erikson explains:

> We're a labor-intensive business. And you're managing employees with a variety of different skill sets. Some perform over 100 percent. Others are maybe 20 percent of what the production standard is, based on timing and how many pieces should get through the system. We need line leads who think outside the box, who enjoy a variety of challenges, and the increased complexity of putting employees in spots where they can succeed. The company only succeeds when we don't create bottlenecks based on somebody's ability.

Line leads need refined soft skills such as attention to detail, having a consistently upbeat attitude, and perhaps most importantly,

> **We don't feel sorry for anybody here. You're here to work. Everyone's treated equally**

patience. Some tasks don't go right the first time, or the second time, or even the third. Patience and a positive attitude keep the workplace moving forward.

Of course, line leads at MDI are constantly caught in a balancing act. While they must be in tune with their employees, they can't lose sight of the business demands, as Jeff Gervais, another operations manager, cautions:

> We don't feel sorry for anybody here. You're here to work. Everyone's treated equally. Unfortunately, we've had a few supervisors we brought in who were so driven to support individuals with disabilities that they lost sight of the business side. You have to balance the money versus mission thing. That's because, as a line leader out there, at the end of the day, if you've got to produce 5,000 pieces, then you've got to have 5,000 pieces produced regardless of who's on your line. And if you don't make that goal, we all need to know why, so we can fix it.

Here are three things MDI does to develop the skilled line leads needed to manage its diverse workforce effectively.

Recognize How the Supervisor's Role Is Different

When managing workers with disabilities, supervisors must be especially aware of who they are working with. Gervais explains:

> Line leads know what accommodations or supports each individual needs. They've got to be constantly attuned to

what's going on. They may look over a production line and see someone becoming disengaged or frustrated with the task. The supervisor will check in with the employee and may pull them off the line or get employment services involved to resolve the issue. Line leads at MDI need to know challenges are coming and constantly come up with creative solutions.

Value People Skills over Technical Know-How

Operations manager Kyle Erickson says the biggest part of his job is bringing in new supervisors who are aligned with the unusual culture of the company. MDI favors new supervisors with more experience managing and motivating a team over ones with a lot of experience in manufacturing. Erikson, for example, hired a former daycare provider who turned out to be one of his best production supervisors. She knows how to handle people and motivate them. Once on board, she learned the technical components of the job. That proved easier to teach than trying to develop a supervisor's people skills.

Use Company's Mission to Attract Talent

Most companies face staffing shortages these days. But MDI has found it easier to hire supervisors who want to work with people with disabilities. This is especially true in rural areas. Erickson notes: "Recruiting and bringing people on board has been a hell of a lot easier because we find folks who prefer a career in an inclusive environment versus just working with your typical assemblers." MDI is able to attract non-disabled workers more easily, too, because plenty of people want more mission-driven jobs.

3. Solve the Scheduling Jigsaw Puzzle

It's challenging to plan work hours for employees on MDI's production line. Many of the company's contract workers who are disabled are only available to work part time. This means more employees are needed to fill out the production line scheduling puzzle.

In addition, those with disabilities usually can't work the second or third shift. Many use public transportation, which isn't available after 8:00 p.m. Or they may have living situations, such as living in a group home, that don't allow for nontraditional work hours. Gervais explains:

> Scheduling is my biggest challenge. Some employees can only work three days a week or just half days. It's a struggle to run our operational floor that way, when we must hit deadlines for our customers, and we don't have full capacity throughout the week. We may have 60 percent capacity on Monday because the individuals we have in our group may fluctuate. We have to do a lot of jumping through hoops and changeovers on the production floor to make sure we meet customer needs.

MDI does several things to meet the scheduling challenges created by accelerated production.

Accommodate More Individual Work Schedules

MDI's managers are creative when designing schedules. For example, the employee who was hired to test the performance of roofing shingles can only work part time. But the company is so happy with the quality of his work that they accommodate his scheduling needs. In other situations, management has agreed to let some employees work only 3 to 7 p.m. on the second shift, so they can leave in time to catch the last bus home. The result of these part-time schedules is

MDI typically overstaffs projects 10–20 percent because they know people will call out sick or there is some other problem that keeps them from working as planned.

Jeanne Eglinton, head of employment services, explains further:

> One thing that sets us apart is we provide schedules that work for people, whether it's full time or part time. We can have 100 different schedules that people work because maybe they don't work all five days or maybe they only work half days, or they work from nine until two. We want to maximize what somebody can do, but we also need to meet our production schedules.

Reorganize Work to Adapt to Unbalanced Shifts

MDI will sometimes redesign work on particular shifts to meet employees' scheduling needs. Management, for example, periodically reorganizes tasks to take advantage of employees who are only available on the first shift. When Gervais needed to scale up production, his team pre-folded totes on the first shift to make better use of that shift's larger labor pool.

> We'd bring people in just to pre-fold the totes, and we'd stack these containers on pallets as a subassembly. That way we have work-in-process waiting for our second and third shifts to weld them. That helps on the second shift where we normally need 16 people to run that line. But we now only need ten because most of the folding has been done on the first shift.

4. Threading the Needle: Mission vs. Money

Increasing output volume means continually balancing the business need to run a profitable operation while also accommodating the needs of workers with disabilities who may be less productive.

Gervais talks about this balancing act in an industry with thin margins:

> We'll be in a management meeting, and I'll remind our line leaders that we're losing money on this contract. But 60 percent of the people on that job may be individuals with disabilities and that's where the problem is. We can't let them go. It's our job to get the most out of our employees. We've got to figure it out. We may not be making money on a contract, but our mission is to employ people with disabilities. I've struggled with this money versus mission for years.

MDI does three key things to manage the tradeoffs between its purpose to employ workers with disabilities and the need to be profitable.

Use Long-Term Projects to Make Lines More Profitable

The company pursues more long-term program work instead of churning through short-term contracts where there is no time to improve the efficiency of the operation. Bigger, long-running projects provide a chance to better train workers and improve efficiency with innovative staffing solutions. Gervais explains:

> When it's the same job every day, like building the same type of tote, we can get people trained and things run much better. We get our efficiencies up because we have more time to get processes figured out, so we can do more training and innovation. People build confidence and competence doing longer-term projects.

Supervisors Manage Team Chemistry to Maximize Productivity

In addition to being creative, flexible and patient, supervisors need another intangible skill to uphold MDI's mission. Gervais elaborates on the challenge:

> If we get the right individuals with disabilities working on a production line, say their skill levels range from 40 percent efficiency up to 70 percent efficiency. If we get the right mix on that line, we can hit performance goals every time. And it runs that way every day. But, as soon as you pull a person out, and put a different worker in, or add a person, the efficiencies drop immediately. And it's very difficult for us to get that line's performance back up to where it needs to be.
>
> There's chemistry there and it sounds like magic. But our supervisors are very skilled at this. They know who works well together, and who doesn't. They know who is not engaged and who needs help staying focused. We rely on our line leads. They're one of our most important assets.

Think More Creatively about Automation

The question of automation is always in the background at MDI, which pursues labor-intensive projects in a world that is increasingly technology-driven. Rather than take an all-or-nothing approach to automation, MDI uses it as a tool to fulfill the company's mission. Here are three ways the company thinks about automating work when looking to scale production.

Implement "no-brainer" automation. Some tasks require automation because the technology is much more cost effective and results in higher quality outputs. For example, MDI has invested in a couple of welding robots to complete the final welds on plastic totes. This last step in the production process had historically been a bottleneck for the operation and made the most sense to automate.

Use automation to improve job quality. Sometimes the way to scale an operation is with supplemental automation that doesn't eliminate people's jobs but makes those jobs easier. Here MDI patiently threads the needle between mission and profits by dedicating significant time to engineering R&D, says Operations Manager Kyle Erickson. "We have to figure out how we can make XYZ product profitable, balancing automation with the skill sets our workers have."

Eglinton agrees. "No one should ever say that people with disabilities can't be involved in automation or running a machine," she says. "Some jobs involving automation could be a better job for somebody with a disability than the job they have right now."

> **In a million years, I didn't think we'd be able to find anyone on the floor able to run our CNC machine**

Marginalized workers can enable some automation. Many companies are being forced to automate parts of their business to survive, given widespread labor shortages. In many situations, of course, skilled workers are still needed to complement automation, and some of MDI's workers fall in that category.

There is a massive shortage of CNC machinists in the US, and training qualified people with disabilities to run complex automated machines can be a big win for companies looking for skilled and loyal talent. (See Classic Wire Cut story in chapter 11 as an example.) In one MDI facility, for example, an employee has been trained on a CNC machine for cutting fabric used in MDI's medical operation. Gervais admits:

> We have that CNC automated cutting machine down on the floor. We struggled with trying to find an experienced operator. We almost gave up. Then we found an individual on the autism spectrum who had some computer capabilities. In a million years, I didn't think we'd be able to find anyone on the floor who would be able to run it. Now he's training other operators on that machine.

Even as MDI explores ways it can automate its commercial business, the federal government's AbilityOne Program provides strong incentives to keep some work labor-intensive. To qualify for large government contracts under the AbilityOne Program, MDI must provide a significant number of direct labor hours to people with documented disabilities.[48] Meeting these expectations creates more job opportunities, but it also limits the pace of automation in some parts of the business.

Emotional Payoffs Make It All Worthwhile

Employing workers with disabilities can support a profitable business, but it can also provide surprising emotional rewards for workers and supervisors alike. Eglinton recalls stories of workers who lacked confidence when they first came to the company:

> They don't talk to anybody at first. But, over time, they start to make friends at MDI. They become more talkative and start participating and joking as one of the guys. They're very different than when they first started. That's because of our culture and how we accept people for everything they bring to the business.

Most mornings, one of Kyle Erickson's employees gets off the bus to work and wanders into Erickson's office to give his boss a hug.

He'll chat with Erickson for five or ten minutes before heading off to work. There's nothing self-conscious or disingenuous about this ritual, the operations manager reflects:

> Our employees create a vibe that makes you want to come to work. Like this guy with a cognitive disability who just wants to talk every morning. It makes work enjoyable, even in the most stressful moments. Suddenly, you have these employees walk by or talk to you, and at the end of the day, they keep everything in perspective. 'Hey, we're just making totes here.' But the big thing is, we're impacting the lives of people with or without disabilities. Every day this job reminds me of that.

CHAPTER 11

Classic Wire Cut: Finding Gold in Neurodiverse CNC Machinists

Classic Wire Cut designs and manufactures medical products used in a variety of practices, such as sports medicine, spinal surgery, and cardiology. Like most manufacturing companies that employ CNC machinists, Classic Wire is always looking for skilled talent to produce high-quality products for its well-known medical device customers. CNC machinists program and operate machine tools, such as grinders, lathes or mills, that are controlled by a computer to produce precision parts.

This is the story of how Classic discovered a remarkable new supply of talent trained by the Uniquely Abled Academy (UAA) at a local community college. UAA is a career training program that gives people diagnosed with level 1 autism the skills needed to work as CNC machinists. This inspiring story shows how one manufacturer learned to integrate workers on the autism spectrum into its high-performing workforce.

Sem Martinez figured it was just a courtesy call. As production manager at a Southern California medical devices manufacturer, he was interviewing some students at the local community college, an institution the company liked to support. But the students Martinez had been slated to meet had been diagnosed with autism spectrum disorder (ASD). He doubted they would have the aptitude to fill CNC machinist jobs in his company, Classic Wire Cut.

Martinez arrived at the school early that day. Sitting in his truck with a hot cup of coffee, he scrolled through his phone as usual. He noticed an older man get out of a nearby car and walk quickly around to the passenger's side. A young man was struggling with his necktie and suit jacket, and the older man stepped in to help. The man beamed with pride as he made the final adjustments, and Martinez realized he was watching a devoted father's excitement for his son, who was about to interview for a job.

Martinez put down his coffee and texted a description of the scene to his wife. He ended the text saying, "Everybody deserves a chance in life. I'm going to give it 100 percent today meeting these guys." Martinez got out of his truck and went inside to meet the newest graduates of the Uniquely Abled Academy (UAA).

Hitting a Talent Jackpot

The young man in the parking lot was among the ten students that Martinez and his HR colleague Angela Bannerman interviewed that morning. They were talking with the first class of graduates from the UAA's training program at College of the Canyons, 35 miles north of Los Angeles. The academy is a 12-week program that trains individuals with autism for entry-level jobs as CNC machinists and machinist trainees. (See sidebar "The Uniquely Abled Academy Creating New Opportunities") Martinez was blown away by what he heard in the interviews.

He and Bannerman raced back to the company's plant and excitedly told their boss, Amy Grant, "We've got to hire all these guys. You're going to love them!"

Grant, Classic Wire's vice president, was stunned by Martinez's enthusiasm. After listening to her

Classic did four things to help its neurodiverse UAA grads become successful employees

managers rave about the students, Grant requested more interviews and a plant tour. The company, which was growing, could use new talent. Classic Wire Cut was fortunate that it didn't have a lot of turnover. But retirements and the frequent promotion of younger CNC machinists created an ongoing need for entry-level talent with the skills and patience to follow Classic's demanding production processes.

The company hired seven new grads from the first cohort of the Uniquely Abled Academy program at College of the Canyons. This was only the beginning of the story. Classic had to do four things to help its neurodiverse UAA grads become successful employees. Their experience can help you learn how to:

- **Explore the potential of people with disabilities**
- **Establish strong partnerships to train and coach nontraditional hires**
- **Effectively onboard and coach workers on the autism spectrum**
- **Educate management on how to work with neurodiverse employees**

1. Explore the Potential of People with Disabilities

Grant and Martinez took the vital first step needed to explore this rich talent pool when they agreed to educate themselves about people on the autism spectrum. Vice President Amy Grant remembers being asked to visit the UAA program:

> The college called and said, 'We have a cohort of Uniquely Abled graduates.' I asked, 'What's that?' And they said, 'Well, it's level one autistic adults, and would you come over and interview them?' I'm thinking I don't know a thing about autism, and we don't have any immediate openings.

> But it sounds interesting. I talked to our production manager and our HR person and asked if they'd go over and interview these young people.
>
> Truthfully, I thought this was a 'Hey, let's do the college a favor exercise.' I never thought we'd have candidates who would get enthusiastic support from our HR person and production manager. When they came back from the college so excited, I was intrigued. I wanted to know what they saw in these guys.

When Grant asked her production manager to interview candidates on the autism spectrum, he was already managing 80 people. Martinez didn't want to take on more difficult staffing challenges, but, eventually, he decided to at least learn about the UAA program. Later, he reflected on what he learned from those first interviews:

> They were really sharp. They understood blueprint reading. They could already program and do this and that. There was no difference from people we normally interviewed. Sure, there were some behavioral things where they were shy, timid, or probably embarrassed because they haven't been exposed to things I took for granted. Maybe I'm their first employer, and I'm listening to this young person just talk about their experiences in the UAA program. I was impressed. I was like, okay, let's give some of these folks a chance. All we can do is give them an opportunity and see what happens.

When Grant interviewed the UAA graduates who had so excited her colleagues, she realized new hires with ASD could be a good fit at the company: "I personally have no experience with autism. But after I talked with them, I thought they're going to change our lives."

Classic Wire Cut hired seven neurodiverse machinists at once. It was a big commitment. Karen Navarro is a supervisor with Jay Nolan Community Services, which supports individuals with autism spectrum disorder. She had coached all the students in the Uniquely Abled Academy training program on the soft skills they would need to get jobs when the program ended. Recalling her experience with that first group, she unexpectedly stops talking. Navarro briefly chokes up as she reflects on the huge commitment Classic made to giving seven young men with autism a chance.

Grant and her colleagues took an essential step when trying to tap a neurodiverse talent pool. They educated themselves about what potential was there and how it might fit in their company.

2. Establish Great Partnerships: A Three-Legged Race

Classic sees the commitment to its neurodiverse hires as a three-legged race. Success requires not only a diligent employer but also a quality training partner, which is the Uniquely Abled Academy at the College of the Canyons. The third leg is a coaching and integration partner. In this story that's Jay Nolan Community Services, a local agency where Navarro works to place candidates with disabilities and keep them employed. Her work at Classic is funded mostly by the California Department of Rehabilitation. "We couldn't have done this without Karen's coaching skills," says Grant.

Unlike the low-skill jobs Minnesota Diversified Industries was filling in the previous chapter, the CNC machinist positions at Classic Wire Cut require significant capabilities. A training resource is essential. This is the role the Uniquely Abled Academy fills.

The Uniquely Abled Academy Creating New Opportunities on the Spectrum

UAA is a career training program created by the Uniquely Abled Project. There are now more than 20 UAA programs licensed to run around the United States.[49] The academy programs are free to all trainees, generally funded by the state vocational rehabilitation agency and federal workforce training grants.

Academy programs are a collaboration between machine technology educators, specialists in educating those on the autism spectrum, social service agencies, and other organizations. They partner to train, support, and provide job placement services that create career opportunities for individuals on the autism spectrum.

UAA programs run 12–16 weeks for young adults with autism. They include 300 hours of in-class instruction and 60 hours of job-readiness training as an entry-level machinist apprentice or CNC operator. Participants learn how to program, set up, and operate CNC machines widely used in manufacturing. They also learn shop mathematics, blueprint reading, and how to use quality control instruments. Before completing the program, students receive soft skills coaching and help with resumes and job interviews. UAA programs have graduated more than 230 individuals and they have a job placement rate of over 90 percent.

A growing number of programs and organizations in the US prepare neurodiverse young adults to work in jobs that take advantage of their unique capabilities. These programs train people with autism and other cognitive disabilities for a variety of good jobs, such as those in IT support, automobile maintenance, and graphic design.[50]

3. Effectively Onboard and Coach Neurodiverse Employees

Classic Wire Cut already had a detailed onboarding process, which helped orient the new UAA hires to become productive. One of the first steps was to create partnerships between each new hire and a veteran machine operator who they could shadow. Management was surprised at how quickly the young machinists learned their jobs.

Martinez recognized early on that his new employees on the autism spectrum lacked any sense of arrogance. Over the years, he had found new machinists often objected to being told how to carry out tasks they thought they already knew. But graduates of the UAA program didn't resist when instructed how to perform various tasks. They just learned and adapted to the Classic way, which Martinez found refreshing—and much more effective. This was particularly important because Classic has very specific and demanding manufacturing processes that require faithful adherence. "You just tell them and they do it that way," said the production manager.

Sometimes, at first, Classic's supervisors were tentative about correcting UAA grads if they varied at all from standard manufacturing practices. But Navarro, a veteran coach who helped with the transition of the new employees, repeatedly impressed upon Classic's management the importance of holding its neurodiverse employees accountable for performance and not tolerating "off-roading" behavior. (That's Classic lingo for cutting corners on well-defined production processes.)

Customized Coaching Is a Must

Integrating workers with cognitive disabilities into an organization like Classic requires customized coaching that takes into account the specific needs of each employee. Navarro continually adapts her approach:

> I only coach people who need coaching. For some people, I'm just sitting next to them and asking questions. Others need more hands-on help. I do a lot of task analysis. One of the guys had a lot of trouble with time management. I

needed to write down the steps of his job. We had to write all that out so he could develop a routine on his own. I'm not here for people to become dependent on me.

The range of self-confidence among neurodiverse employees varies significantly despite their similar training. Grant's team discovered this early on. Some UAA grads were excited to take on the challenges of running one or several CNC machines immediately. Others didn't have the self-confidence to operate any machine at first, even though tests showed they had the skills needed. These new hires were initially assigned tasks where they would be more comfortable, such as deburring newly machined parts (i.e., checking for defects), which requires very fine motor skills and great attention to detail.

Working with Unconventional Habits

Navarro spent about 24 hours a week coaching the seven new employees on different shifts at Classic in the first few months. Among other things, she helped new hires address quirky habits, such as their phone addictions, which affect individuals with autism more than most.[51] One employee with autism, for instance, was preoccupied with reading on his phone and sometimes disappeared for 45 minutes while lost in a book. Although he was more productive than many of his colleagues, Navarro worked with him to curb this behavior.

> **Not every neurodiverse hire works out, of course. Two had sleeping problems.**

There were a few other unusual problems. One employee had trouble writing legibly, and when he had to sign an official form confirming he had attended a mandatory training session, his signature was outside the lines on the form, which an FDA inspector noted in his report. Grant rolled her eyes at that one. They had to coach this young employee on the importance of his signature being completely between the lines.

In the last few years, Classic has hired 15 graduates from the UAA program. Not every neurodiverse hire works out, of course. Two had sleeping problems. Management tried everything with these guys, from changing to splitting up shifts—anything to get them to work on time or to keep them from falling asleep on the job. Eventually, the company had to let these two machinists go. Another moved away, but 12 are still with the company.

Good Coaching Enhances Management

Some unusual obstacles must be overcome to make sure neurodiverse employees are effective in their new jobs. Having a competent transition coach to address these challenges is a huge benefit for supervisors and managers.

Navarro worked closely with supervisors on both day and night shifts, helping them get comfortable with new employees. Because she understood the ins and outs of the machine shop environment, her tutoring around specific tasks was right on target.

This allowed Martinez, the production manager, to stay focused on the overall operation and to work with other departments instead of just attending to the challenges of integrating new neurodiverse employees. Navarro and Classic's supervisors were taking care of that. "Our supervisors, along with Karen and her Jay Nolan team, made it possible for me to become much more relaxed and to believe in this program," says Martinez.

No Screaming Children in This Machine Shop

After six years working in grocery stores, Harrison needed a change, as related in chapter 1. The unpredictable retail environment, with its annoyed customers, screaming children, and harried bosses, had proved frustrating and emotionally demanding for this smart guy with level 1 autism. Fortunately, his mother heard about the UAA program at a nearby community college.

Harrison was used to working with his hands. But the Uniquely Abled Academy was different. When he finished the 12-week training program, he had the skills to work in manufacturing. But he'd also had the skills for the grocery store job. Would manufacturing be a good fit?

After some COVID-related false starts, Harrison landed a job as a machinist at Classic Wire Cut. For more than two years, Harrison has programmed a wire machine that cuts metal parts for tools used for endoscopies. He describes his work this way:

> Most of the time, I'm setting up jobs to run on about four machines I'm in charge of. Once they're running, I inspect each part as called for. My department has about 20 of the same machines. So, when my machines have a long run time, I may bounce to other machines that need attention.

In every job he's had, Harrison has struggled to work out what his colleagues and his boss mean when they ask him something. Sometimes he can't quite discern if the words they're saying mean one thing or another. "People at Classic know my condition beforehand so they're a lot more forgiving than my previous employers," he says. "It was still a challenge figuring it out with my coworkers."

Working at Classic Wire has been a great fit for Harrison and the other UAA graduates the company has hired. With two thumbs up, he says:

> The biggest thing for me is enjoying how my coworkers are very friendly and nice and they're willing to hear what it is you need to do your job. Unlike my past jobs in grocery stores, it's great working at a place where the customers aren't complaining, and you don't have to hear screaming children all the time.

4. Educate Managers to Work with Neurodiverse Talent

Coaching neurodiverse employees was one thing, but Grant and Martinez also needed to teach managers and supervisors how to work with their new hires. They brought Navarro in to lead a meeting with Classic's production leaders and supervisors. Grant recalls:

> We needed to know how to give these guys the softest landing possible in the company. But a lot of us were afraid we were going to hurt people's feelings. We wondered, *How are we supposed to behave?* Karen was very frank saying, 'Don't treat them any differently. They're adults. They're in your company and they need to follow your rules.'

In the following months, Navarro continued to coach the company's managers and supervisors informally. "We kind of went in cold turkey," says Martinez. "We bring these seven guys on board, and no one understands how to communicate with them. A lot of us had never had any interactions with people on the autism spectrum. What is autism? What does it mean? And what level of autism are we working with?" Grant saw it, too:

> Initially, we handled them with kid gloves. We treated them like they were—I hate to say it—disabled. I think it's because they're different. We didn't want to hurt their feelings, but honestly, it's just ignorance. We didn't know how to deal with them.

Navarro gave Classic's supervisors lots of tips on how to integrate UAA grads into the company. Her mantra was "differences don't mean deficiencies." One of Navarro's biggest challenges was teaching supervisors how to hold the young machinists accountable.

"Some guys should have been fired," Navarro says frankly, "if they kept showing up late, or were calling out sick. I had to work with Sem [Martinez] to get a little tougher. I'd say, 'Discipline them. Write them up. They're not going to break.' And if they get fired, that's OK. It's part of life." Martinez confesses these were important lessons for management:

> We came to realize what this program is about, that these new hires are uniquely abled. In fact, they're smarter than a lot of us in many ways. A lot of them are living alone. They're paying rent. They pay bills. They have independent lifestyles. They make important decisions. And we have to treat them like any other employee. Karen really helped us understand that.

At the same time, Navarro had to show that accommodations are sometimes necessary when working with neurodiverse employees.

One young machinist she was coaching did not have the manual dexterity to loosen a bolt on a grinding tool. His boss, a new supervisor, kept insisting that he had to do it. The machinist was very nervous and flustered as he struggled with a task he couldn't complete. Navarro knew some other female employees who couldn't loosen the tool relied on a male colleague to do it for them. As the night shift supervisor continued to insist that the young machinist complete this task, Navarro went to the production manager and said:

> 'Look, there are things my guy might not be able to do, and this might be where he needs an accommodation. Can he get someone to loosen the tool for him? The UAA grad can do the job. He just can't loosen that tool. And that shouldn't stop him. Could we just accommodate him?' Classic was phenomenal. Martinez asked me to come talk to their supervisors, so they understood what accommodations are and where they should step in. That to me was

like a dream. When do you hear employers say, 'Teach us to be better employers?'

Employing individuals with level 1 autism exposed a paradox. Classic's managers have learned not to treat their UAA hires as fragile or different from other employees, yet they are likely to need some accommodations to be effective. But the payoff is worth it.

Everybody Wins! Benefits of Neurodiverse Talent

Leaders at Classic have no trouble pointing to the major benefits of their decision to invest in UAA grads on the autism spectrum.

Increased Productivity

Classic's veteran production manager is unequivocal in recounting the value of his nontraditional employees:

> I just didn't anticipate we were going to get the productivity we're getting. I thought they were going to be, sadly, more handicapped, and just not able to do certain things. But I was blown away. Just seeing after two or three days of learning, they were on their own, and the productivity was just off the charts. I really underestimated this.

More Quality Focus—Less Off-Roading

When I spoke with Grant, she had just had a CNC line leader in her office saying what a great employee this UAA grad was. "He follows every direction. He remembers everything," said the line leader. "Where can you get me more of these guys?"

Like most manufacturers, Classic has ongoing challenges making sure workers follow strictly prescribed production practices. But its neurodiverse employees turn out to be much better than most at adhering to validated manufacturing processes. "With the UAA grads we don't have to deal with that," says Martinez. "Once you set the expectations and the guidelines, they follow directions exactly. It doesn't get any better than that."

Polite, Punctual, and Perfectionists

Another benefit of tapping this market of neurodiverse talent is the quality of the people Classic has brought into their company. Sometimes talent brings a lot of difficulties with it. There is an old saying, "Strong people have strong weaknesses." In the neurotypical world, people who are brilliant or highly competent in one area often really screw up another part of their lives. But Classic's management has been amazed by the qualities UAA grads bring to the job. "In general, these are some of the most pleasant human beings you'll ever meet," says Grant.

Our entire workforce is very comfortable now dealing with people with autism

Navarro is even more passionate when extolling the virtues of her neurodivergent protégés:

> You're getting an employee who's probably never going to leave you if you invest in them. Poaching is huge in the CNC world right now. But people with autism don't like to switch from job to job to job. They're not going to get poached. In general, they're going to be punctual, and they have an attention to detail that's fantastic.

Amy Grant is Classic's champion in its push for neurodiversity. She frequently repeats what Martinez texted his wife the day of his first UAA interviews: "Everyone deserves a chance in life." She concluded our interview by saying,

I'm so proud of our company and our culture. This experience has really enriched us. Our entire workforce is very comfortable now dealing with people with autism. And it's gotten everybody to think a little differently about people who aren't the same as us. I believed we could have people come in here and be successful. It could change their lives and their parents' lives. It has certainly changed ours.

CHAPTER 12

How Heartland Systems Corporation* Maintains Data Quality Across the Spectrum

Many technology and information-driven companies have discovered the value neurodiverse employees bring to their businesses and have made significant investments in recruiting, training, and employing this talent.[52] *Employing people on the autism spectrum, in particular, has become a common practice in finance, tech, and data intensive businesses.*

There is a popular saying in the autism community "When you meet one person with autism, you've met one person with autism." Even though they share common traits, such as difficulty in communication and social interactions, individuals diagnosed with autism spectrum disorder (ASD) have unique personalities, likes, and dislikes.[53] *This means, as with neurotypical employees, they must be managed as individuals. Some with ASD can handle changes in the schedule better than others, for example. Others manage stress more readily.*

That said, businesses are learning a lot about the ongoing challenges and obstacles that must be addressed to make investments in neurodiverse talent pay off. Hiring workers with disabilities is a long game, especially when these employees are performing high-value tasks that are hard to fill with neurotypical talent. This chapter looks at data intensive companies that have employed workers on the autism spectrum over time and the opportunities this talent pool presents in the long term.

MAINTAINING DATA QUALITY ON THE SPECTRUM

In March 2020, the COVID-19 pandemic disrupted the lives of millions of US workers, including a small group in Minneapolis. Locally, Heartland Systems Corporation (HSC)* employed half a dozen workers on the autism spectrum when this large financial services company closed its Minneapolis office and asked its staff to work remotely. For workers on the autism spectrum, who are very uncomfortable with rapid change, this overnight change to work from home was an extremely unsettling period.

HSC is one of a growing number of companies that have employed workers with developmental disabilities as contractors in partnership with Mind Shift. This staffing agency trains and places people with autism, who they call "specialists," for sustainable jobs in fields such as manufacturing, non-clinical healthcare, and data/technology roles.

Working with employees who have developmental disabilities is a journey. If this talent is going to make a difference in a business, they need help coping with the inevitable changes that occur on the job. Below are five steps companies have taken to make sure their partnerships with agencies like Mind Shift continue to add value for the business, as well as for the specialists they employ:

- **Continually identify important tasks in hard-to-fill jobs that draw on the skills of neurodivergent workers.**
- **Help employees with developmental disabilities navigate changes in the workplace.**
- **Invest in the capabilities of neurodivergent workers to enhance their value to the business.**
- **Enhance supervisory skills to match the needs of employees with disabilities.**

---

*This company name is disguised. Some details have been changed to protect confidentiality of Mind Shift's client. But management lessons and the story of their experiences are true.

- Draw on customized coaching to support neurodivergent staff.

1. Identify Hard-to-Fill Jobs for Workers Who Are Neurodivergent

EY, the huge global professional services firm, has dozens of neurodiverse employees doing sophisticated work on AI, blockchain, and data analytics projects. "We really wanted to invest in that space. It allows us to have an even bigger playing field of talent," says Karyn Twaronite, EY's global vice chair of DEI.[54]

Like EY and every information-intensive business today, Heartland Systems Corporation faces challenges maintaining quality data for use in decision-making. This regional company initially hired Mind Shift specialists to perform data cleansing work and report generation that was being done by overqualified actuaries and other highly paid staff. Highly-educated professionals can find this work mind-numbing because it is very repetitive and requires incredible attention to detail. Nevertheless, maintaining data quality is essential to business performance.

> Data quality tasks performed by Mind Shift specialists at HSC have evolved

With data quality tools continuing to improve over time, HSC has increasingly automated as much data cleansing work and report generation as possible, according to Oscar Denton, vice president of data analytics. This means some of the tasks originally performed by workers on the autism spectrum have gone away, but there are still anomalies in HSC's data files that confound even the smartest computer systems. These require painstaking human intervention.

HSC uses some cheaper offshore resources to review problematic data records, but the results are often lacking. Specialists with ASD hired through Mind Shift, however, are extremely detail oriented. They are unmatched in identifying problematic patterns in the data and in determining what information needs to be associated with which record. With this persistence and attention to detail, proper human intervention continues to produce the best solutions.

The data quality tasks performed by Mind Shift specialists at HSC have evolved, and they continue to draw on the unique skill sets of people on the autism spectrum. The key is finding a match for these competencies—attention to detail, focus on precision, and high tolerance for repetitive actions. In a society increasingly defined by short attention spans and addictions to entertainment and erroneous information, these competencies will almost always add value. (See sidebar "Level 2 Autism: Finding Talent at Another Level.") As work tasks continue to evolve with the rapid evolution of technologies, business leaders should anticipate new ways to effectively use the skill sets of individuals who are neurodiverse.

2. Help Neurodivergent Staff Cope with Unexpected Changes in Business

The COVID-19 pandemic presented a huge challenge for HSC's workers who are on the autism spectrum. "COVID was a big change for them," says Oscar Denton, vice president of data analytics. "They went from working with each other face-to-face where they had managers and a Mind Shift coach who could help, if needed. Once they went home, they were pretty isolated. They lost that comradery with others in the office and that amplified their anxiety."

With the shift to remote work, HSC found some unexpected challenges in supervising employees with autism when not operating face-to-face. Monika Reinhardt is the IT business analyst at HSC who supervises Mind Shift specialists remotely. She learned some team members were not comfortable on Zoom video calls from home. Reinhardt quickly stopped using the video, so specialists just heard her voice on their regular status calls. But when they couldn't see her, she discovered they were more likely to misinterpret the emotions behind her words.

"Body language makes a lot of difference," says Reinhardt. So she became more aware of her tone and how the group was interpreting what she said, working hard with the specialists to help them transition into their evolving roles.

Changes in the business environment and the organization are inevitable today. Every worker must cope with them. Neurodivergent employees, however, are more likely to be rattled by unanticipated changes in ways that affect their performance. "They like work schedules that don't have sudden changes," says Reinhardt. "If I go in and tell them, 'OK, you're not doing this today. You're doing something else.' I know they will do it, but it's really going to upset them. I can't do that."

In reality, stimuli and sources of change often come from outside the workplace. The murder of George Floyd in May 2020, for instance, was emotionally devastating for the nation, but particularly for residents in the Minneapolis region. For some on the autism spectrum, this kind of emotional event was even more traumatic and made it very difficult to work.[55] Indeed, management has learned it must provide extra care for some neurodivergent workers who can be extremely sensitive to non-work events.

Managers at HSC have learned to accommodate these emotional reactions wherever possible. "You're going to have bumps in the road," says Denton. "The attitude is let's work through it and get you back on the right track."

3. Expand the Capabilities of Workers on the Autism Spectrum

Like neurotypical team members, to get the most value from employees with developmental disabilities, you have to invest in their professional growth. That means increasing their independence, leadership skills, and in some cases, their workday from part time to full time. Sometimes, this can also mean protecting them from other departments that may not understand their unique talents, work styles, and the accommodations needed to maximize productivity (such as a workspace with less harsh overhead lighting or headphones to block out ambient noise).

Develop Leaders to Promote More Independent Work

Reinhardt, the HSC supervisor, and Mind Shift coach JoLynn Larson have collaborated to increase the independence of the Mind Shift specialists. "Now we just give them supportive guidance," says Larson. "They're managing themselves instead of us being on them all the time. We just support them to give them confidence. That's their team now."

To increase independence, HSC has worked to develop leadership skills among its specialists. Larson explains:

> We have one guy who was schlepping boxes at Federal Express when we found him. We wondered why he was doing that when he's so gifted and talented in a data cleansing role. He's now the leader of the team. Tom is super responsible. He keeps the team on track, making sure the group is running well day to day. He gets the other specialists and understands them.

Reinhardt and Larson meet with Tom regularly and coach him on leading the team in the coming week. Creating a sustainable program has meant looking for leadership where they could find it.

Adjust Work Hours

Many people on the autism spectrum can only work part time when they start employment. There are a variety of reasons for this. Some can only tolerate sensory inputs in a work environment (e.g., noise and lighting levels) for so long. Others must manage additional physical or cognitive conditions they live with.

Often, however, the limitations can be financial. People who are receiving government benefits because of a disability have limits to their income. Losing benefits, such as government-supported health insurance, is often too big a risk for people with disabilities and their families, so they will only work part time. If those income limits are exceeded, the government benefits are taken away and are very difficult to get back. Full-time work, especially if one needs to find another job, is too risky for some.

> **Employing people with developmental disabilities means being open to schedule changes**

Sometimes, however, after working part time, individuals with ASD discover they are capable and eager for more time on the job. One specialist at HSC didn't want to work more than six hours a day when he started. But then Larson approached Edward, suggesting that he might increase his hours and asked what he thought about the idea:

> He said, 'Let me think about it. I think I can do that now.' Today he's up to 40 hours a week. He's really happy. He has taken on some data-cleansing tasks that originally he didn't do. He's also picked up on some quality assurance work. And he's working on his own independent data files now with very little review.

Employing people with developmental disabilities means being flexible and open to schedule changes mandated by their physical, cognitive, and financial needs. Often, people on the autism spectrum find specific job settings to be too demanding to allow them to work full time.[56] But in the right situation with appropriate accommodations and an understanding boss, neurodivergent employees can sometimes take on more than they expected. Success with this talent pool requires adapting to an individual employee's needs and potential.

Manage Emotions Across Organizational Boundaries

In big organizations, different departments or functions can have different subcultures that shape expectations about getting work done. Neurodivergent workers are likely to be more successful in smaller groups or teams if they can't work independently. EY has created 23 Neurodiverse Centers of Excellence around the world that support workers with autism, dyslexia, ADHD, and other cognitive differences. These offices provide work environments tailored to the professional development needs of the firm's neurodivergent employees.[57]

EY has invested heavily in training all employees about diversity and inclusion as cultural values. But sometimes, work in high-performing companies naturally crosses departmental boundaries where this understanding of differences may be less accepted. In this case, managers must negotiate with those in the company who are not attuned to the benefits and challenges facing people with developmental disabilities.

At HSC, managers on Denton's team have learned to defuse friction that can arise between software developers in other departments and the Mind Shift specialists doing data quality work. Because some individuals with ASD can be very sensitive to criticism, even when it is constructive, supervisors will always be present to moderate conversations that might raise questions about why certain specialists aren't producing outputs faster. It's a balancing act of making sure the Mind Shift team achieves their monthly goals in terms of outputs without triggering negative emotional reactions that can derail their productivity.

4. Enhance Supervisory Skills to Maximize Neurodivergent Talent

SAP, the enterprise software company, has over 200 employees diagnosed on the autism spectrum. At both SAP and EY, these employees have a retention rate of over 90 percent. Part of that success comes from investing in the education of all employees on the importance of understanding and accepting individual differences. Genevieve Koolen, HR director at SAP Africa, believes this training is essential for success. "Regular awareness sessions help employees develop a deeper understanding of neurodiversity and encourage empathy with those who may view the world differently."[58]

When she began supervising the team of Mind Shift specialists at Heartland Systems, Monika Reinhardt had no experience with autism. She admits she didn't know what she was getting into since she had never interacted with people on the spectrum. Here are five ways she altered her management style to work with her neurodivergent team.

Adapt Communication Styles

Reinhardt laughs when she describes herself as someone who talks quickly, snapping her fingers to indicate the pace she prefers. "I like to get things done in a very quick, efficient manner," she says. But Reinhardt soon realized she had to adapt her approach when leading her team of neurodivergent analysts.

Shortly after she started, Reinhardt gave her specialists a data analysis task and told them to get it done in a week. But nothing happened and no one on the team asked for help. She learned later the specialists were worried she would think they were not doing their job, but they were too stressed to ask for help. Reinhardt had to change the way she communicated with the group. She couldn't talk to them assuming everyone comprehended what she was saying in her rapid-fire, just-get-it-done style. She had to continually check in to make sure her messages were being understood.

Put Your Job in Jeopardy! Finding New Ways to Connect

Effective supervisors learn how to connect in nontraditional ways with their neurodiverse team members. Reinhardt wanted to build her team's comradery and create an environment that was fun and not all about work. One way she did this was by playing a daily game of Jeopardy! with her group as they worked remotely. Specialists looked forward to getting the "answers" each day and trying to come up with the questions that made sense. They enjoyed the competition and the specialist who got the most correct answers each month received a gift card from Reinhardt. "They look forward to the games every day," she said. "I always try to keep them engaged."

Monitor Assumptions about Neurodivergent Training

Reinhardt still ran into surprises that reminded her to check assumptions about how the Mind Shift team would understand her instructions. Early on, she tried to convince the group to use the company's calendar system to notify colleagues when they were unavailable. Reinhardt gave the specialists cursory instructions on how to use the calendaring system. To her surprise, this temporarily caused chaos in office scheduling when the team misunderstood what to do and inadvertently started blocking their colleagues' meetings. She recalls with a smile:

> I shouldn't have done that because they weren't familiar with how the software worked. Calendaring was very new to them. I should have shared my screen and shown them exactly step by step what needs to be done so they didn't block other people's calendars.

Reinhardt knows she can't succeed by throwing half-trained neurodivergent specialists into a new task. Managing people on the autism spectrum requires making sure they have the tools they need to succeed in doing a job and that they're trained correctly. They also need a very clear picture of what is expected and what needs to be done. Task steps and the specific outcomes must be unambiguous from the specialist's perspective.

Expect Things to Take Longer

Patience is particularly important when onboarding a specialist to the company or a specific task. Reinhardt says:

> In an ideal world that should be done for all new hires. But sometimes we just send an email and tell them to go through this document and take care of that form. But for Mind Shift specialists, we make sure to list everything out and complete all the trainings before we put them in any job. We have one person support them completely until they're ready.

Challenge Expectations about Neurodivergent Potential

As Reinhardt got to know the specialists, she realized they had more potential than she had expected. For one thing, they didn't need as much "handholding" as she had anticipated. Reinhardt slowly stopped attending meetings with the analysts every day. They liked the extra freedom and were fine with their new independence.

The irony is that even though their behavior was highly individualized, their connection as team members was more intense than normal. For example, one team member's frustration with a particular task could impact the attitude of the entire team. But if they were confident about the work they were doing and believed they were doing the right thing, then they're happy doing even the most repetitive job. Reinhardt has been surprised at the impact her Mind Shift team has had on her personally:

> I love working with them. I've learned to have more patience, which is something I always needed to work on. And I've learned to watch my tone when I am talking. I tend to come across as very intimidating. They're the most gentle folks. Sometimes I think they're much better human beings because they're true to themselves and they're very honest. They don't like to hurt anyone. It's been a wonderful experience.

5. Invest in Customized Coaching to Meet Individual Needs

A stable external coaching partner like Mind Shift is essential for a company that seeks to tap a neurodivergent talent pool over time. Other organizations that provide training services include the Stanford Neurodiversity Project and The Precisionists. Finding a partner who can provide ongoing, customized coaching for *both* the individuals and managers in the business is essential. Here are three ways external coaches add value.

Find and Train New Candidates

Mind Shift continues to identify new employees on the autism spectrum to fill roles at HSC and with their other clients. Heartland

Systems Corp needs this ongoing partnership to source neurodivergent talent who have the social skills and motivation to work in its professional environment. Mind Shift coaches help with the transition when onboarding new specialists. They may alert the company about any accommodations an individual needs to work effectively, such as reduced noise or special lighting. This personal connection between the coach and the specialist is important to help the transition go smoothly.

Coach Through Difficult Situations

Workers on the autism spectrum sometimes run into unexpected obstacles to their continued employment, but continuity in coaching can help manage these disruptions. In these situations, a solid, established relationship is everything. Lucas Espinoza is a data warehouse director at HSC and Reinhardt's boss. He recognizes the nontraditional situations the company must handle:

> We have to give our specialists the leeway to work at their own pace. Some work faster than others. Sometimes they have outside challenges like family situations or there were challenges around COVID. From a company standpoint, that's where working with Mind Shift coaches helps make sure they feel comfortable. And if they need to take time off or need to do something to get back on track, we give them that leeway.

Coach Managers on Managing Change

Supervisors and managers also need occasional coaching on how to keep their neurodivergent talent productive. Staffing changes, reorganizations, and redesigned work tasks can throw people with ASD for a loop, and managers sometimes need help minimizing the emotional disruptions these changes can cause. JoLynn Larson, employment services manager at Mind Shift, says:

> My advice is always to catch specialists before they go to their work in the morning. Let them know that a change has happened. That's because even if you give them a little notice before they start work, it's better than them having no notice at all and being surprised by the change.

Economics and Passion Win Out

It is one thing to hire a couple of workers with developmental disabilities and another to sustain their valuable contributions in today's fast-changing business environment. HSC has developed a realistic approach. They recognize the tasks where Mind Shift specialists can continue to add the most value. Although the company employs offshore resources to do basic data quality work, they reserve the most important challenges for their Mind Shift specialists, who are more meticulous in finding and resolving complicated data problems.

"Frankly, it's high-value work for the organization, yet it's relatively low skill. It's a very good niche for their skill set," says Oscar Denton, vice president of data analytics. "They provide value at a reasonable cost."

That's the economic argument for investing in workers with disabilities. Another is about diversity: "[Clients] don't want a homogeneous group of people trying to solve their problems," says Karyn Twaronite, EY's global vice chair of DEI.[59]

But for the supervisor working most closely with the Mind Shift team, the reasons are more personal. "I love working with them," Reinhardt says. "And I'm proud to be part of a company that is trying to give equal opportunities to everyone, making sure they're part of something big and important."

More and more companies are recognizing this is a journey worth taking.

Level 2 Autism: Finding Talent at Another Level

Individuals on the spectrum are often classified as level 1, 2, or 3, although there is some controversy about this labeling system.[60] Those diagnosed as level 1, or high functioning, have been most readily recruited by a growing number of employers. They may require some support, but they live relatively independent lives. These employees are widely recognized for their latent talent and above average intelligence.

But many employers are missing the boat by ignoring a different group of talent on the autism spectrum. Those diagnosed as level 2s can be the real asset when it comes to staffing hard-to-fill positions with loyal, high-performing workers.[61] Those diagnosed as level 2s on the autism spectrum require more training and support than those identified as level 1s. But with some relatively minor accommodations, they can be loyal and productive employees. JoLynn Larson, employment services manager at Mind Shift, a staffing agency that trains and places people diagnosed with ASD, says:

> The autism population that is completely missed is the middle, the individuals who are not necessarily your most high functioning. But they have important skills, and with the right coach and in the right business, they can be productive almost immediately. This level 2 group really wants to work and give back. And they are dedicated to their jobs. But businesses have to change how they think about hiring.

Individuals on the spectrum categorized as level 2s are good for certain types of hard-to-fill jobs like hands-on-work in manufacturing and inventory management roles where they can operate productively but at an independent pace.[62] Larson explains how they are different from level 1s this way:

Level 2s need additional coaching to get set up in a job. They also might need a coach stepping in from time to time to help regulate some behavior or to make sure they're communicating well with their manager. Also, they often still live at home with their parents, or in a group home, so they're less independent that way.

From Cleaning Toilets to Helping People Live Longer

Winters in Minnesota can be crazy cold. Nick didn't mind. He was warm inside the Boston Scientific facility outside of Minneapolis, where he worked as part of a team assembling and shipping medical devices around the world. Then, one day, the fire alarm went off.

Everyone trooped outside immediately, as dictated by safety procedures. Nick instantly felt the cold. It had to be below zero. His co-workers decided it was a false alarm. He called to them as they headed back inside to get warm, chiding them for not waiting longer. In a moment, he was the only one still standing outside in his lab gown, wearing light disposable gloves. Nick's fingers felt like they were freezing off. But he knew the rule said to wait until after the alarm cleared. "I should have gone back inside instead of choosing to get numb," he says, recalling that day with a slight smile.

It is not evident at first, but behind his pleasantly earnest demeanor, Nick has been diagnosed as level 2 on the autism spectrum. This means he needs extra support in the workplace, but he definitely delivers. With coaching from Mind Shift, he's worked a couple of jobs at the Boston Scientific plant outside of Minneapolis. Most days, Nick carefully packs boxes of vein catheters, used in different medical procedures, for shipment as far away as Malaysia.

He creates about 60 packages a day with dozens of catheters in each order. Nick is unusually patient and careful at his job. He likes what he does because he's helping people around the world live longer, better lives.

But Nick wasn't always this content. After finishing school and getting some training, he found jobs working in a gym and then at a brewery, mopping floors and cleaning toilets. "I was the second greatest janitor in the world," he says sarcastically. But he and his coach, JoLynn Larson at Mind Shift, knew he could do more.

Finally, with coaching and encouragement, he landed a job at Boston Scientific. Nick doesn't mind getting to work at 6 a.m. because it's worth it to be "impacting millions of lives," he says. His supportive parents drive him to work, but his goal is to get his own car by the time he is 26. That's next year.

When asked about his biggest challenges at work, with little hesitation or emotion, he says, "It's dealing with other people and noise from the nearby radio in the lab."

Nick knows his colleagues are just having fun, but the noise gets too distracting for him to do his work. "I've just got to deal with it," he says matter-of-factly. "That's why I have earplugs to drown out the radio. And did I forget to mention my station is like a busy traffic lane? I got to be careful of others walking behind me!"

Meeting people of different nationalities is another aspect of work Nick enjoys. He quickly adds, "The food in the cafeteria is pretty good, except the pizza. They serve good soup there, too. And why are all the healthy foods more expensive?" You can tell this is a man with distinct tastes. He also points out that his lunch break is 24 minutes, not 25!

Getting serious at another moment, Nick confides, "I'm highly respected at work because of all the stuff I get done. And my charm. I don't play around. I'm like the hall monitor of my station."

When asked what he likes most about coming to work, Nick confides that this job is a huge change from all the other ones he's had, in no small part because of his long list of responsibilities. But again, it's the mission that counts. "The best part is helping people live longer, better lives, serving people around the world," he says. "I take pride in my employment. I'm doing so much more than before. It's almost indescribable."

To find this level 2 neurodiverse talent, employers should do three things.

1. Tap Networks in the Autism Community

First, you need to find a partner organization in the community that identifies, screens, and trains individuals with ASD who have been identified as level 2. You can contact your local Autism Society or get a referral from another employer to an agency or nonprofit that works with people on the spectrum.

Find a partner who is screening and preparing level 2s for part-time or full-time employment. Ask for references of other companies who have hired neurodivergent talent from this organization. People diagnosed in the mid-range on the autism spectrum may not appear motivated to work by traditional standards. But with some probing and by connecting them to the company's mission, that motivation spark can often be ignited in powerful ways.

For example, Mind Shift has placed product assemblers at Boston Scientific's medical devices division in Minnesota. These workers are not motivated by money or the prestige of working for a well-regarded company but by helping to fulfill the company's mission of saving lives around the world. A good partner will help show potential employees how they will contribute to the larger impact of your organization's mission.

2. Change Recruiting, Interviewing, and Onboarding Processes

Identifying jobs or tasks that are a good fit for people with level 2 ASD is another essential step. This often means jobs that require careful attention, such as inventory management or product packaging, are very repetitive, and are not highly integrated with the tasks of other workers. For example, an assembly line may not be a good fit because of the pressure neurodivergent workers can feel to keep up with their colleagues. Working at an independent pace is preferred.

The biggest change for employers trying to hire level 2s on the autism spectrum is reinventing their hiring processes. The key is designing a job interview that is comfortable for the applicant, not the hiring manager. This may mean giving the candidate room to walk around or pace *during* a job interview. And don't judge them on their eye contact or the quality of their small talk. It may also mean avoiding direct questions such as "What motivated you to apply for this job?"

Traditional interview questions can fluster a candidate on the autism spectrum. They are unlikely to have canned answers ready. Instead, you could ask if they have researched the company. If so, you might explore what excites them about the business. This may help you uncover ways they can contribute to its mission. Larson, who has coached many job candidates with autism, says:

> Employers really miss the boat by overlooking those level 2 individuals who don't interview well. Maybe the job isn't a position they're interested in. Maybe their interest in working for you comes from another place. It might be, 'Hey, I researched the company, and I like that you make a difference in the world.' But they can't eloquently talk about their interest in the job because that's not what they care about. This means changing how you look at the candidate and how the candidate looks at the job.

Too often, the hiring manager will turn down a candidate with autism and select the next neurotypical applicant who walks in the door. That's only because they can sit still and answer standard interview questions in the traditional manner. Unfortunately, the new hire will be bored with the job in six months and quit. In the meantime, your neurodiverse candidate would still be excited to come to work and perform the job's detailed and repetitive steps at a highly productive level.

Onboarding is another part of the hiring process that needs to change. Giving people with level 2 autism a full tour of where they would be working is the only way you're going to know if they can do the job. Showing candidates what the workflow looks and feels like is essential for these hands-on learners.

3. Find Sources of Individual and Business Coaching

To integrate people with autism into your workplace, you need the right level of coaching both for the new employees and their supervisors.

Ask whether your potential partners can provide coaching for the business to effectively employ workers on the spectrum. Where will this ongoing support come from, and how is it being paid for? Mind Shift supplies workers with ASD as contractors. Contracts with companies like Boston Scientific and Accenture are renewed annually. This staffing agency also charges businesses a separate fee to provide coaching to managers on how to work with neurodivergent talent. This is essential when engaging with neurodivergent employees who need additional support. Larson advises:

> If you're going to direct hire these individuals, who's supporting you? The local Vocational Rehab office might say, 'You'll get a job coach.' The problem is the job coach is not there to train the business. The question is, 'Who's going to support my business, my managers, my team, so we can be successful in hiring them?'

If you can find quality training partners and adapt your hiring process, then the talent pool of quality workers on the autism spectrum gets much larger for you. And the payoffs can be great. Larson concludes:

> The reliability and loyalty of our level 2 workers is incredible because they're so excited to have a real career. When you find the right ones, they're going to be there long term for you. They're like family.

CHAPTER 13

Lessons Learned From Employing People with Disabilities

The talent pool of people with disabilities is vast, complex—and underemployed. Although this book cannot discuss all the nuances of various disabilities, we can draw some cautious conclusions about the similarities and differences between the experiences of the three companies in the previous chapters. This chapter integrates lessons learned from these stories and from my interviews with other thoughtful leaders who have deep expertise in working with disabled employees. If you are a busy manager, this framework, built around six critical success factors, can help you decide whether to more proactively seek to employ those with disabilities and how to do it successfully.

The three previous chapters told the stories of companies that have found great value employing workers with a range of disabilities in very different jobs. These chapters also showed lessons the companies have learned from pursuing these innovative talent solutions.

Leaders at Minnesota Diversified Industries (MDI) understand it takes special creativity, patience, and persistence to lead production teams that include individuals with disabilities. Classic Wire Cut has adapted its hiring and onboarding processes to bring on more than a dozen autistic CNC machinists. And a supervisor at Heartland

Systems Corporation, who manages a team of data analysts on the autism spectrum, has learned not to underestimate the potential of her team members. There is much to learn from the experiences of these companies, but the following six areas demand special attention.

1. **Identify opportunities to employ workers with disabilities**
2. **Clarify the executive sponsor's role in leading this type of initiative**
3. **Build effective partnerships to source and train candidates**
4. **Adapt hiring and onboarding processes**
5. **Train supervisors to work effectively with employees who have disabilities**
6. **Rethink work design and scheduling practices**

1. Identify Opportunities for Your Organization

Identifying the role workers with disabilities could play depends first on your organization's business needs and previous experiences. If you already have experience employing people in this talent pool, you may be thinking, "What's the big deal? We know how to do this." But maybe you can learn from others. Things are always changing.

Walgreens began actively employing people with disabilities in 2007 when it needed to staff a new distribution center in South Carolina. Since then, the company has hired more than 1,000 team members with disabilities across its US distribution system. Sephora, the global cosmetics company, was responding to a similar business need when it launched its "All Abilities Hiring Initiative" in 2017 to staff its distribution centers.[63] There are businesses out there with plenty of experience, but sometimes with turnover in leadership or changing business structures and priorities, the know-how can be lost. And, of course, there are others who have only recently started to pursue this option.

Classic Wire, for example, only began recruiting more highly trained job candidates

> **Big tech companies like Microsoft, SAP, and EY already draw on the talents of those with level 1 autism**

with disabilities when they became available in their region in recent years. With the chronic shortage of CNC machinists across the US, Classic recognized that the special training program at a nearby community college could be a goldmine of new talent. Like all data intensive businesses, Heartland Systems (disguised) struggled to find employees skilled and persistent enough to perform tedious but critical data cleansing tasks. In 2017, they started hiring contractors on the autism spectrum as data analysts when they learned about the training and coaching programs of Mind Shift, a staffing agency that trains and places people diagnosed with ASD.

In practice, folks with disabilities can fill a range of roles from entry-level or low-skill jobs on MDI production lines to middle-skill jobs as CNC machinists. Of course, big tech companies like Microsoft, SAP, and EY have already shown they can draw on the talents of level 1 autistics to tackle complex tasks where the individual's focused intelligence is a distinct advantage.

Where does your organization fit on this map? Are there roles or tasks where you could be proactively investing in people with disabilities? Here are some questions you can ask to get started:

- **Do you have routine jobs that are particularly hard to fill?**
- **Do you have jobs that have lots of turnover because they are so repetitive and boring?**
- **Who in your organization has experience with family members or friends with disabilities?**

- **Are there any training programs in your region that might adequately prepare candidates with disabilities so they could be considered for positions you need to fill?**

2. Clarify the Executive Sponsor's Role

Like all initiatives involving change, investing in marginalized workers is more likely to pay off if you have a committed and passionate executive sponsor. That passion comes from different places. Sometimes there is a family member involved. Bill Morris founded Blue Star Recyclers, a Colorado-based electronics recycler that employs people with disabilities. Morris grew up with an older brother who was developmentally disabled. Randy Lewis, who has an adult son with autism, was director of global supply chain when he championed disability employment at Walgreens starting in 2007.

Sometimes, the connection to the cause is less personal. Amy Grant, vice president at Classic Wire Cut, and production manager Sem Martinez became passionate about hiring graduates of the Unique Abled Academy training program only when they got to know these young men with ASD. Patrick McIntyre, CEO of OneOme, a healthcare genetics testing company, was encouraged by his wife to learn more since she had worked in the field of developmental disabilities for many years. McIntyre first saw the value workers with ASD could bring to a business when he worked in another company. Soon after joining OneOme, McIntyre encouraged his colleagues to identify areas where people with ASD could be a good fit in their business.

MDI's CEO Eric Black recognizes that the chief executive is not always best positioned to champion an initiative around hiring people with disabilities. So, he has another suggestion for developing sponsors. These programs are much more likely to get started by people who have lived experience with disability unemployment. He adds:

It's not about making it a huge corporate initiative. The thing may start with a mother, brother, cousin, or a friend who sees the challenge that a person they love can't get a job. And they know this person absolutely can do this. And they can do the job better than the able-bodied guy down the hall.

> **We don't need you to become the expert on employee disabilities**

These employees with lived experiences want to do something. The CEO hears about it. And you've got two choices. One is saying, 'That's not what we do.' You take a blanket, throw it over the flame to snuff it out. Or you just blow gently. Let it start to grow where the interest is because those people who care will create some success.

That's the best thing a CEO can do. We don't need you to become the expert on employee disabilities. But when it happens, just encourage it and let it grow. Let it have enough freedom to be successful. Then you can hold it up as 'We want to do more of what Paul did, or what Carly did.' And this isn't the mailroom job. It's somebody doing something functionally important for our organization, and they're an individual with a disability.

3. Build Effective Partnerships to Source and Train Candidates

It is hard to imagine an employer venturing into the world of disability hiring without a strong partner. The type of partner you'll want depends, in part, on who is operating in your region and the types of jobs you are filling. Classic Wire works closely with Jay Nolan Community Services to hire and onboard new graduates of the local Uniquely Abled Academy. Heartland Systems Corporation contracts with Mind Shift, which helps businesses employ neurodiverse talent who need some extra coaching. Classic Wire and Heartland Systems both are connected with focused partners who provide the talent and coaching they need.

On the other hand, MDI reaches out to a broad spectrum of recruiting agencies in Minnesota. These agencies work with individuals who have a variety of disabilities. Sometimes MDI approaches traditional staffing agencies to see if they know of potential applicants with a disclosed disability who might be a good fit for production jobs at the company. Both MDI and Walgreens have their own internal coaching capabilities so they don't need external help with onboarding.

Level of Commitment: Employee or Contractor?

Partners can also play the role of legal employer, with workers hired only on a contractor basis to simplify the employment relationship and make it easier for the business to deal with fluctuating labor demand. MDI lacks the HR infrastructure necessary to meet rapidly shifting staffing needs, so they use staffing agencies to supply employees as contractors. Sometimes, these "seasonal" workers become full-time employees at MDI. Of course, the company is very sensitive to the challenges workers with disabilities face if they must look for another job, so they try to limit layoffs as much as possible.

Heartland Systems hires contractors from Mind Shift, who coaches its autistic "specialists" to work in a variety of companies. Businesses like Target, Accenture, and Boston Scientific regularly tap into this talent pool. When specialists prove to be a great fit for a business, they may be hired by the company as permanent employees.

Clarify Coaching Services and Costs

One striking feature of the successful stories at MDI, Classic Wire, and Heartland is the quality of the coaching provided both for employees with disabilities and for supervisors and managers. Coaches like Karen Navarro at Jay Nolan Community Services and JoLynn Larson at Mind Shift are savvy, empathetic, skilled experts who understand the needs of their clients—both the individuals with disabilities and the businesses they serve. With a skilled, purpose-built HR team, this same work can be done internally. Jeanne Eglinton, vice president of employment services at MDI, is a great example of an experienced and skilled internal resource. She works with her team to coach employees through challenges both routine and unusual. Don't try this with an inexperienced HR team.

If you're looking to engage an external partner, ask pointed questions about the quality of coaching that will be available to your employees *and* to your managers. Often, agencies expect to provide coaching just to those with disabilities that they are sending to you. Know who will be a resource for your managers when supervising neurodiverse workers, and be skeptical about the quality of this coaching at first. Too often, coaches are underpaid and undertrained.

Another important question is who pays for the coaching. Sometimes government funds are available. At Classic Wire, coaching for new CNC machinists with ASD is funded by the California Department of Rehabilitation. In other cases, a business like Heartland Systems pays an agency like Mind Shift to provide coaching for both the employees and the business. MDI, on the other hand, has developed coaching capabilities within its business as a social enterprise.

Use Partnerships to Create a Talent Pipeline

If your business finds success in hiring people with disabilities, you may want to create an ongoing pipeline of talent. Good partnerships are key to creating this. Classic Wire solidified its links with the Uniquely Abled Academy and Jay Nolan Community Services to continue hiring new graduates from this training pipeline for CNC machinists. Mind Shift, on the other hand, has offices in Minneapolis, Milwaukee, Denver, and Fargo (North Dakota). Businesses in those regions can use Mind Shift to continually search out new sources of talent with ASD.

Blue Star Recyclers is a Colorado-based electronics recycling social enterprise. It has continued to grow since it started in 2009, creating jobs for people with developmental disabilities. Founder Bill Morris learned early on that he would need a talent pipeline if he was going to continue to expand the business. Initially, a savvy vocational rehab counselor did a good job referring candidates who were a good fit for the recycling business. But her successor continually referred people who were not viable for employment. Morris learned quickly that government-funded agencies are often too focused on just referring candidates to employers without considering the actual fit or the follow-up transition coaching needed.

To address this, Morris developed his own pipeline. He partnered with a large local high school district to create a miniature Blue Star center. Qualified students now train in the center for as long as it takes to acquire and demonstrate the skills needed to work at Blue Star. It may be a month or three years. When ready, these candidates are referred to Blue Star for employment.

4. Adapt Hiring and Onboarding Processes to Identify Hidden Talent

Companies that successfully hire neurodivergent talent learn to reinvent their hiring and onboarding processes. Here are three questions any manager should be thinking about:

- How do I decide who to hire?
- How should I be thinking differently about new hires who have disabilities?

- How do we onboard and train these new hires so they are productive as soon as possible?

In many situations today, an applicant may have a disability they are not comfortable disclosing in an interview (e.g., depression, dyslexia, diabetes).[64] In this book, I am only addressing situations where the applicant's disability is diagnosed, disclosed, and mutually acknowledged (at least implicitly) by the employer and the job candidate. The following tips can help you reinvent your hiring and onboarding process to better serve people with diagnosed and disclosed disabilities.

Skip the Formal Interviews

MDI, Walgreens, and Blue Star Recyclers all dramatically changed their interviewing and hiring process once they were committed to hiring candidates with disabilities. The first step was throwing the traditional interview format out the window. Instead of asking questions across the desk, hiring managers emphasize "touring and talking," showing the candidate the actual work setting to see if they would feel comfortable there. Is the lighting okay? The sound level? The general pace of the work?

They are trying to find answers to these questions:

- Would the candidate be comfortable in the actual work environment?
- Is it a job that is a good fit for their capabilities?
- What reasonable accommodations would need to be made for the new hire?

Jeanne Eglinton, vice president of employment services at Minnesota Diversified Industries, frequently hires new workers with disabilities for the company's production operations. She says:

> A tour is a way of giving them information about us, like what type of schedule they would have, how many days a week they need to work. We get all that information out there. And, most importantly, part of the tour is going out on the floor and actually seeing the work. That's key for both sides.

At Walgreens, Randy Lewis is equally passionate about changing the hiring process for people with disabilities who staff some of the company's 12 distribution centers. He says:

> We don't interview them and we don't care about their work experience. That's because we know they're going to have been underemployed or unemployed. The question is, can they do the work? That's where we start. There's no discussion about your credentials. It's not a job interview. We simply say, 'This is what needs to be done on the job. Can you do these things?' And we have ways to test for that. Of course, there may be some communication issues. But as long as you're not disruptive and you can do the work, it doesn't make any difference.

When hiring neurodiverse candidates, the key is avoiding traditional interviewing protocols and expectations. Don't look for good eye contact and snappy answers to questions like "Why do you want this job?" People on the autism spectrum may need to walk around while they talk to an interviewer. They're also unlikely to have rehearsed answers to routine interview questions like "Why should we hire you?" and "Can you tell me about a big challenge you have overcome?" You have to let go of this traditional interviewing approach.

The consistent mistake managers make is hiring the neurotypical candidate who performs well in a standard job interview, but who will be totally bored in the job within six months and headed out the door. If you can accept non-standard behavior and embrace the neurodiverse candidate's other qualifications, you open the business to new hires who will still be excited about coming to work in six months and continue to improve their performance.

Think Differently about Workers with Disabilities

Bill Morris, founder of Blue Star Recyclers, which has employed dozens of workers on the autism spectrum, is passionate about changing the way neurodiverse people are viewed. Once his new hires discover what they are good at, they often confess they had no idea they would be so good at a particular skill Blue Star needs. "That's because no one ever looked at them as assets!" says Morris emphatically. He adds:

> Government-funded programs were created and designed to focus on the diagnosis and deficits of people with disabilities, which I believe is working on the problem. Working on the solution is focusing on the discovery and development of assets with the goal of competitive employment and greater independence. From my experience, the root of this problem is how the disability services sector is funded. The only financial incentive for them is to create consumers of their services and keep them in services for as long as the funding is available. This is why the attitude of most service providers I've met is, "We're not paid to recognize talent. We're paid to deliver services."

Morris may be a little harsh here and overgeneralizing a bit. But there is no denying that most of us are guilty of focusing too much on deficits and not enough on assets when it comes to evaluating the employment potential of those with developmental disabilities.

This attitude comes in part from the uncertainty managers and supervisors feel about how to treat their neurodivergent new hires. Working with a variety of employees, veteran job coach Karen Navarro has a mantra she continually shares with supervisors: "Differences don't mean deficiencies." Navarro has struggled at times to teach supervisors to hold young autistic CNC machinists accountable. She has had to work on management to get a little tougher on them. "Discipline them. Write them up. They're not going to break," she says. Navarro has helped Classic Wire's managers understand they have to treat machinists with ASD like any other employee.

> **We wanted to go after people who could never otherwise hold down a job**

Ultimately, managers at Classic Wire and Walgreens have had to fire some workers with disabilities. Randy Lewis, former head of global supply chain for Walgreens, says this was a barrier at first because his managers were worried about making a mistake. To ease this tension, he recalls:

> We said we're going to have to fire some people with disabilities because not everybody's going to be able to perform. We wanted to go deep into that pool, not just skim off the top with people who have disabilities and who are easy to employ. We wanted to go after people who could never otherwise hold down a job.
>
> So we knew there were going to be some who couldn't perform well enough. And we want the standards to be the same because we need to demonstrate to the business that this is not a charity. You don't have to lower standards. That meant we were going to have to let some people go. But we wanted to sleep well at night. So our approach with managers was "Just give it your best."

How to Become a Company with a Heart

Firing workers with disabilities is a sensitive matter, even with expectations in place. Randy Lewis talks about how Walgreens changed its approach:

> We started to ask what happens if we fire this person, and they can never get hired anywhere else? So why don't we consider the circumstances that led to it? Maybe there were extenuating circumstances. What is the cost of the damage? And what is the likelihood they'll do it again? Plus, what is the likelihood they could ever get another job? That was a new approach, and people saw that it made things more human for everybody.
>
> That flexibility turned out to be good because nobody wants a company without a heart. It changed the culture of the building. And it brought humanity in. Managers talk about not just being better managers, but also better people.
>
> Hiring a significant number of employees with disabilities can make cultures "softer" and more human. That was a common theme in the companies I studied. This doesn't mean they were less productive. They were just nicer places to be.

Onboarding: How to Get Neurodivergent Hires Productive Faster

Supervisors learn quickly that training has to be more thoughtful and thorough for people with disabilities. You can't throw people on the autism spectrum into the fire and expect them to figure things out.

Neurodiverse new hires need a clear picture of all the steps for performing specific tasks, and outcomes also must be unambiguous from the employee's perspective. In practice, this should be done for all recent hires, but in today's frantic, resource-starved work environments, many new employees are thrown into the fray. They're told to review some online documents or training program and to figure things out. This is not always a viable option when working with neurodiverse employees.

Paradoxically, neurodiverse workers may take longer to master a new job but often perform far beyond expectations. Classic Wire's production manager is unequivocal about the value his CNC machinists trained by Uniquely Abled Academy have brought to the business. He says he severely underestimated the productivity the company would get from this new infusion of talent. Their productivity is "off the charts," he raved.

Bill Morris at Blue Star labels the unspoken perception of those with developmental disabilities as "the tyranny of low expectations":

> Their whole lives everybody has been telling them what they can't do. Parents are understandably trying to prepare their sons and daughters for disappointment, and no one's asking anything of them. All we did at Blue Star was provide an opportunity for their assets to surface and set goals. We'd set reasonable expectations for our team members and ask, 'Could you do this?' And, of course, they blew past those new goals.

5. Train Supervisors to Work Effectively with Employees Who Have Disabilities

New hires with disabilities aren't the only ones who must adapt. Workers and managers without disclosed disabilities also need coaching initially to work effectively with neurodiverse employees. Depending on the context of your business and where workers with disabilities are being brought in, companies take different approaches.[65] Many bigger firms, like EY and SAP, have trained thousands of their employees on values, norms, and behaviors that support a culture more oriented to DEI+B. This is sometimes referred to as sensitivity training. It has been a hot topic in recent years but has seen mixed success.[66]

SAP has hundreds of employees diagnosed with autism. This enterprise software company has invested in the education of all employees on the importance of understanding and accepting individual differences. In contrast, when Heartland Systems first decided to bring on a team of data analysts with ASD in 2017, the head of the division had Mind Shift do an afternoon training of about 20 Heartland employees who would be working with the new autistic data analysts. The program's sponsor wanted them to know what to expect and how best to interact with their new colleagues.

Mind Shift's head coach provided sensitivity training so Heartland employees would be more aware of how people on the spectrum might feel and behave, how they would approach certain assignments and how they might interact socially. This helped when one new Mind Shift specialist turned out to have a strict routine of noisily shaking a cup of iced tea every morning for five minutes. A Heartland executive recalled:

> This ice shaking sound would reverberate through the office. But we'd had this training, so people reacted more like, 'Okay, this is just his thing.' If we hadn't had the training and someone was doing that, I could see people getting irritated. But we got ahead of it, so people were sensitive about some of the quirkier things we saw from the Mind Shift guys.

Coaching on Accommodations vs. Accountability

It's one thing to attend a training about working with employees with ASD. It is another to manage them on a daily basis. Classic Wire was lucky to have Navarro informally coaching their managers and supervisors. Having a competent transition coach to address these obstacles was a huge benefit for supervisors and managers at Classic Wire—and the coaching expenses were covered by the California Department of Rehabilitation.

This kind of coaching is more important if your staff has no experience with individuals on the autism spectrum. On working with these new hires at Classic, Grant confesses:

> Initially, we handled them with kid gloves. We treated them like they were—I hate to say it—disabled. I think it's because they're different. We didn't want to hurt their feelings. But honestly, it's just ignorance. We didn't know how to communicate with them.

Classic's supervisors had to learn to avoid overprotecting their new autistic machinists. However, they also had to recognize that sometimes accommodations are necessary. One supervisor wouldn't accept the fact that her new machinist, though otherwise capable, couldn't loosen a bolt on a grinding tool. He struggled with the task and became increasingly nervous and flustered. Recognizing the disconnect between the supervisor's perception and the employee's capability, Classic's production manager asked the coach to meet with all the supervisors and help them better understand what accommodations are and where they should be used.

New Skills for Supervisors

To effectively employ workers with disabilities, businesses ultimately need supervisors who can manage variation among their team members. More specifically, they need to be flexible and patient. MDI, for example, now favors line leaders who have more experience managing and motivating a team over ones with a lot of experience in manufacturing. A former daycare provider has turned out to be one of their best production supervisors. MDI learned they can teach technical skills more easily than building competence in soft skills.

Supervisors must also be able to adapt their communication styles. The supervisor at Heartland Systems overseeing a team of neurodiverse data analysts had to adjust her rapid-fire speaking style because it led her colleagues with ASD to think she was angry with them. She has learned to speak more slowly and ensure she has been understood by all her team members. A willingness to adapt communication styles is an essential capability for supervisors working with employees on the autism spectrum.

Helping neurodiverse employees negotiate constant changes in the workplace is another essential skill for managers and supervisors. Changes are inevitable, whether in personnel, restructured work tasks, or new technologies. Employees with ASD are more likely to be emotionally rattled by unexpected changes in ways that affect their performance. Says a supervisor at Heartland Systems, "If I go in and tell them, 'OK, you're not doing this today. You're doing something else.' I know they will do it, but it's really going to upset them. I can't do that."

JoLynn Larson, employment services manager at Mind Shift, says her advice is to always catch neurodivergent workers before they get to their job at the start of their shift. Tell them about the change, even if it is just a few minutes before they would be unexpectedly confronted with it on the job. A little notice is better than being surprised about a reorganization in their department, layoffs, or significant changes that affect their work routine.

6. Rethink Work Design and Scheduling

When accessing the talent pool of people with disabilities, businesses need to rethink the design of jobs, uncovering new ways that important tasks can be accomplished. At the same time, employing those with disabilities can create major scheduling challenges due to their work availability.

Revisit Work Design and Job Requirements

At MDI, management has rethought the prerequisites of certain jobs to find more ways to employ people with disabilities. In some cases, MDI dropped degree requirements. In others, they focus on flexible hiring, prioritizing training people to do a specific job, instead of insisting that candidates already have the skill set before being hired. When they needed someone to work on validating the performance of clients' products, for example, they placed a recent hire into the position, even though he had no experience in the area. He's now considered a "rock star" in the job.

Blue Star Recyclers tries to minimize the impact of traditional job descriptions when hiring people with ASD. Founder Bill Morris says:

> The HR department wants to write job descriptions and put people in boxes. But we put aside this traditional way of hiring and bring people in for a working interview. It's a two or three hour visit. Our job is to uncover and discover the assets that everyone brings.
>
> So, the interview is designed to discover innate interests and skills. That might translate into taking computers apart or fixing them, sorting electronic materials for recycling, or just shredding hard drives. We let them try different things until you see the light go on. It's wonderful. And, if they can articulate it, they'll often say, 'I had no idea I was going to be good at this.' That's because with this neurodivergent workforce no one's ever looked at them for their assets.

Hiring from this talent pool can have another benefit. At Classic Wire Cut, management has found that newly graduated CNC machinists with ASD are most open to being taught very specific ways of doing a job. This was unlike experienced neurotypical machinists who often resist being told how to carry out specific tasks they think they already know. A willingness to follow standard practices is critical for Classic because they have very specific and demanding manufacturing processes that require faithful adherence. In this company's experience, workers with disabilities are more likely to follow standardized work practices.

Solving Workforce Scheduling Puzzles

"Scheduling is my biggest challenge," says Jeff Gervais, operations manager at MDI. That's because some employees with disabilities can only work half days or just three days a week. In addition, those with disabilities often rely on public transportation, so they can't work second or third shift, or they live in a group home, where nontraditional work hours are not viable.

In addition to logistical issues of transportation and housing, those with disabilities often have to manage specific physical or cognitive conditions that can limit their availability to work. They may be able to tolerate certain sensory inputs, such as noise or lighting levels, at work for only so long. More often, however, the factor that shortens the workday is the need to limit income earned to continue receiving vital government benefits. Companies like MDI and Blue Star work to address the need for limited work hours by breaking positions into two jobs. For some jobs they will employ two people roughly half time so they don't work too many hours. Bill Morris at Blue Star Recyclers says, "If it were up to me, we probably would have another 50 percent of our employees working full time with a livable wage and benefits." But losing government benefits, such as Social Security Disability Insurance, is a risk many families can't take.

Scheduling can be a challenge when employing workers with disabilities, but the upsides are worth it, particularly when it comes to company loyalty. One operations manager at MDI told me he had a neurotypical worker call out, saying he couldn't make it to work in his four-wheel drive jeep because of the three-inch snowstorm overnight. This manager laughed knowing that same morning he had workers with disabilities who would show up after taking three buses in their two-hour commute to the plant. Who would you want on your team?

Workers with Disabilities Will Surprise You

Despite the challenges inherent in working with this talent pool, a consistent theme in my interviews was how often individuals with developmental disabilities surprise management and take on more complex, more valuable jobs than the company expected.

Of course, like neurotypical employees, new hires with ASD will vary in their level of self-confidence. At Classic Wire, some recent graduates from the Uniquely Abled Academy didn't have the confidence to operate CNC machines at first, even though they had the training needed. Another new hire was surprisingly adept at overseeing six machines at once.

MDI unexpectedly found a current employee with ASD who they could train to run their CNC machine. Operations Manager Jeff Gervais was astonished at how this outcome exceeded his expectations, saying, "We struggled to find an experienced operator and almost gave up. Then we found an individual on the autism spectrum who had some computer capabilities. In a million years, I didn't think we'd find anyone on our production floor who would be able to run that machine."

> **...there's so much talent in this workforce that's hidden**

Surprise is a theme that comes up repeatedly when talking to leaders about their employees who have diagnosed disabilities. Bill Morris, founder of Blue Star Recyclers, has spent several years training other electronics recyclers how to employ a neurodiverse workforce. He had been telling his counterparts in the industry how productive his workers are:

> They said, 'Hey, Bill, you're just a social worker type and we have a real business to run.' But when they finally come to see the Blue Star operation and witness our team at work, their jaws often drop and they say, 'Oh my God, these guys aren't just really good. They're definitely outperforming the workers we have. They stay on task. They don't come in late. They follow all the safety protocols and standards.' By the end of the tour, these managers all want what we have.
>
> It's been such a great learning experience for me that there's so much talent in this workforce that's hidden. If an employer will take the time to identify it and develop it, they'll just be blown away.

SECTION 4

A Practical Path Forward: Which Marginalized Workers to Employ and How to Do It

Hiring marginalized workers offers both businesses and individuals terrific benefits. This final section summarizes the opportunities—and challenges—that come with employing the different types of marginalized talent. It will help you decide which group—formerly incarcerated, refugees, or people with disabilities—might be a good fit, given your workforce needs. Along the way, you'll be reminded why hiring from these overlooked talent pools is good for everyone involved.

Chapter 14 shares stories of three individuals who have overcome substantial barriers to sustainable employment. This chapter can help you become clearer on which group or groups you are most interested in exploring. It can also provide insights into possibilities you may be overlooking.

Chapter 15 shows how to overcome the potential barriers you will face in accessing any of these talent pools. It also summarizes the critical success factors that must be managed, along with the pitfalls to avoid with each step. Finally, this chapter concludes with a detailed framework that can be used to build a business case for employing refugees, the formerly incarcerated, and people with disabilities. As I was told over and over, "This is not charity. These hiring decisions are good for business."

CHAPTER 14

Finding Your "Why": Three Stories to Inspire and Clarify Who You Might Hire

This chapter is built on three stories of people who have overcome great obstacles to land in good jobs with a promising future. A painful ski accident sent Luisa spiraling into serious substance abuse and crimes that landed her in prison. It has been a long journey back, but today she is in a promising entry-level sales position for a sophisticated global tech firm. Solange walked across the country for three months to escape a civil war in her native Central African Republic. She then spent ten years in a refugee camp in Africa before coming to the US. Today she works for one of the country's most prestigious hospitals. Diagnosed with autism spectrum disorder, Tucker faced less dramatic but no less challenging issues. He has gone from appeasing annoyed customers waiting to ride the roller coaster at Six Flags to working as a CNC machinist, producing high-quality machined parts used in medical procedures. All three of these stories can help you understand why hiring traditionally marginalized workers like these may be worth a try.

Randy Lewis is the former head of the Walgreens global supply chain and a leading expert in disability employment. He's learned a lot by helping companies employ workers with disabilities:

"People act on emotion but justify their decisions and actions based on 'facts.' We think it's facts that drive us to act," says Lewis, "but when I start to tell people the facts of how to employ people with disabilities their eyes glaze over. There has got to be a story."

One of the key findings in my research for this book was the strong emotional connection leaders felt for the marginalized workers they had hired. They know that they and their company are making a major difference for people who normally don't get a chance at sustainable employment in good jobs. Simultaneously, most of the leaders I spoke with saw this feel-good result as a pleasant side benefit. I heard it over and over: "This is not charity. It is good for our business."

In the next chapter, I provide a summary of the "facts"—the critical success factors in creating long-term practices to employ marginalized workers, along with the business benefits of making these investments. But, first, I want to share the stories of three more individuals to remind you of the challenges they had to overcome to succeed in the workplace.

When reading these stories, notice which ones resonate with you. Maybe you will learn something that will broaden your interest in exploring talent pools you hadn't considered. Keep two questions in mind:[67]

1. **What is it about this particular story that inspires or touches you?**
2. **Do you have past experiences or relationships that make you more empathetic toward refugees, the formerly incarcerated, or people with disabilities?**

True Grit: From Heroin to High Tech

Luisa was terrified to apply for a sales job at Precisely. Six years in prison because of your heroin addiction saps your confidence and makes you question what story you should tell.

It didn't start this way. Seven years ago, Luisa had a good job in a big retail call center. Okay, her relationship with her partner of seven years hadn't worked out, and maybe she was a little lost. But she had a young daughter. She was taking college courses. On a trip to Colorado, she tried snowboarding with friends and hurt her back. At a pain management clinic, the doctor prescribed pain pills. Want to guess the end of this story? She quickly became addicted to the pills.

Luisa fell into another unhealthy relationship and had a second daughter. In the process, she and her soon-to-be ex-boyfriend became addicted to heroin. As a single mother with no family support, Luisa committed crimes to support her children and her all-consuming heroin use. When she was arrested, police charged her with 24 felonies. Three years after falling on a ski slope, she was sentenced to more than six years in prison.

She had fallen so far so fast. The drugs had been a way of numbing herself out of the chaos in her life. Worst of all, she felt she had abandoned her daughters. Prison was a wakeup call. She was determined never to be in this place again.

> **When I applied at Precisely, I worried I'd be questioned about my criminal past**

Fortunately, Luisa was accepted into the Televerde program in the Perryville prison (see chapter 2). While behind bars, she developed sales leads on software products for well-known companies. She met Brenda Kay during one of the software sales executive's visits to the prison. Kay invited Luisa to apply for a job at Precisely after she was released.

Luisa went through the standard interview process for Precisely's entry-level sales position. A friend coached her to make sure she was highlighting the right skills and managing her anxiety. Luisa recalls:

> Transitioning from my sentence to the "real world" and losing battles to regain custody of my kids, I had no confidence at all. I wondered if I was even capable of the job, even though I'd been doing the same job I was interviewing for while in prison. I still doubted I had the skills to be successful.
>
> When I applied at Precisely, I worried that I'd be questioned about my criminal past, and that the managers interviewing me wouldn't understand. I'm a nervous person, so I was completely sweaty during the interviews. I always feel I'm not as good as other people who didn't lose the rights to their kids and didn't have to learn the hard way through a six-year sentence. The coaching and my experience working for Televerde got me through it.

Today Luisa works as a business development rep digging up leads to help her team sell complex software. She is continually learning and expanding her skills, which has boosted her confidence and motivation to do the work well:

> I've realized I have a talent for sales that comes naturally for me. But there is so much more to the sales operation. I come to work every day with an open mind and just try to learn everything I can about the business. I want to turn my job into a career where I'm happy every day.

Most of all, Luisa is grateful for the financial security the job has brought to her family life:

That stability is huge. It's allowed me to build relationships with my daughters. I have my house and bought a car. I'm no longer a burden on my family because I support myself. I still have a lot of emotional growth to do as a result of the trauma I went through. This job gives me the foundation to do that.

A Refugee Who Always Passes the Test

Solange arrived at a high school near Boston on a chilly Monday morning in March. The school had a special academy designed to support recent refugees or immigrants. She spoke almost no English, having just arrived as a refugee from the Republic of the Congo. On her first day at school, a teacher told Solange she would have to join her new classmates two days later to take the state's standardized educational assessment test. Solange had no idea what that meant.

Later that week she sat in a crowded classroom staring at the test's questions. The questions, written in English, meant nothing to Solange. She approached a teacher hesitantly and asked if she was allowed to borrow a French/English dictionary.

Back in her seat, Solange used the dictionary to slowly translate the English questions into French, a language spoken in her native country. Writing in French, she then used the dictionary to translate her brief answers back into English. When the results came back a few days later she had passed the exam! Solange graduated from high school a year later. It isn't surprising Solange found ways to survive at her new school, given the challenges she had already faced.

Her mother had passed away when Solange was just a little girl. Soon after, she fled the ongoing civil war in the Central African Republic with her aunt's family. Solange still remembers walking for three months as a small child to escape death threats. They settled as refugees in the Republic of the Congo, a neighboring country. After

10 years there, Solange and her aunt finally had a chance to immigrate to the US under the auspices of Catholic Charities.

She had no work experience when she arrived in the US. But after school Solange took a job in a small Boston restaurant. Most employees there spoke only Spanish. It was impossible to develop her English skills.

She moved to another restaurant where she worked for three years, getting promoted to assistant manager despite her limited English. The high cost of housing forced her family to live far outside the city, so she endured a 90-minute commute each way. When COVID hit, the restaurant closed.

Solange and her aunt had been taking work readiness English classes at Boston Jewish Vocational Service, a workforce development agency that partners with many Boston employers to provide immigrant talent.

After learning about the research operations training program at Boston Children's Hospital (see chapter 6), Solange decided to apply despite feeling unsure about the job. The training program had prepared her: she learned how to work in a professional environment and how to communicate with supervisors via email. She also learned more job-specific English.

When she got the job, Solange's biggest hurdles were multi-tasking and interpreting feedback from her supervisors. However, she was eager to learn the role and anxious to find a stable career with growth opportunities.

Three months after being hired, Solange was promoted to team trainer at the hospital. Later, she became an advanced technician. She now has dreams far from surviving a three-month trek to escape civil war. Solange will no doubt find a way to pass her next test:

> I want to finish my BA in biology at UMass Boston and then apply to medical school. I want to be a pediatrician.

I'm not worried about taking on a new job. I love trying new things.

From Six Flags to Stainless Steel: Finding a Fit in Machining

Tucker worked a variety of jobs at Six Flags Magic Mountain in suburban LA, but staffing the Flash Pass office was his least favorite. In that job, he fielded complicated questions from guests about the benefits of spending extra money to cut in line for the park's popular thrill rides. Guests sometimes got angry when they didn't like the answers he gave, and Tucker had no one to turn to for help in those stressful moments. He hated that.

Diagnosed with autism spectrum disorder (ASD), Tucker enrolled at a local community college after high school, majoring in filmmaking. After a couple of years, he realized he liked learning about films more than he liked making them, so he became a computer science major. Along the way, he picked up a part-time job stocking shelves for a pharmaceutical company. Why? "To get money, I guess," he says ambivalently.

Then he majored in business, but that didn't feel like a good fit either. Eventually, Tucker burned out on school. But there was always Six Flags. Sometimes he managed lines for rides like Apocalypse or Canyon Blaster. Other times he supervised games. Still, none of it felt right. Tucker was smart, but he had no idea what a comfortable workplace would feel like.

Then he heard about the Uniquely Abled Academy at College of the Canyons, where he and others with ASD could learn about machining. He recalls:

> Before UAA, machining was definitely not something that I thought I would be going into. There are so many jobs that you don't know about that those of us with autism

can do. We tend to work by ourselves and we're very detail oriented. I never thought beforehand that could be applied to something like machining.

The Academy's intense program ran eight hours a day, five days a week for three months. But that didn't deter Tucker, who stopped working at Six Flags. He liked learning machining terminology and using math skills he hadn't practiced since high school.

Soon after graduating, he was among the first group of UAA graduates hired by Classic Wire (see chapter 11). Tucker started in the deburring department, putting the finishing touches on newly machined parts before they were sent to assembly. He has since been trained on several machines used in the plant, allowing him to bounce around to where his skills are most needed. His favorite part of working at Classic Wire is being able to see progress in his work, something not possible at Six Flags. "Everything there was either virtual or counting money, so I didn't get to see what I was producing," he says.

> **The production manager told me I don't produce as many scrap parts as some of the other guys.**

Tucker has learned he loves that sense of completing things. As a machinist, he can see what is coming in the queue, as well as the parts he has completed. It's very different from managing endless lines of riders at Six Flags.

He has three suggestions for managers who hire people with ASD:

1. **Be patient.** He says, "People with autism do tasks slower. But we also tend to be more focused, more detail oriented. The production manager told me that I don't produce as many scrap parts as some of the other guys. That's because I take my time to inspect what I'm doing to make sure I'm doing

it right. Even though it takes us a little bit longer, you'll get better quality and more quantity if you're patient."

2. **Expect a lot of questions.** Tucker says he and his colleagues with ASD are likely to ask a lot of questions because they need to make sure they are clear about the instructions they were given.

3. **"If you see us struggling, don't be afraid to ask if we need help," says Tucker.** Even though people with autism spectrum disorder may ask a lot of questions, sometimes they don't ask enough. "Occasionally, we're too scared to ask for help," he says.

The help available at Classic Wire makes Tucker's job a great fit. And it's a long way from the emotional roller coaster at Six Flags:

> My co-workers and the supervisors here are very nice. They'll always help me if I need it. So if there are a lot of jobs I need to do, and I am getting overwhelmed, the supervisor helps me out or has another coworker help me. So I don't get stressed out about having too much to do. Just the idea of being able to ask someone for help, and knowing they won't say, 'You should be able to do this on your own.' That's a feeling I really like.

Questions to Fuel Discussion

Here are questions to consider as you and your colleagues reflect on the stories of Luisa, Solange, and Tucker.

- **Are you more passionate than you realized about second chances, new starts for resilient refugees, or providing big breaks for people with disabilities?**
- **Why would you like to give folks from this talent pool a chance?**

- **Do others on your team have emotional connections to people in these groups? Are they willing to share their stories?**
- **Can you think of related stories of people in these talent pools who you have known and respected and who deserved a chance at a good job?**

Of course, some stories may be too personal to share, such as those about a family member who is in prison or a child with a disability. We must respect that and only ask colleagues to share stories when they are comfortable. But in the end, stories about possibilities and potential are central to motivating change in how your organization thinks about employing workers who have traditionally been overlooked. Use these stories to start a conversation.

CHAPTER 15

"Yes, You Can Work Here"
A Practical Framework for Employing Marginalized Workers

When I asked Eric Black, CEO of Minnesota Diversified Industries (MDI), what advice he would give other executives about hiring people with disabilities, he said frankly, "People don't listen to advice on things they don't think about. It's just noise until you're ready to do something."

Talk about hiring marginalized workers may have been just "noise" to you until now. But if you've gotten to this chapter, you're probably thinking more seriously about hiring from these underused talent pools, or expanding what you are already doing. This last chapter is the final push, providing some inspiration to move forward and a guide to overcome potential barriers you may face. You'll also find a detailed review of the business benefits these three talent pools—refugees, the formerly incarcerated, and those with disabilities—can provide.

No matter which group you are trying to access, five critical factors will determine your success:

- **Define your strategic context for uncovering hidden talent**
- **Build more effective partnerships**
- **Expect employee resistance to a more diverse workforce**
- **Adapt recruiting, hiring, and onboarding practices**
- **Invest in coaching resources**

1. Define Your Strategic Context for Uncovering Hidden Talent

Any potential workforce initiative has boundaries dictated by staffing needs and resources. Here are five decisions you need to get right.

Do You Need a Pilot Program?

Be realistic about the scale of what you want to do. Are your staffing needs big enough to warrant a pilot program, or are you just filling a couple of positions? Boston Children's Hospital ran a successful pilot before committing to an elaborate training program to help dozens of refugees fill jobs as research operations technicians. At the other extreme, HDF Painting simply hired two Haitian refugees to paint houses to fill an immediate need.

Are You Clearly Communicating the Skills and Attributes Needed For Each Role?

Companies usually know what their staffing problems are, but they often don't realize when they've failed to communicate the specific skills, capabilities, and attributes they need new hires to have. Wes Jurey of the South Dallas Employment Project runs into this problem often. He must continually ask employers to be more specific about the skills they need for candidates to fill entry-level logistics jobs. For example, it may be that the skills an employer needs can be taught in brief certification programs for roles such as forklift driver or logistics technician.

Before they implemented Open Hiring (chapter 3), management at The Body Shop assumed they needed to hire people with previous retail sales experience. But Open Hiring taught them they could train inexperienced candidates to be successful with computer-based training and on-the-job coaching. Continually check the assumptions you are making about the competencies needed to fill specific jobs or to perform basic tasks. Are you communicating those clearly to partners who might supply applicants?

Do Your Jobs and Geography Line Up?

Are you making practical assumptions about transportation challenges workers may face? Your options for finding viable candidates depend in part on the location of the jobs you need to fill. Are the jobs in a city like Minneapolis or Boston with a sizable population and a decent transportation system? Are they in the suburbs of LA or Akron, where transportation could be a problem? Or is your business in a more rural location where there is no viable public transportation and a more limited pool of workers to draw from? Precisely's business development representatives and Heartland's data analysts can work from home, which expands the talent pool they can tap into. But remote work, of course, presents other challenges, particularly in managing workers.

Which of Your Internal Stakeholders Must Be Involved?

This is a polite way of asking how complex and bureaucratic your business is. Face it, if you are a world-class hospital or large financial services company, a lot of stakeholders will be included in any initiative like this—line management, HR, legal, and more. The situation is different in a family-owned manufacturing plant or a house-painting business. Many large organizations committed to diversity and inclusivity, like Sephora, Microsoft, EY, and SAP, have worked through these complex challenges. Involving colleagues with different perspectives and responsibilities is essential for many businesses—and much more time-consuming. Check your assumptions about which stakeholders to involve before you start.

Do You Have a Committed Executive Sponsor?

Every company discussed in this book had a resolute leader who wanted to try employing marginalized workers. Randy Lewis was the former global supply chain lead at Walgreens, where he championed a successful program to hire people with disabilities. He insists initiatives like this cannot be led by human resource managers alone. The main champion must be an operations manager or executive responsible for the function where the employees will work.

The innovations discussed in this book happened because some leader or leaders outside of the human resources department got behind the idea of hiring refugees, people with disabilities, or those who have been incarcerated. But what happens when these executives move on or retire, leaving behind successors who are not as passionate about the initiative? The stories of JBM Packaging, Main Street Gourmet, and Heartland Systems show that effectively employing marginalized workers is a journey requiring reinvention and recommitment over time. Long-term success is not assured without continued leadership and emotional commitment.

Main Street Gourmet's "Lunch with Leaders" (see chapter 8) is an example of a program that continually educates new managers in the company about the value its foreign-born workers bring to the business.

2. Build More Effective Partnerships

The jobs you need to fill determine the types of workforce partners required. Often, however, how you address your staffing needs will be driven by what local partners can provide. The support of a strong regional workforce agency may create innovative staffing opportunities that would not otherwise exist. Here are four ways to sustain more productive relationships.

Look For Great Partners in Your Area

Classic Wire Cut's vice president didn't even know about the CNC machinist training program until she got a call from the local college; she certainly would not have hired seven autistic CNC machinists if the program training them was 200 miles away. Boston Children's Hospital needed a strong regional partner in Boston Jewish Vocational Service to recruit and train candidates for its research technician jobs. Finally, the Body Shop found local staffing agencies around the country to work with nearby stores and distribution centers to support Open Hiring.

Evaluate Whether Your Partners Produce Viable Candidates

Finding candidates with the capabilities and skills needed to fill specific positions requires different types of partners. Precisely and Boston Children's Hospital needed agencies that could carefully screen and train job candidates. Clampco and The Body Shop, on the other hand, expect to train any new hires themselves, so they didn't require as much from their partners.

The reality is competition for marginalized workers has intensified in recent years as the labor pool has become more depleted. Companies like MDI and Main Street Gourmet are competing with more and more firms trying to tap into these historically overlooked talent pools. While there are still plenty of good candidates out there, agencies serving those with disabilities, the justice-involved, and refugees now have to work harder to find coachable applicants they can prepare for a successful job search.

Before collaborating with a workforce nonprofit or staffing agency, check their track record related to job placement. Get references. Talk with people from companies they have worked with. Ask challenging questions: Can you tell us where you have placed clients recently? What kind of jobs did they take?

Employers tend to treat their relationships with workforce and staffing agencies in a transactional manner, considering them simply as suppliers of entry-level workers. In this case, flexibility, patience and grace are not characteristics employers need when it comes to staffing decisions. Another option is to treat these talent sources as true partners, collaborating with them to help their candidates be successful. Remember the coach at JBM Packaging who took donuts to a favorite recruiter just to stand out a little bit? In the long term, building relationships can create better opportunities for engaging with marginalized workers, but it also requires more resources and patience. It's your call.

Plan to Regularly Recalibrate Partnerships

JBM had to reeducate partners who began sending unqualified candidates for interviews. The Body Shop planned to review partner relationships annually. Boston Children's Hospital, on the other hand, avoids potential communication breakdowns by holding a weekly team meeting with their counterparts at Boston JVS. This core team discusses any problems or changes needed with the current cohort in training, as well as with technicians who have recently started on the job. This regular meeting helps ensure a highly collaborative effort where details don't get missed and training and retention problems are caught early.

Create Partnerships Through Individual Relationships

Blue Star Recyclers had a vocational counselor who referred strong candidates with disabilities because she understood the type of worker Blue Star needs. When this counselor left, however, the pipeline of new employees dried up because her successors didn't understand the particular attributes Blue Star needed. Recruiters at JBM Packaging recognize they are often building relationships with individuals at recruiting agencies, not whole organizations. Those personal relationships must be nurtured, and their limitations understood. Turnover in partner organizations can, unfortunately, change the quality of potential job candidates referred to you.

3. Expect Employee Resistance to Having a More Diverse Workforce

It's important to think ahead about how you will help managers and veteran employees adapt to the changes that come with expanding the diversity of your workforce. This includes discovering their biases as well as your own. To prepare your organization to be more inclusive of nontraditional talent, consider how many new employees are coming on board and the types of marginalized workers you are hiring.

Process Resistance to Change

Don't be surprised if you face initial opposition to workforce changes. The Body Shop experienced this as current employees wondered aloud about what it would mean to work next to someone with a criminal past. Letting employees express their concerns is part of the process of surfacing biases and giving people a chance to check the validity of their fears. One thing you can do is keep reminding employees about the benefits of adding additional staff. At Clampco, hiring a group of refugees took pressure off the second shift and reduced the need for overtime.

Whose Story is it to Tell?

If you are hiring formerly incarcerated candidates, you must abide by legal restrictions in your state (or city) about what you can ask and share about an individual's history of justice involvement. At Precisely, the hiring manager may be aware of a candidate's former incarceration, but it is up to the employee whether they share that information with colleagues. "It's their story to tell" is management's attitude in this global tech firm.

On the other hand, if you are hiring people with disabilities, it may be necessary to spend time with current supervisors and employees to explain how to work effectively with their new colleagues. That was the approach taken at Classic Wire and Heartland Systems, who both brought in a coach to lead a workshop about what to expect from new employees who have been diagnosed with ASD.

Refugee Impacts May Be Unplanned

When refugees were brought into companies I studied, education for veteran employees and managers actually happened *after* the new hires were working in the company. Problems or challenges, such as around communication, sometimes precipitated complaints from supervisors or colleagues about extra work and training required to integrate the new arrivals. Education beforehand is likely preferable, but in smaller companies, employing refugees may be an unplanned initiative. If management doesn't feel pressure to provide practical inclusivity or communication training until it is clearly needed, be aware this could be a potential problem.

4. Adapt recruiting, hiring, and onboarding processes

No matter which group you are hiring, you will have to adapt your hiring and onboarding processes to make staffing decisions and transitions successful. Each talent pool requires somewhat different accommodations. Here are five mistakes to avoid.

Don't Depend on Generic Sources of Applicants

You are usually better off with agencies that specialize in particular types of marginalized workers. They can more deliberately screen applicants appropriate for your business. For refugees, you might work with an agency or nonprofit like Boston Jewish Vocational Service, which carefully vets immigrants and refugees before presenting them as candidates for training at Boston Children's Hospital (chapter 6). JVS knows the questions to ask refugees to determine whether they are good candidates for working in a demanding healthcare environment. Heartland relies on Mind Shift, an agency that recruits and trains people with ASD to identify viable candidates for its data cleansing team.

Try to Minimize the Risks of Isolation

Isolation is always a risk when hiring just one person from a particular group. Cluster hiring is one way to avoid this with foreign-born workers. Main Street Gourmet has done this by hiring groups of refugees from Nepal and Afghanistan. Hiring folks who speak the same language increases the chances of successful transitions because language familiarity increases employees' comfort level and sense of belonging. There is also a greater chance that at least one of them speaks some English and can sometimes serve as a translator for the group. This is what happened at Clampco (chapter 11).

Whenever Possible, Avoid Traditional Job Interviews

The more you can create an interaction where the candidate is comfortable, the more likely you are to discover the applicant's strengths. Thus, the key to interviewing those with developmental disabilities is to forget about traditional job interviews. At MDI, they've traded standard interviews across a desk for a "touring and talking" approach (chapter 10). The idea is to get the candidate out on the production floor so they can see the work environment and determine whether it feels like a good fit. This kind of informal interaction is also a good way to exchange information about the job, work hours, and other requirements while learning more about the candidate. This approach also makes sense when interviewing refugees, whose limited English comprehension makes it very difficult to discuss the realities of a particular job.

Don't Hide That You are Open to Second-Chance Hires

Hiring candidates who were previously incarcerated presents different challenges. The actual job interview may seem routine, but lingering in the background for the candidate is the question of whether the company knows about past criminal convictions and how that figures into the ultimate hiring decision. JBM Packaging is very upfront about being a felon-friendly company and invites candidates to provide whatever information they are comfortable sharing. Be open about your company's policies on hiring justice-involved individuals, and be sure to comply with local laws in guiding these discussions.

Don't Confuse Longer Onboarding with Lower Performance

For foreign-born workers and people with disabilities, employers should expect a more prolonged onboarding process. In both cases, check in frequently to make sure each new task and its expected outcomes are clearly communicated. Be particularly in tune with smiling and nodding by your new hires, which can be motivated by a desire to please the boss rather than to confirm understanding during training.

Hiring managers consistently make the mistake of rejecting neurodiverse candidates or refugees because they don't perform well in a standard job interview and will take longer to onboard. Instead, they hire the neurotypical candidate who speaks good English and interviews well. Unfortunately, this new hire is often less likely to stay at your company for more than six months because they become bored with the job and start looking elsewhere. If you can accept unconventional behavior in the hiring process, and if you recognize when candidates are qualified in other ways, you open yourself up to new hires who are still excited about coming to work in six months and continuing to improve their performance.

Investing in Marginalized Workers When You Have Limited Time and Resources

So you don't think you have the time or money to recruit, train, and manage marginalized workers? Tackling these opportunities with limited resources can look like a real challenge for small and middle-market companies, especially when it comes to providing more onboarding support for refugees and people with disabilities and helping second-chance hires address needs outside of work.

But research shows managers routinely underestimate their ability to get more out of the resources they have.[68] Here are four ways to think differently about employing marginalized workers when resources are limited:

1. Challenge your assumptions about innovative staffing solutions. Dan Frost at HDF Painting thought it was going to be difficult to hire refugees out of a local shelter, yet he had two new painters working within a week. It won't always be this easy, but check your expectations about how demanding and time-consuming the process actually will be. Classic Wire Cut discovered their new CNC machinists on the autism spectrum were productive much faster than expected.

2. Treat any new initiative as a pilot. You don't have to go big when hiring marginalized workers. We're not talking about a company transformation here. Many of the organizations in this book tested the waters first. The Body Shop and Boston Children's Hospital explicitly tried pilot programs that showed a payoff before making a bigger investment. Main Street Gourmet hired one refugee to start, not knowing what would happen.

3. Don't overlook the financial savings. A consistent finding in my research is that hiring marginalized workers produces loyal employees, reducing the costs of constant turnover. This means fewer resources are needed to continually recruit and onboard a steady parade of new hires. Boston Children's Hospital, for example, no longer has to conduct endless training for new research operations technicians. And by hiring refugees, Clampco was able to reduce overtime and fill major staffing gaps in the plant's second shift, significantly increasing production.

4. Use lessons from your organization's past experiences. It's easy to forget what someone in the company has already tried. An innovation may not be as time consuming as you think because others in the business already know important steps. Maybe you already have a connection with a workforce-development partner who can provide second-chance job candidates.

The incredible pace of business and rapid employee turnover results in the loss of valuable resources—notably, practices and know-how—that could impede your efforts with new marginalized workers.[69] "Forgetting" what you've already learned about recruiting, developing, and retaining marginalized workers somewhere in the business limits the value of resources you already have.

5. Invest in Coaching Resources—Four Mistakes to Avoid

The perceptions of coaching and the role it plays will vary when helping marginalized workers be successful. The key is to anticipate the need for it, as well as the potential costs. Here are four mistakes to avoid if you plan to employ refugees, the formerly incarcerated, or people with disabilities.

Mistake #1: Failing to recognize coaching is essential

Marginalized workers must overcome so many obstacles to stay on the job and be effective that it is almost impossible to expect them to succeed without support. Miscommunication caused by language barriers or cognitive processing differences is common, but coaching can mitigate this issue. Sometimes the challenges are logistical. New hires may need help accessing services outside of work to meet needs for housing, transportation, childcare, and legal assistance.

Coaching must always be highly customized to meet individuals' needs. The more complex the job, the more coaching will likely be needed. Training and onboarding research operations technicians at Boston Children's Hospital would not have been possible without skilled, attentive coaches from JVS who check in regularly with trainees and new hires.

Mistake #2: Assuming supervisors don't need coaching

This can be another costly assumption. As the Fair Chance program took hold at JBM Packaging, it became clear to management that its supervisors were not empathetic enough to help formerly incarcerated employees succeed. Supervisors didn't understand the experiences second-chance hires had in prison or after their release. This was addressed with a new program for supervisors.

Supervisors and managers often need extra coaching because leading marginalized workers often forces them to confront challenges they've never faced before. For example, coaches at Mind Shift helped Heartland Systems supervisors learn to direct employees on the autism spectrum through significant changes in the workplace. Unexpected changes, like reorganizations or new work processes, can be very disruptive for people with ASD. Heartland's supervisors had to learn new ways to help their workers handle these transitions.

Mistake #3: Expect workforce agencies to provide all the coaching you need

Partners often coach job candidates they bring to an employer, but that coaching is usually not enough. Agencies also rarely coach the supervisors and managers who will have to work with new nontraditional hires. Be skeptical about the coaching you are promised by an outside agency, and check with other companies who have worked with the agency to validate the agency's coaching skills.

Great coaches are a huge asset, but they may be hard to come by. Many are also underpaid and lack the necessary experience. A key question for staffing sources is, "Where will our managers get the coaching they need to work effectively with their new employees?" See how the agency responds to this. If you need funds for coaching, see if government funding is available. Classic Wire Cut found the California Department of Rehabilitation funded most of the coaching work done by a local agency that helps candidates with disabilities transition to new jobs.

Mistake #4: Assume experienced employees will make extra efforts to onboard new hires

Be sensitive to how much extra work you ask of supervisors and other team members when marginalized workers join their team.

There are wonderful stories in my research of employees going out of their way to help refugees, those with disabilities, and second-chance hires succeed in their new jobs. But the extra effort needed, if it goes too far or is unrecognized, can alienate experienced workers, demoralize them, and even lead to unwanted turnover.

Overall, coaching will be increasingly critical in future workforce development, and its costs should be considered when drawing on talent pools of marginalized workers. Be sure to ask frank questions about the coaching resources you can expect from your partners.

A Framework for the Benefits of Hidden Talent

Implementing any program designed to employ marginalized workers will be much more successful if you regularly connect it to the benefits your hiring initiative brings to the business. If investments in marginalized talent don't make sense for the business, they won't be sustainable. As they say at JBM Packaging, "No money, no mission."

The case studies in this book point to three types of advantages for businesses: financial benefits, improved productivity, and intangible but still critical benefits.

1. Is this initiative a good financial decision?

Below are several questions to determine the value of your investment in these new sources of talent.

Will new employees be taking on hard-to-fill jobs or positions that have continual and costly turnover? In virtually every company profiled in this book, the jobs being filled were difficult to staff. Whether technicians at Boston Children's Hospital, machine operators at JBM Packaging, or CNC machinists at Classic Wire, the costs of recruiting, training, and retaining people in these roles is high. Hiring marginalized workers into these roles helps these companies contain or reduce those expenses.

Are marginalized workers a cost-effective investment in talent? The Body Shop's Open Hiring approach (chapter 3) minimizes hiring costs because it eliminates interviewing and resume processing steps. Even if a significant portion of new hires don't work out, the company has invested very little to bring them on board. At the other end of the spectrum, Boston Children's Hospital (chapter 6) carefully vets and trains its foreign-born new hires, which has significantly increased its retention of research operations technicians and made the hospital's $6,400 cost per trainee a worthwhile investment. Heartland Systems, on the other hand, hires data analysts diagnosed with ASD to perform relatively low-skill and tedious data-cleansing tasks. This allows the company to dedicate its highly-trained neurotypical data analysts and actuaries to focus on more complex and high-value activities.

How will marginalized workers impact turnover? Workforce turnover depends largely on compensation, professional development opportunities, and work-life balance needs. When marginalized workers land a job that's a good fit, however, they tend to stick with it. Precisely, JBM Packaging, Boston Children's, and Classic Wire all explicitly mentioned the connection between hiring marginalized workers and reduced turnover. At JBM Packaging, turnover dropped from 68% to 31% when the company reinvented its Fair Chance hiring program after the COVID-19 pandemic.

Will this initiative create a new talent pipeline? Committing to hiring refugees, the formerly incarcerated or those with disabilities has greatly reduced uncertainty about labor for many companies. Boston Children's Hospital moved from a standard train-and-pray model to a talent pipeline model to train competent research operations technicians. The hospital now knows it is hiring qualified candidates who can support critical research programs for years to come. It is also now trying to replicate this model for other entry-level positions that necessitate some training but don't require a specific credential. This can make jobs accessible to people who can't afford to pay for pre-employment training.

Precisely likewise has gained more certainty about its labor supply by recruiting from Televerde, a nonprofit workforce development agency that provides incarcerated women in five US prisons with telemarketing training. Meanwhile, the Uniquely Abled Academy program is offered at College of the Canyons outside of Los Angeles. Its graduates, who all have ASD, have become a steady source of new CNC machinists for Classic Wire Cut.

Hiring marginalized workers doesn't automatically create a new talent pipeline, of course, but an initiative can lead to a more dependable source of talent if you have partners able to source candidates, provide high-value training, and collaborate with employers to coach and successfully transition trainees into sustainable jobs.[70]

2. How will our organization's productivity be affected?

My research suggests performance standards are rarely compromised when hiring marginalized workers. In fact, the opposite is more likely to be true; expectations were consistently exceeded in most companies I studied. For instance, at Clampco, management found that the refugees they hired consistently outproduced their US-born counterparts. "It's made us realize we can be more efficient than we thought," says Vice President Jason Venner.

Sem Martinez, Classic Wire Cut's veteran production manager, is unequivocal when describing the productivity of his CNC machinists with ASD:

> I just didn't anticipate we were going to get the productivity we're getting. I was blown away. Just seeing after two or three days of learning, they were working on their own, and the productivity was off the charts. I really underestimated this.

Except in unusual cases, such as when MDI hires workers with significant disabilities, performance and productivity standards are rarely negatively affected by hiring marginalized workers. Even in these situations, MDI's managers and supervisors figure out a way to bring overall team performance up to a profitable standard.

3. What are other important intangible benefits of these initiatives?

The more you reflect on the payoffs of hiring individuals from marginalized talent pools, the more likely you'll recognize less quantifiable benefits that may actually be the most valuable.

Become a more purpose-driven organization

Diversifying your workforce by hiring more foreign-born workers, people with disabilities, or those who have been previously incarcerated is itself an advantage. At JBM Packaging, CEO Marcus Sheanshang recognizes his company today is a more purpose-driven business because of their Fair Chance hiring program. This was not his objective when the company adopted this practice. He says,

> We make everyday products, but trying to help those coming out of prison and being part of their journey has been very gratifying. I didn't fully appreciate how much our other employees would become invested in the program. It makes coming to work each day more fun.

At both JBM and MDI, the commitment to giving marginalized workers an opportunity has had another unexpected benefit in recruiting. Both companies insist they now attract better managerial and supervisory talent. Experienced candidates sometimes come aboard, instead of taking higher paying jobs elsewhere, because they are inspired by the company's mission.

Support diversity, equity, inclusion, and belonging (DEI+B) objectives

It may be part of the plan or an afterthought, but hiring from marginalized talent pools can help companies achieve their goals for DEI+B initiatives. Main Street Gourmet didn't have a grand plan to be a DEI+B leader when they hired their first refugee in 2008. They simply pursued this strategy of recruiting foreign-born workers because they knew it would give them a competitive advantage in the business. Today, the company's employees speak at least one of nine languages in addition to English. Main Street has since been recognized as a diversity and inclusion leader in the baking industry.

A few years ago, Precisely began proactively hiring formerly incarcerated business development reps who were trained by Televerde while in prison. Precisely soon recognized this actively supported the company's commitment to diversity, equity, inclusion, and belonging goals by increasing the racial, ethnic, and socioeconomic diversity of its salesforce. The order here is notable. They didn't hire these entry-level salespeople because it was good for their DEI goals; they did it because it was good for the business.

Create a culture that actively supports the inclusion of marginalized workers

Maybe the most important benefit of these initiatives is the longer-term payoff of creating a company culture that welcomes nontraditional employees. Workforce shortages are going to be with us in many sectors for decades.

Creating a culture that embraces this change will be a serious competitive advantage. The Body Shop began working on that shift by implementing an Open Hiring approach. For example, at its North Carolina distribution center, the acceptance of a more diverse workforce means some employees became comfortable openly wearing their ankle monitoring bracelets. Workers would leave to see their parole officer or take a call from them during the day. Team members in the distribution center weren't prepared to deal with this before, but it became part of daily life.

At MDI about 45 percent of employees have a documented disability. Jeanne Eglinton, vice president of employment services, sees the impact of the company's culture when integrating new employees who have a disability. She says these workers often lack confidence when they first come to MDI:

> They don't talk to anybody at first. But over time at MDI, they start to make friends. They become more talkative and start participating and joking as one of the guys. They're very different than when they first started. That's because of our culture and how we accept people for everything they bring to the business.

Classic Wire Cut is another company that has seen a change in its culture. Vice President Amy Grant is Classic's champion in its push to increase the neurodiversity of the firm's workforce. She says,

> I'm so proud of our company and our culture. This experience has really enriched us. Our entire workforce is very comfortable now dealing with people with autism. And it's gotten everybody to think differently about people who aren't the same as us.

A bonus benefit—changing lives

Some leaders are only focused on the value workers from normally marginalized groups can bring to the business. Others, like MDI's CEO Eric Black, JBM Packaging's CEO Marcus Sheanshang, and Brenda Kay, SVP at Precisely, also know that their firm's job offer can change a person's life. Regardless of their motives, every company in this book is changing people's lives.

For example, Nick, who packages medical devices at Boston Scientific, has been diagnosed with autism spectrum disorder. Before taking this job, he was cleaning floors and toilets at a brewery. Now he marvels at the responsibilities he has been given to "help people live longer better lives." He says, "I take pride in my employment. I'm doing so much more than before. It's almost indescribable."

Solange spent 10 years in a refugee camp in the Republic of the Congo after fleeing a civil war in her home country. She now works as a research operations technician at Boston Children's Hospital and has dreams of going to medical school.

At The Body Shop, store manager Jennifer Crespo learned that the benefits of hiring traditionally marginalized workers go well beyond business performance:

> We often talk about the metrics, but really, a lot of it has to do with just giving people the opportunity to have a job that not only impacts them but their families and the direction of their lives. It's really eye-opening and humbling to know we had such a big impact on someone's life by simply saying, "Yes, you can work here."

The Next Step Is Yours

My purpose for this book was to give innovators and early adopters a voice about what they've learned from employing the formerly incarcerated, refugees, and people with disabilities. The question is: Where are you on this innovation curve? You may be an innovator who is already onto the next phase of recruiting and employing marginalized workers. Or you might be an early adopter like most of the companies in this book.

Or maybe you will be part of the majority who are more skeptical, still wondering whether hiring marginalized workers is a practical business decision. "What's in it for us?" you ask. "Is it really worth the trouble?" Anyway, figure out where you want to be on this innovation adoption curve.[71] You can still be part of the early majority if you move now. However, the workforce and demographic trends spelled out in the book's introduction suggest it would be a mistake to be late to this party.

In the end, keep these benefits in mind when exploring the opportunity to employ refugees, people with disabilities, or the formerly incarcerated. Your initiative can:

- Staff hard-to-fill jobs
- Be a cost-effective investment in talent
- Improve productivity
- Enhance recruiting by being more purpose-driven
- Support DEI+B goals
- Build a more inclusive culture to broaden the talent pool for your workforce
- Change lives

These benefits are compelling, but nothing you have read in this book will impact your business performance—or culture—unless you start hiring differently. As you have seen, other companies are doing it. You can too.

If you do it well, employing historically marginalized workers may be one of the most important—and impactful—workforce initiatives you've ever tried. Getting there won't be easy. If it was, every business would be pursuing this talent already. Given the workforce shortages facing organizations today, the rewards can be huge—for your organization, for the individuals involved, and for the community. I hope this book has given you the tools and inspiration to get started.

Acknowledgments

Most authors will confess it takes a great team to produce a good book. *Hidden Talent* would have been absolutely impossible to write without the incredible contributions of scores of people who I interviewed and re-interviewed to tell their stories and provide the valuable lessons I tried to relate in the book. I can't thank these people enough for sharing their precious time, experiences and insights with me. They made the lessons in *Hidden Talent* possible.

I am especially grateful to the leaders and staff in the organizations that I profiled in the book. (A few have chosen to remain anonymous.) Among those folks who were *immensely* helpful were Brenda Kay, Jennifer Wale, Eric Black, Kristin Driscoll, Karen Krueger, Susan Schafer, Mandy Townsend, Devi Shiwnath, Amy Grant, Sem Martinez, Karen Navarro, Bill Morris, Ed Hennings, Jason Venner, Jeanne Eglinton, Katie Johnson, Jeff Gervais, Kyle Erickson, Jen Crespo, Joy Dice Kieffer, JoLynn Larson, Kelly Loebick-Frascella, Miranda Rosado, Dan Frost, Marcus Sheanshang, Amanda Hall, Valerie Plis, Allison Steele, Brian Frawley, Michelle Cirocco, Nick Carney, Cindy Alcantara, Pat McIntyre, Joe Kenner, and Peter McDermott.

Hidden Talent would have been a much less useful book without the generous contributions of my first readers Michael Tamasi, John Konsin, Jaimie Francis, John Cain, Jeffrey Korzenik, Jeff Thielman, Beth Vause, Ed Hurley-Wales, Wendy Swallow and Bob Nicosin.

Others who also contributed valuable ideas that found their way into the book are:

Gregg Croteau, Ivan Rosenberg, Wes Jurey, Pete Leonard, Randy Lewis, Gabriella Priest, Ashley Furst, Anthony Martinez, Yaron Schwartz, Jeannie Hebert, Lisa Lourie, Alex Beck, Angela Shoe, Annette Underwood, Becca Collins, Ben Gilman, Bill Mueller, Rob Hebert, Sue Gunderman, Catherine Jones, Crissy Vicendese, Dylan Lundgren, Ellen Parlee, Emma Tobin, Esther Leonard, Froswa' Booker-Drew, Genevieve Martin, Sara Marcus, Jacquie Gallo, Jacquelyn Carpenter, Rick Thomas, Jeff Williams,

Caitlin Codella Low, Niki DaSilva, Peter Beard, Kami Welch, Jamal Feerasta, Jessica Trepcos, Jeff Bernick, Jennifer Luebke, Kat Maudru, Jerry Rubin, Jim Hodges, Jina Krause-Vilmar, John Cummings, John Klem, John Peterson, John O'Neil, John Wheeler, Julie Brekke, Kami Welch, Katie Smith Milway, Kim Jedlicki, Laurie Mays, Liddy Romero, Liz Brown, Ricardo Febles, Jefferson Alvarez, Melissa Kleder, Mike Bastine, Nancy Lambert, Nicole Lake, Willie Cordero, Randy Lusk, Tom Krivickas, Elaine Katz, John O'Neill, Tanya Rylee, Ben Theis, Marcia Ballinger, Marcia Proto, Cammie McGovern, Wade Rubenstein, Deb Broberg, and Nate Mandel. I am very grateful to all these people and a few others I may have missed for their time, insights and encouragement.

Every book inevitably involves a production team who are critical for turning a book manuscript into a finished product. Essential members of my team who got me over the finish line include my editor Jesse Winter, Cristina Smith, Debby Englander, Geoffrey Berwind, Christy Day, Becky Robinson, Kelly Edmiston, Sandy Blood, Mark Stein, Gregory Manousos, Paige Gilbert, Madeline Mahoney, Bob Plaskon and Judy Wolff.

Finally, most authors drag their patient friends and family along on this arduous journey of getting a book written and published. Among those who have been most supportive in this venture are Paul and Leslie Mahoney, Michele Bograd, Deborah Miller, the guys in my poker posse and my men's group at church, along with Bob Brown, Phil Morris, Pat and Betsy Goodman, Doug and Becky Gladstone, and Sean Crowe.

Finally, my family has been the most important part of this adventure. *Hidden Talent* is dedicated to my wife Sue whose work at UTEC, a non-profit working with young adults coming out of prison, opened my eyes to the complex challenges marginalized populations face in finding sustainable employment. Our daughter Anna has provided constant emotional support and guidance around appropriate language based on her experience teaching students with learning disabilities. Finally, our daughter Sara was my most demanding editor and cheerleader, continually challenging me to rethink the language I used and the messages I conveyed when promoting the value overlooked talent pools can bring to employers. This book is truly a product of the love and relationships I have been blessed with. Thank you all.

Notes

1. "The Biggest Future Employment Crisis: A Lack of Workers," by Roy Maurer, Society of Human Resource Management, October 19, 2021.

2. "Labor Force Crisis: Employers Losing Patience," Connecticut Business & Industry Association, August 18, 2023. https://tinyurl.com/3wjurywn

3. Maurer op. cit., "The Biggest Future Employment Crisis," 2021.

4. For a more detailed summary of the statistics on incarceration in the US, see *Untapped Talent: How Second Chance Hiring Works for Your Business and the Community* by Jeffrey Korzenik, HarperCollins Leadership, 2021.

5. "Felon History and Change in U.S. Employment Rates," by Ryan Larsen et al., *Social Science Research*, March 2022. https://pubmed.ncbi.nlm.nih.gov/35183305/; "America's Invisible Felon Population: A Blind Spot in U.S. National Statistics," Nicholas Eberstadt, American Enterprise Institute, May 22, 2019, https://tinyurl.com/49z5sfdd

6. "How Much Do States Spend on Prisoners?" *USA Facts*, March 28, 2023. https://tinyurl.com/2jz967d5; "Economics of Incarceration," Prison Policy Institute, December 21, 2023. https://www.prisonpolicy.org/research/economics_of_incarceration/

7. "Immigration Rebound Eases Shortage of Workers, Up to a Point," by Lydia DePillis, *New York Times*, February 6, 2023. https://www.nytimes.com/2023/02/06/business/economy/immigration-labor.html; "New Census Projections Show Immigration is Essential to the Growth and Vitality of a More Diverse US Population" by William H. Frey, Brookings Research, November 29, 2023, https://tinyurl.com/2t8a6ssk; "Barriers to Career Advancement Among Skilled Immigrants in the US," by Cassie Arnita, Ballard Brief, BYU Marriott, December 2022.

8. "One Big Reason Migrants Are Coming in Droves: They Believe They Can Stay," by Miriam Jordan, *The New York Times*, January 31, 2024. https://www.nytimes.com/2024/01/31/us/us-immigration-asylum-border.html. "Migration: This Time

It's Different," by Mark A. Green, Wilson Center Blog, January 23, 2024. https://www.wilsoncenter.org/blog-post/migration-time-its-different. "How Temporary Protected Status Has Expanded Under the Biden Administration," by Mohamad Moslimani, *Pew Research Center*, March 29, 2024.

9. "People With Disabilities Buck Cooling Trend, Reaching New Employment Highs," Kessler Foundation, nTIDE November 2023 Jobs Report, December 8, 2023. https://kesslerfoundation.org/press-release/ntide-november-2023-jobs-report-people-disabilities-buck-cooling-trend-reaching-new

10. "Disability rates among working-age adults are shaped by race, place, and education" by Martha Ross and Nicole Bateman, May 15, 2018, Brookings Institute Blog. https://www.brookings.edu/articles/disability-rates-among-working-age-adults-are-shaped-by-race-place-and-education/

11. "Why Are Middle-Aged Men Missing From the Labor Market?" by Jeanna Smialek et. al., *The New York Times*, December 2, 2022. https://www.nytimes.com/2022/12/02/business/economy/job-market-middle-aged-men.html

12. "Understanding America's Labor Shortage" by Stephanie Ferguson, U.S. Chamber of Commerce, January 9, 2024. https://www.uschamber.com/workforce/understanding-americas-labor-shortage

13. "The Demographic Outlook: 2022–2052, Population Used to Project the Labor Force," Congressional Budget Office, July 2022. https://www.cbo.gov/publication/58347#_idTextAnchor007; "The Mystery of the Declining U.S. Birth Rate, by M. Kearney et al., EconoFact, February 15, 2022. https://econofact.org/the-mystery-of-the-declining-u-s-birth-rate.

14. "Older Workers Stay if You Invest in Them," by Adi Gaskell, Forbes, February 21, 2023. https://www.forbes.com/sites/adigaskell/2023/02/21/older-workers-stay-if-you-invest-in-them/?sh=70bc09e26858#:~:text=It%27s%20a%20problem%20that%20is,market%20and%20in%20public%20finances.

15. "Migrants, Immigrants, Refugees, Asylum-Seekers, Parolees: Understanding the Key Differences," International Institute of New England, September 15, 2023; https://iine.org/2023/09/migrants-immigrants-refugees-asylum-seekers-parolees-understanding-the-key-differences/

16. For more on the concepts of "neurodiversity" and "neurotypical" see "Neurodiversity as a Competitive Advantage," by Robert Austin and Gary Pisano, *Harvard Business Review*, May-June 2017. "What is Neurodiversity?" by Nicole Baumer and Julia Frueh, Harvard Health Publishing, November 23, 2021; https://www.health.harvard.edu/blog/what-is-neurodiversity-202111232645.

17. Recidivism is a complicated and controversial statistic with a variety of definitions. What matters is that a relatively high percentage of former inmates return to prison at some point, which is always bad for your resume. It makes the possibility of gaining sustainable employment increasingly difficult. For more details see articles like: "The Misleading Math of Recidivism" by Dana Goldstein. https://www.themarshallproject.org/2014/12/04/the-misleading-math-of-recidivism and "Why Do So Many Ex-Cons End Up Back in Prison," by Leon Neyfakh, *Slate Magazine*, October 29, 2015. https://slate.com/news-and-politics/2015/10/why-do-so-many-prisoners-end-up-back-in-prison-a-new-study-says-maybe-they-dont.html

18. "nTIDE May 2024 Jobs Report: People With Disabilities Succeeding in Finding Jobs," Kessler Foundation, June 7, 2024; "Persons With a Disability — Labor Force Characteristics 2022," Bureau of Labor Statistics, February 23, 2023, https://www.bls.gov/news.release/pdf/disabl.pdf.

19. "Insights," Diability:IN, https://disabilityin.org/country/united-states/#:~:text=However%2C%20people%20with%20a%20disability,than%20people%20with%20no%20disability.

20. For more information about Televerde's work in prisons contact Michelle Cirocco, chief impact officer, Michelle.cirocco@televerde.com. https://www.televerdefoundation.org/about-us/

21. For more information on these programs, see: The Last Mile: https://thelastmile.org; Prison Entrepreneurship Program. https://www.pep.org; Persevere Now: https://www.perseverenow.org/.

22. For a compelling story about the difficulties faced by the formerly incarcerated who are trying to reenter society and the workplace I highly recommend *The Many Lives of Mama Love: A Memoir of Lying, Stealing, Writing and Healing* by Lara Love Hardin, Simon & Schuster, 2023.

23. "Imagine a Hiring Process Without Resumes" by David DeLong and Sara Marcus, *Harvard Business Review Blog*, January 5, 2021. https://hbr.org/2021/01/

imagine-a-hiring-process-without-resumes; For more about how the Greyston Foundation shares its experiences with Open Hiring, see their website at https://www.greyston.org.

24. For more on the important concept of psychological safety see "What is Psychological Safety?" by Amy Gallo, *Harvard Business Review Blog*, February 15, 2023; https://hbr.org/2023/02/what-is-psychological-safety; *The Fearless Organization: Creating Psychological Safety in the Workplace for Learning, Innovation and Growth,* by Amy Edmondson, Wiley, 2018, https://www.getabstract.com/en/summary/the-fearless-organization/35444#:~:text=Leadership%20expert%20Amy%20Edmondson%20defines,ideas%2C%20feedback%20and%20constructive%20criticisms.

25. For more information on "Ban the box" laws in your state see "Ban the Box — State Laws on Criminal Records," *Workplace Fairness. https://www.workplacefairness.org/privacy-criminal-ban-the-box/#ME;* "States, Advocates Push Beyond Ban-the-Box for Hiring Ex-Felons," by Khorri Atkinson and Chris Marr, *Bloomberg Law,* January 23, 2024. https://news.bloomberglaw.com/daily-labor-report/states-advocates-push-beyond-ban-the-box-for-hiring-ex-felons

26. "Shaping Wellness Workplace Programs With Employees," July 26, 2023. B Lab Newsletter, https://usca.bcorporation.net/zbtcz7z23zshaping-workplace-wellness-programs-with-employees/

27. "Learn How CliftonStrengths Assessment Works," Gallup.com, https://www.gallup.com/cliftonstrengths/en/253676/how-cliftonstrengths-works.aspx

28. "Are You Experiencing Compassion Fatigue?" by Rebecca A. Clay, American Psychological Association, July 11, 2022, https://www.apa.org/topics/covid-19/compassion-fatigue.

29. *Untapped Talent: How Second Chance Hiring Works for Your Business and the Community,* Jeffrey D. Korzenik, HarperCollins Leadership, 2021; "How Employers Can Set Formerly Incarcerated Workers Up For Success," Jeffrey Korzenik, *Harvard Business Review,* Digital Article, October 3, 2022.

30. "Work Opportunity Tax Credit Frequently Asked Questions," IRS. https://www.irs.gov/businesses/small-businesses-self-employed/work-opportunity-tax-credit.

31. *The Power of Positive Deviance: How Unlikely Innovators Solve the World's Toughest Problems* by Richard Pascale et. al., Harvard Business Review Press, 2010; *A Path Appears: Transforming Lives, Creating Opportunity* by Nicholas D. Kristof & Cheryl WuDunn, Vintage Books, 2014.

32. Interview with Willie Cordero, head of Laz Parking's Second Chance Program, October 19, 2021; "A Laz Story on Second Chances," Alan Lazowski, Facebook, July 30, 2021, https://www.facebook.com/watch/?v=364020631762756

33. "I Have a Bean" video is available at: https://www.ihaveabean.com/pages/about-us-1.

34. Dave Dahl and his famous bread company is one of best known success stories in the second chance hiring world. https://www.youtube.com/watch?v=IZgfg-vSdHA.

35. UTEC works with some of the most challenging justice-involved youth who are dealing with many challenges (e.g. unstable housing, no work experience, and past drug involvement) that make it difficult to succeed in the workplace. https://utecinc.org/our-mission/

36. "Workforce Development: What it is and Why It Matters," Taproot Foundation, August 13, 2020. https://tinyurl.com/4u8zbkca.

37. "Recruitment Agency vs. Temp Agency: What's the Difference?" Welcome to the Jungle, October 24, 2022. https://www.welcometothejungle.com/en/articles/difference-between-recruitment-and-temp-agency.

38. South Dallas Employment Project Info Session, Wise Resource Development, July 15, 2021, accessed 7/25/23: https://www.youtube.com/watch?v=zO-4Me5hKU0

39. For more information on certifications that can help your partners prepare and qualify second chance candidates for specific jobs see "Career Onestop Job Search Help for Ex-offenders: Certifications." https://www.careeronestop.org/ExOffender/GetTraining/TypesofTraining/certifications.aspx; also Texas has done some of the most sophisticated work on Industry-Based certifications. See "Industry-Based Certifications for Middle-Skill Step Occupations in Texas," Texas Workforce Investment Council, November 2018. https://gov.texas.gov/uploads/files/organization/twic/2018-Industry-Based-Certifications.pdf.

40. "How Second Chance Employees Can Boost a Bottom Line: The Nehemiah Manufacturing Success Story" by Micah Solomon, Forbes Magazine, August 8, 2021. https://www.forbes.com/sites/micahsolomon/2021/08/09/how-second-chance-employees-with-proper-support-can-boost-a-bottom-line-the-nehemiah-manufacturing-success-story/?sh=6fc006553dc7

41. "Ex-Prisoners Face Headwinds as Job Seekers, Even as Openings Abound" by Talmon Joseph Smith, *New York Times*, July 6, 2023. To shop for some cool work shoes or to learn more about Ed Hennings' motivational programs see https://edhenningsco.com.

42. "U.S. Employer's Guide to Hiring Refugees," Tent Partnership for Refugees, January 2024, https://www.tent.org/wp-content/uploads/2024/03/Tent_US-Hiring-Guide_2023_singles_Mar12.pdf]

43. "For a Concord Small Business, Haitian Migrants Get the Job Done," by Marcela Garcia, *The Boston Globe*, May 20, 2024.

44. "The Demographic Outlook: 2023 to 2053," Congressional Budget Office, January 2023. https://www.cbo.gov/publication/58612

45. "Upward Momentum: Refugee Employment Programs Offer Pathway to Stability and Self-Sufficiency," by Amelia Compton Wolff, *Insight on Manufacturing*, November 15, 2023. https://tinyurl.com/26r8h939. "Refugees Find Way to Success Through a Regional Team," by Anya Kelley, *Oshkosh Herald,* August 30, 2023. https://oshkoshherald.com/wp-content/uploads/2023/08/August-30-2023-Oshkosh-Herald.pdf

46. "Bridging Language and Work: Solutions to Invest in Immigrant and Refugee Talent," guide book by Tent Partnership for Refugees and Jobs For the Future, February 2022. https://www.tent.org/wp-content/uploads/2022/02/Tent_BridgingLanguageWork_2.7.22.pdf

47. "Innovative Transportation Solutions for Refugee Employment," Podcast, Chris Chancey, founder of Amplio Recruiting and author of *Refugee Workforce* interviews Seye Onabolu, founder of Sona Circle. November 18, 2022. https://www.youtube.com/watch?v=wG52npvWNNg

48. For more information about AbilityOne see https://tinyurl.com/3zh7a7ur.

49. For more information about current and future Uniquely Abled Academy programs around the country, see their website: https://uniquelyabledproject.org/academy-locations/

50. Other organizations who do both training and provide work themselves include: Aspiritech (https://aspiritech.org); TACT (https://www.buildwithtact.org) ; Auticon (https://auticon.com/us/); Exceptional Minds Studio (https://exceptional-minds.org); NeuroTalent Works (https://www.neurotalentworks.org); or check out this networking organization in the field: HAAPE (https://haape.org)

51. "Autism and Screen Time: Special Brains, Special Risks," by Victoria Dunckley, *Psychology Today*, December 31, 2016. https://www.psychologytoday.com/us/blog/mental-wealth/201612/autism-and-screen-time-special-brains-special-risks

52. For more information on different initiatives see "Neurodiversity Hiring Initiatives and Partnerships," Employer Assistance and Resource Network on Disability Inclusion, https://askearn.org/page/neurodiversity-hiring-initiatives-and-partnerships.

53. "When you meet one person with Autism, you've met one person with Autism," Healis Autism Centre, July 14, 2020. https://www.healisautism.com/post/when-you-meet-one-person-with-autism

54. "How EY is Focusing on Neurodiverse Talent — and Why It Benefits Everyone," by Leah Carroll, BBC, March 21, 2024. https://www.bbc.com/worklife/article/20240320-ey-karyn-twaronite-neurodiversity-bbc-executive-interview#:~:text=We've%20since%20expanded%20our,have%20a%2092%25%20retention%20rate.

55. "George Floyd, Justice and Equality Through an Autistic Lense," by Sam Farmer, The Hill, June 15, 2020. https://thehill.com/changing-america/opinion/502752-george-floyd-justice-and-equality-through-an-autistic-lens/

56. "Why Working is Harder Than It Looks for Many People with Autism," by Kay Lomas, Organization for Autism Research, September 5, 2018. Online: https://researchautism.org/blog/why-working-is-harder-than-it-looks-for-many-people-with-autism/.

57. Carroll op. cit., BBC "How EY if Focusing on Neurodiverse Talent..," March 21, 2024.

58. SAP News op. cit., "Transparency, Empathy Key to Supporting Neurodiversity in the Workplace," March 1, 2024.

59. Carroll op. cit., BBC "How EY if Focusing on Neurodiverse Talent..," March 21, 2024.

60. "Levels of Autism: Everything You Need to Know," *Medical News Today*, January 23, 2024. https://www.medicalnewstoday.com/articles/325106; "Autism Severity and It's Relationship to Disability," by E. Waizbard-Bartov, et. al, *Autism Research*, April 2023. https://onlinelibrary.wiley.com/doi/10.1002/aur.2898

61. "An Employer's Guide to Supporting Workers With Autism," by Keith Wargo and Chet Hurwitz, *Harvard Business Review*, March 5, 2024. Digital article. https://hbr.org/2024/03/an-employers-guide-to-supporting-workers-with-autism.

62. To complete the spectrum, those diagnosed as level 3 require continuous high-levels of support and have trouble completing routine tasks. They are unlikely to be viable candidates for employment in a for-profit business.

63. "Walgreens Transitional Work Group Sets Standard in Disability Hiring," by Sarah Cason, Walgreen's Boots Alliance, December 8, 2022. "Sephora: Enabling a Workforce With Disabilities," *Employer Assistance and Resource Network on Disability Inclusion*. https://askearn.org/employerprofile/sephora-enabling-a-workforce-with-disabilities#:~:text=Driven%20by%20a%20need%20to,Southeast%20Regional%20Distribution%20center%20in

64. "Why People Hide Their Disabilities at Work" by Pooja Jain-Link and Julia Taylor Kennedy, *Harvard Business Review Blog*, June 3, 2019. https://hbr.org/2019/06/why-people-hide-their-disabilities-at-work

65. There are myriad of good sources on "sensitivity" — or related training to create more inclusive and productive work environments for employees with disabilities. Some places to start are: "Disability Sensitivity Guide," National Disability Institute, 2017. https://tinyurl.com/54cjta4c; "Working Together: Ensuring People With Disabilities Feel Welcome and Included in the Workplace," Employer Assistance and Resource Network on Disability Inclusion, https://askearn.org/page/disability-etiquette.

66. "The Failure of the DEI-Industrial Complex," by Lily Zheng, *Harvard Business Review Blog*, December 1, 2022. https://hbr.org/2022/12/

the-failure-of-the-dei-industrial-complex ; SAP News op. cit. March 1, 2024. Leah Carroll, BBC op. cit, March 21, 2024.

67. The questions in this chapter were inspired by *Find Your Why: A Practical Guide for Discovering Purpose for You and Your Team,"* by Simon Sinek, David Mead and Peter Docker, Penguin/Random House, 2017.

68. For more insights on overcoming resource constraints, see *Stretch: Unlock the Power of Less* by Scott Sonenshein, Harper Business, 2017; *Subtract: The Untapped Science of Less* by Leidy Klotz, Flat Iron Books, 2021.

69. For more on improving knowledge retention, see my previous book, *Lost Knowledge: Confronting the Threat of an Aging Workforce*, Oxford University Press, 2004.

70. The US Chamber of Commerce Foundation has been a leader in developing methodologies for Talent Pipeline Management initiatives for a decade. To learn more about their work with marginalized groups, see "Opportunity Knocks: Lessons Learned From Leveraging Opportunity Talent," by David DeLong and Jaimie Francis, US Chamber of Commerce Foundation, 2022. For more general information about the Chamber's role in supporting Talent Pipeline development, see "Talent Forward: Stories by State," US Chamber of Commerce Foundation, https://www.forwardontalent.org/map/.

71. "Leveraging the Innovation Adoption Curve" Faster Capital, June 2, 2024. https://www.fastercapital.com/content/Leveraging-the-Innovation-Adoption-Curve.html

Index

A
AbilityOne Program, 201
Accenture, 168, 237, 243
Afghan refugees, 163–165
Alcantara, Cindy, 48, 52–53, 55, 95, 100
Amcor, 168
American Job Centers, 84
Asia Services in Action, 159
asylees. *See* asylum seekers
asylum seekers, 4, 12, 17–18, 109, 117, 151, 170-171
    See also immigrants; refugees
autism spectrum disorder (ASD), 13, 184, 205–206, 218, 232–237
    See also neurodiverse employees

B
Baby Boomers, 6
background checks, 29, 30, 47, 55, 103
Bajra, 17–18, 123–124
Bannerman, Angela, 204
"ban the box" laws, 64, 104
Ben and Jerry's, 45
benefits of hiring marginalized workers, 285-291
Better Lives Program, 68
biases, confronting, 43–46, 55
Bike Connector, 178
birth rate, U.S., 5
Black, Eric, 186, 188, 241–242, 271, 290
Blue Star Recyclers, 241, 245, 246, 248, 255
The Body Shop
    ankle monitoring bracelets, 56, 290
    biases and, 43–46, 55
    decoding needs, 49–53

    Inclusive Leadership course, 54–55, 95
    joyful collective form, 52–53, 100–101
    Open Hiring initiative, 41–57, 90, 91-94
    partnerships and, 85, 86
    pilot projects, 46–49
    psychological safety, 50–51
    recruitment partners, 47–48
    training reinvention, 47, 49–50, 53–55
Boston Children's Hospital (BCH)
    coaching and, 115, 121, 126–128, 132
    cohort model, 115, 128, 129
    getting buy-in, 116
    job-specific English training, 114, 115, 122
    paid training, 115, 122, 132
    surprises and, 179
    weekly team meetings, 115, 126
    See also Jewish Vocational Service of Boston (JVS)
Boston Scientific, 233–234, 235, 237, 243, 291
Bounce Back program, 102
Bray, Matthew, 168
business development reps (BDRs), 24, 25, 27, 35–36, 38, 40

C
California Department of Rehabilitation, 207, 244, 253, 284
call centers. *See* Televerde
Career Resources, Inc., 85
Carney, Nick, 43–45, 49, 55, 56, 93, 94
case studies
    Bajra, 17–18, 123–124
    Charles, 15–16, 60–61

Harold, 49–50, 56
Harrison, 18–20, 212
Luisa, 2–3, 261, 263–265
Lusata (Papa), 144–145
Lynn, 188–189
Maria, 39
Mu Soe, 156–158, 160–161
Nick, 233–234, 291
Solange, 2, 261, 265–267, 291
Tucker, 2, 261, 267–269
Valerie, 32–34
Victor, 41–42, 55
certifications, 89
change management,
 culture change, 46, 50-52,146-147, 166, 217, 289–290
 executive sponsor's role, 29–32, 38, 134-136, 139–142, 241–242
 getting buy in from management and employees, 29, 43–46, 89-93
 HR practices, 113, 148, 232, 235-237
 managing change with neurodivergent talent, 222, 230-231, 254
 personal change, 15-16, 19, 26, 61, 76, 81, 100, 145, 207, 212, 227
 resistance to, 87, 96, 219, 277
Charles, (case study) 15–16, 60–61
Cheshire Correctional Facility, 81–82
CityLink, 85
Clampco Products
 career paths and, 148
 cluster hiring, 133, 136
 communication breakdowns, 146–147
 Congolese refugees, 133–134, 135, 144–145, 173, 178
 English language training, 137–138
 finding best fit jobs, 142–144
 Ohio Resettlement Bureau (ORB), 135, 139–140
 transportation problems, 138–139, 178
Classic Wire Cut
 about, 9, 183, 203
 coaching managers, 213–215, 252–253
 customized coaching, 209–210, 211
 onboarding process, 208–209
 Uniquely Abled Academy (UAA), 203, 204, 205–208, 211, 213
Clifton Strengths Assessment, 71
CNC machinists, 200–201, 203, 204, 205, 208
coaching
 accommodations *vs.* accountability, 213–215, 252–253
 customized coaching for neurodiverse employees, 209–210
 mistakes to avoid, 283–285
 for new refugee hires, 126–128, 132, 175–177
 on-the-job coaching, 101–102
 outsourcing of, 103, 243–244
 soft skills enhanced by, 62, 208, 251-252
 specialized employee assistance coaching, 102
 of supervisors, 230–231, 283–284
 transition coaching, 211
College of the Canyons, 204, 205, 207
communication, 146–147, 254
 See also language barriers
compassion fatigue, 72–77
convicted felons. *See* formerly incarcerated
COVID-19 pandemic, 5, 42, 58, 71, 77, 155, 156, 163, 219, 221
Crawford, Lisa, 29
Crespo, Jennifer, 41–42, 47, 53–54, 55, 56–57, 91, 291
Croteau, Gregg, 97

D
Dave's Killer Bread Story, 82

Debray, Nicolas, 90
DEI+B (Diversity, Equity, Inclusion and Belonging), 8, 39, 168–169, 220, 225, 231, 251–252, 274, 289, 292
Democratic Republic of Congo, 135, 144
Denton, Oscar, 220, 221, 231
disabilities, people with
  AbilityOne Program, 201
  accommodations for, 164, 187, 192–193, 197, 214–215, 223, 225
  benefits of hiring, 201-202, 215–217, 231, 237, 257-258
  executive sponsor's role, 241-242
  firing of, 211, 249–250
  Harrison (case study), 18–20, 212
  HR processes, changing, 235-237, 245-251
  job coaches and, 191
  identifying opportunities, 239-241
  learning curve and, 192
  Lynn (case study), 188–189
  Nick, (case study), 233–234, 291
  nontraditional interviews with, 246–248, see also interviewing
  onboarding and, 250–251
  part-time work and, 224, 256–257
  partnerships, 242-245
  person-first language, 13
  scheduling problems, 256-257
  statistics, 5
  surprises, 258
  training supervisors, 251-254
  Tucker (case study), 267–269
  unconventional habits, 210–211
  undisclosed, 246
  See also neurodiverse employees
Disposable Employee Model, 80
Driscoll, Kristin, 112–116, 122–127, 129–132

E
early adopters, 46, 79–80, 91–92
Eglinton, Jeanne, 187–188, 190–191, 192–193, 197, 200, 201, 244, 246–247, 290
Elevate, 70–71
employee assistance coaching, 102
employment agencies, 84, 87
Erikson, Kyle, 193, 195, 200, 201–202
Espinoza, Lucas, 230
ex-offenders. *See* formerly incarcerated
EY, 220, 225, 226, 240, 251, 274

F
Find your "why," 81-83, 162, 247, 261–262, 269
Floyd, George, 222
foreign-born workers
  navigating US job system, 109, 130–131
  onboarding tips, 160–162
  See also asylum seekers; immigrants; refugees
formerly incarcerated
  background checks and, 29, 30
  "ban the box" laws, 64, see also interviewing
  barriers to employment, 16
  benefits of hiring, 38-40, 56-57, 77–78
  challenges faced by, 62
  Charles, (case study) 15–16, 60–61
  coaching for, 101–103
  deciding to do second-chance hiring, 107-108
  diversity, equity, inclusion, goals supported, 39
  finding your "why," 81–83
  firing, 72–73
  halfway houses, 15–16
  language and, 11–12
  Luisa, (case study) 2–3, 261,

263–265
obstacles to hiring, 28-29, 30-31, 60
performance standards and, 36, 44–45, 93–94
protecting privacy of, 34–35, 95
recidivism, 17, 297n17
reentry checklist, 86–87
setting boundaries, 103
statistics, 3–4, 17
surprises, 38
telling your story, 34, 50–51, 278
trauma and, 70
types of convictions, 103
Valerie, (case study) 32–34

Frost, Dan, 151–154, 171
Frost, Harrison, 151–153

G
G3 Consulting, 54
Gallo, Jacquie, 81
Gervais, Jeff, 185–186, 194–195, 196, 197, 198, 199, 200–201, 256, 257–258
getting started hiring marginalized workers,107-108, 179-181, 258, 291-292
Grant, Amy, 204–207, 211, 213, 215, 216–217, 241, 253, 290
Greyston Bakery, 45–46, 52, 92

H
Haitian refugees, 151–154
halfway houses, 15–16
Hall, Amanda, 58–59, 60, 62, 63, 64, 66, 70, 73, 77
Hardy, Jason, 82
Harold, 49–50, 56
Harrison (case study), 18–20, 212
HDF Painting, 151–154, 168, 171
Heartland Systems Corporation (HSC)
about, 9, 183, 219
data cleansing work and, 220–221

developing leaders, 223
hard-to-fill jobs and, 220–221
Mind Shift, 219, 220–221
See also Mind Shift
Hennings, Ed, 87, 97–100
hiring practices
biases and, 43–44
cluster hiring, 115, 128, 129, 133, 136, 170, 279
collaborative interviewing process, 63–65, 104
employee *vs.* contractor, 243
finding best fit jobs, 187–188
firing, 249–250
neurodiverse hires, 245–251
nontraditional interviews, 246–248, 279–280
onboarding, 31–32, 192–193, 208–209, 236–237, 243, 250–251
online process, 166
transparency, 190
human resources
changing processes and practices, 31–32, 35–37, 47, 52–55, 48-50, 62–66, 67–71, 100–105, 112–115, 119–122, 130–132, 136–137, 278–281
coaching, 101–103
collaborative interviewing process, 63–65, 104
identifying needed support, 100–101
retention strategies, 148, 164,
humor, 146-147

I
I Have a Bean, 81, 82, 95–96, 108
immigrants, See also refugees
English-language proficiency and, 17–18
lower-skilled jobs and, 18
number of, 4
obstacles for, 17–18
refugees *vs.*, 117–118

terminology and, 12
transportation and, 18
Indeed.com, 59, 60
Inmate to Boss, interviewing formerly incarcerated, 97-100
International Institute of New England (IINE), 172
interviewing, 30, 31, 34, 42, 63, 65, 66, 89, 98-100, 104,108, 115, 120-121, 131, 160, 187-188, 204, 235-236, 246-248, 255, 264, 279-281

J
Jay Nolan Community Services, 207, 211
JBM Packaging
  Better Lives Program, 68
  CityLink and, 85
  collaborative interviewing process, 63–65, 104
  community referrals and, 66–67, 88, 89
  compassion fatigue, 72–77
  Fair Chance program, 58–60, 72, 77–78
  feedback scorecards, 68–69, 94
  life coaches, 61, 62, 66, 67–68, 101, 102
  peer assessment process, 64–65
  RoadMap2Wheels program, 68
  second chance hiring and, 9, 58, 80
  Talent Tuesdays, 65–66
  trauma-responsive training, 70–71
Jewish Vocational Service of Boston (JVS)
  analysis of staffing challenges, 113
  coaching, 115, 121, 126–128, 132
  interview practice, 120
  pilot program, 122, 124–126
  previous work experience, 121–122
  training program, 114–117, 122, 128, 130
  weekly meetings, 115, 126

See also Boston Children's Hospital (BCH)
Jurey, Wes, 88-89, 272
justice-involved. *See* formerly incarcerated
JVS. *See* Jewish Vocational Service of Boston (JVS)

K
Kay, Brenda, 23–40, 81, 90, 92, 94, 102, 105, 106, 263, 290
Koolen, Genevieve, 226
Korzenik, Jeffrey, 80, 82
Krueger, Karen, 113, 116, 131–132

L
Lambert, Nancy, 102
language, author's note on labels used, 11–14
language barriers
  coaching and, 283
  language training solutions, 136–138, 173–175
  software and, 147–148
  translators, 152, 161, 165, 170, 174–175, 279
  use of visual cues, 147, 175
Larson, JoLynn, 223, 224, 231, 232–233, 234, 236, 237, 244, 254
Last Mile, 28
Lazowski, Alan, 81–82
LAZ Parking, 81–82
leadership sensitivity, 70–71
learning disabilities, 49–50
learning from experience, 48–49, 105-107, 144, 173, 227, 247, 249, 257, 258, 281, 283-285, 292
Leonard, Pete, 81, 96
Lewis, Randy, 241, 247, 249–250, 261–262, 274
Loebick-Frascella, Kelly, 156–157, 158, 159, 162, 166
Love Hardin, Lara, 83

Luisa (case study), 2–3, 261, 263–265
lunch with leaders, 162
Lusata/Papa (case study), 144–145
Lynn (case study), 188–189

M

Main Street Gourmet
   Afghan refugees, 163–165
   COVID-19 pandemic and, 155, 156, 163
   diversity and, 166
   Lunch with Leaders, 162, 274
   Mu Soe (case study), 156–158, 160–161
   Nepali refugees, 156, 159–160, 165
   referrals and, 163
   training and, 158, 161
   workforce shortages, 155–156
The Many Lives of Mama Love (Love Hardin), 83
marginalized workers
   about, 3, 6, 7
   emotional connection to, 25, 81–83, 262
   language and, 11, 13–14
   Open Hiring and, 42, 48
   See also names of specific groups
Maria, 39
Martinez, Sem, 203–204, 205, 206, 209, 211, 213–214, 216, 241, 287
McIntyre, Patrick, 241
Microsoft, 240, 274
migrants, 12
Mind Shift
   about, 219, 240, 242–243, 245
   attention to detail, 221, 284
   Boston Scientific and, 235
   coaching and, 230–231, 237, 244
   data cleansing work, 220, 279
   employees as contractors, 237
   increasing independence, 223
   sensitivity training, 252
   talent pipeline, 229–230
   See also neurodiverse employees
Minnesota Diversified Industries (MDI)
   about, 9, 183, 185–186
   company tours, 187–188, 246–247, 280
   finding best fit jobs, 187–188
   good job coaches, 191
   line leads, 193–195, 199
   mission *vs.* money, 186, 197–198
   nonprofit partnerships, 190, 243
   onboarding process, 192–193, 243
   scheduling challenges, 196–197
   supplemental automation, 199–201
   team chemistry, 199
   transparency and, 190
mistakes, *See* learning from experience
Morris, Bill, 241, 245, 248, 251, 255, 256–257, 258
Mu Soe (case study), 156–158, 160–161
Myanmar, 156

N

Navarro, Karen, 207, 209–210, 211, 213–214, 216, 244, 249, 252
Nehemiah Manufacturing, 92
Nepali refugees, 156, 159–160, 165
Neurodiverse Centers of Excellence, 225
neurodiverse employees
   accommodations for, 214, 223, 225, 230, 253
   benefits of, 215–217
   coaching and, 209–210
   described, 13
   Harrison (case study), 18–20, 212
   language and, 184
   onboarding, 208–209
   patience and, 228, 229
   remote work and, 219, 221–222
   sensitivity, 222, 225–226
   unexpected change and, 222, 254

INDEX   311

unique skill sets of, 221
See also autism spectrum disorder (ASD); disabilities, people with
neurotypical individuals, 13, 216, 218, 236
Nick, (case study), 233–234, 291
nonprofit workforce development organizations, 84, 85, 87, 88, 170–172, 190, 274

O
Ohio Resettlement Bureau (ORB), 135, 139–140, 163, 171, 174
onboarding, 31–32, 192–193, 208–209, 236–237, 243, 250–251
OneOme, 241
on-the-job coaching, 101–102
Open Hiring
  benefits of, 56–57
  described, 41–42
  performance standards and, 44–45
  training and, 273
  See also The Body Shop
Outside In, 82

P
Parlee, Ellen, 172
Parlee Farms, 172
partnerships, workforce
  building effective partnerships, 275–277
  different types of, 83–84
  finding partners, 85–86, 190
  holding accountable, 89
  qualified candidates and, 66–67
  resettlement agencies, 170–172
  for sourcing and training, 242–245
  for talent pipeline, 244–245
  workforce readiness training, 87–88
performance management, 68–69, 93–97, 191, 199, 209, 222, 280, 287-288

Perryville Women's Prison, 23–24, 26, 28–29, 33, 81
Persevere Now, 28
Pfizer, 168
phone translation apps, 152
pilot programs, 46–49, 122, 124–126, 272, 282
Pitney Bowes, 24, 26, 33
  See also Precisely
Plis, Valerie, 59–60, 70–71, 73–74, 76, 77
Precisely
  about, 24, 26
  career paths and, 36
  emotional connection, 81
  interviews and, 30, 31
  on-the-job coaching and, 101–102
  referrals and, 32
  remote work and, 35–36, 273
  turnover and, 39
  See also Televerde
The Precisionists, 229
Prison Entrepreneurship Program, 28
psychological safety, 50–51, 298n24
publicly funded agencies, 84
Pursuit Aerospace, 81

R
refugees
  about, 4, 12
  Afghan refugees, 163–165
  Bajra, (case study), 17–18, 123–124
  benefits of hiring, 128-130, 148–150, 177
  best job fit for, 172–173
  coaching and, 175–177
  Congolese refugees, 133–150, 265–267
  cultural differences, 146–147, 159–160, 164–165
  getting started, 179-181
  Haitian refugees, 151–154
  immigrants *vs.*, 117–118
  language barriers, 168, 173–175

Lusata, (case study), 144–145
Mu Soe, (case study) 156–158, 160–161
Nepali refugees, 156, 159–160, 165
obstacles to employment, 17–18, see also interviewing
open-mindedness, 153
patience, 153
resettlement bureaus, 135, 139, 144, 156-157, 159, 163, 164, 170-171, 176, 179
Solange, (case study) 2, 261, 265–267, 291
surprises and, 125, 179, 278
training and, 154, 158, 161
translators, 152, 161, 165
transportation challenges, 152, 165, 177–178
See also immigrants
Reinhardt, Monika, 221–222, 223, 226–229, 231
remote work, challenges 35-36, 221-222, 273
resettlement bureaus, 159, 170–172, 179
resource constraints, overcoming, 281-282
returning citizens. *See* formerly incarcerated
Rogers, Josh, 26–27, 29, 39, 90
Rosado, Miranda, 160–161, 164, 165

S
SAP, 226, 240, 251, 252, 274
Schafer, Susan, 112, 128, 132
Schwartz, Yaron, 117–118
The Second-Chance Club (Hardy), 82
second-chance hiring. 9, 12, *See* also formerly incarcerated
getting buy in, 43-46
obstacles to, 28-32, 34-38
HR practices, 31-32, 36-37, see also interviewing
sensitivity training, 251–252

Sephora, 239, 274
Sheanshang, Marcus, 58, 62, 77–78, 82, 92, 96–97, 102, 107, 288, 290
Shiwnath, Devi, 114–115, 118, 119, 120–121, 127–128
soft skills, 54–55, 95, 141, 160, 194, 207, 208
Solange (case study), 2, 261, 265–267, 291
South Dallas Employment Project (SDEP), 85–86, 88–89, 272
specialized employee assistance coaching, 102
staffing agencies, 84, 88, 174, 190, 276
Stanford Neurodiversity Project, 229
Steele, Allison, 64, 65, 66–67, 69, 71, 72–73, 74, 75, 76, 77, 96
strategic context for hiring marginalized workers, 272-274

T
Target, 243
Televerde
  about, 23–26, 27–28, 85, 87
  background checks and, 30–31, 37
  benefits of program, 38–39
  emotional connection, 81
  flexibility and, 38
  recruiting, 30
  training and, 25
  See also formerly incarcerated
temp agencies, 84, 134, 138, 140, 190
Tent Partnership for Refugees, 117, 174
Townsend, Mandy, 113, 131
training
  certifications, 89
  for foreign-born workers, 154, 158, 161
  manager training, 47, 54–55, 213–215
  reinvention of, 49–50, 53–55
  sensitivity training, 251–252

supervisor training, 251–254
trauma-responsive management training, 70–71
translators, 152, 161, 165, 170, 174–175, 279
transportation challenges, 68, 138–139, 146, 152, 165, 177–178, 273
Tucker (case study), 2, 261, 267–269
Twaronite, Karyn, 220, 231

U
Undifferentiated Model, 80
Uniquely Abled Academy (UAA), 203, 204, 205–208, 211, 213
Untapped Talent (Korzenik), 80, 82
Upwardly Global, 169
U.S. birth rate, 5
US Chamber of Commerce Foundation, 7, 296n12, 303n70
US Rubber Recycling, 102
UTEC, 97, 299n35
UTEC: Trading Violence and Poverty for Social and Economic Success, 83

V
Valerie (case study), 32–34
Venner, Jason, 133–150, 171, 173, 179, 287
Victor (case study), 41–42, 55

W
Wake Local Reentry Council, 47–48, 85, 86, 103
Wale, Jennifer, 43, 44–45, 46, 47–49, 50–52, 56, 92, 93, 105, 106
Walgreens, 239, 241, 243, 246, 247, 249–250
Whole Foods Market, 45
WIOA (Workforce Innovation and Opportunity Act), 84
workforce development nonprofits, 84, 85, 87, 88, 170–172, 190, 274, 284
workforce shortages, 1–2, 5–6, 42, 58-59, 119-120, 134-136, 151, 155-156, 185-186, 205
workforce turnover, 59, 78, 286
Work Opportunity Tax Credit, 80

About the Author

For more than 30 years, author, speaker, and consultant Dr. David DeLong, has helped leaders implement practical solutions to address critical skill shortages and improve knowledge retention in a fast-changing, technology-driven economy. Today, David focuses solely on helping organizations tap into the underutilized talent pools described in this book.

As an author, David is also known for his widely-praised book, *Lost Knowledge: Confronting the Threat of an Aging Workforce* (Oxford University Press). He co-authored *The Executive Guide to High-Impact Talent Management* (McGraw-Hill) and also wrote *Graduate to a Great Job: Make Your College Degree Pay Off in Today's Market*.

A veteran researcher, David has spent over two decades studying the strategic impacts of changing workforce demographics and knowledge loss on organizational performance. He served on the research staff at both MIT's Sloan School of Management and Harvard Business School and taught "Managing Organizational Change" as an adjunct professor at Babson College.

He has consulted with and spoken for many organizations such as Microsoft, MasterCard, the U.S. Chamber of Commerce Foundation, Kraft Foods, Lockheed Martin, The Conference Board, American Organization of Nurse Executives, Council of Manufacturing Associations, Michigan Works, and the Council of State Chambers. His work has been widely cited in *The New York Times*, *Fortune*, *The Wall Street Journal*, *The Financial Times*, the *Harvard Business Review* blog, and *CIO* magazine. David holds a master's in public administration from Harvard's Kennedy School of Government and a doctorate in organizational behavior from Boston University's Questrom School of Business.